HUMAN PSYCHOLOGY THROUGH BIOLOGY

EMPHASIZE ABOUT HUMAN BEHAVIOUR

MRUGANK TRIVEDI

Copyright © Mrugank Trivedi
All Rights Reserved.

ISBN 979-888606509-1

This book has been published with all efforts taken to make the material error-free after the consent of the author. However, the author and the publisher do not assume and hereby disclaim any liability to any party for any loss, damage, or disruption caused by errors or omissions, whether such errors or omissions result from negligence, accident, or any other cause.

While every effort has been made to avoid any mistake or omission, this publication is being sold on the condition and understanding that neither the author nor the publishers or printers would be liable in any manner to any person by reason of any mistake or omission in this publication or for any action taken or omitted to be taken or advice rendered or accepted on the basis of this work. For any defect in printing or binding the publishers will be liable only to replace the defective copy by another copy of this work then available.

This book is dedicated with love and affection

TO MY MOTHER AND FATHER

AND TO ALL THOSE PERSONS WHO THROUGHTOUT THE

LONG PAST

AGES HAVE CONTRIBUTED TO LITTLE JOY OF LIFE

THROUGH THEIR EMBRODERIES

Contents

1. Neuro Transmitters (a View Into Biology Of Psychology) — 1
2. Evolution : The Boundary Of Psychology — 60
3. Social Psychology : How We Interact With Other Sector — 141
4. Cognitive Psychology : How Things Processed In Mind — 210
5. Personality Psychology : Who Am I ? & What Is Me ? — 295
6. Spiritual Psychology : What Is My Relatioship With Myself — 350

How Experiments Are Done — 371

How To Read Scientfic Paper — 379

I
NEURO TRANSMITTERS (A VIEW INTO BIOLOGY OF PSYCHOLOGY)

Neurotransmitters :-
From a fixed of biological bases For a variety of psychological process take place in thoughts. It means hormones goes to neurons.

The concept is very simple that some thing taking place inside the frame of mind which affects thoughts, behaviour and understanding system.

Spiritualist and Self- help guys don't considered biological strategies or they may be coded.

that is simply visible wondering that folks who don't deliver sufficient notion (thought) to idea.

How BIOLOGY performs function in psychology ?

For this we must understand the simple chess analogy. because we are able to communicate about 6 hormones or five elements of mind however behaviour are endless and it goes to all one of a kind route. (endless version)

There are general 6 sorts of happiness, how we are able to attach them handiest to dopamine ?

How is it if biology is the basis of psychology ?

PSYCHOLOGY IS INFINITE BUT BIOLOGY IS FINITE

And for that we want to recognize easy chess rule.

Biological psychology, additionally called physiological psychology, is the have a look at of the biology of behavior; it focuses on the frightened system, hormones and genetics. organic psychology examines the connection between mind and body, neural mechanisms, and the have an impact on of heredity on conduct.

The biological technique believes conduct to be because of our genetics and body structure. it is the best method in psychology that examines mind, emotions, and behaviors from a organic and consequently physical point of view.
consequently, all this is mental is first physiological. All mind, feeling & conduct in the end have a biological reason. A organic attitude is relevant to the study of psychology in 3 ways:

1. Comparative approach: one of a kind species of animal may be studied and in comparison. this can help in the seek to understand human behavior.
2. Body structure: how the apprehensive system and hormones paintings, how the brain functions, how changes in structure and/or feature can have an effect on conduct. for example, we should ask how pharmaceuticals to deal with melancholy have an effect

on behavior via their interplay with the apprehensive system.
3. Research of inheritance: what an animal inherits from its mother and father, mechanisms of inheritance (genetics). as an example, we would need to understand whether or not high intelligence is inherited from one generation to the following.

Research of Inheritance

Dual research offer geneticists with a form of herbal experiment in which the behavioral likeness of same twins (whose genetic relatedness is 1.0) may be in comparison with the resemblance of dizygotic twins (whose genetic relatedness is 0.5).

In different words, if heredity (i.e., genetics) impacts a given trait or behavior, then equal twins must show a more similarity for that trait in comparison to fraternal (non-identical) twins.

There are types of twins:
Monozygotic = equal twins (percentage one hundred% genetic statistics).
Dizygotic = non-same twins (proportion 50% genetic records, similar to siblings).

Research the use of dual studies looks for the degree of concordance (or similarity) among same and fraternal (i.e., non-equal) twins. Twins are concordant for a trait if both or neither of the twins exhibits the trait. Twins are stated to be disconcordant for a trait if one shows it, and the alternative does not.
same twins have the same genetic, and fraternal twins have just 50 percentage of genes in common.

Thus, if concordance rates (that could range from 0 to one hundred) are appreciably higher for equal twins than for fraternal twins, then this is proof that genetics play an important role in the expression of that specific conduct.

Bouchard and McGue (1981) performed a overview of 111 international studies which as compared the IQ of family individuals. The correlation figures beneath constitute the average diploma of similarity among the 2 humans (the better the similarity, the greater similar the IQ rankings).

equal twins raised together = .86 (correlation).
equal twins raised apart = .72
Non-equal twins reared together = .60
Siblings reared together = .47
Siblings reared aside = .24
Cousins = .15

But, there are methodological flaws which reduce the validity of twin studies. as an example, Bouchard and McGue covered many poorly done and biased studies of their meta-evaluation.

additionally, research evaluating the conduct of dual raised aside have been criticized as the twins regularly percentage similar environments and are sometimes raised through non-parental family member.

Methods of analyzing the brain

It is vital to understand that the human brain is an exceptionally complex piece of biological machinery. Scientists have most effective just "scratched the surface" of know-how the many capabilities of the workings of the human brain. The brain can have an effect on many varieties of conduct.

in addition to reading brain broken sufferers, we will find out approximately the working of the brain in 3 other approaches.

kids start to devise sports, make up video games, and initiate sports with others. If given this opportunity, children increase a experience of initiative and experience at ease in their capability to steer others and make decisions.

1. Neuro surgical procedureWe know so little approximately the brain and its functions are so intently integrated that brain surgical treatment is usually handiest tried as a ultimate inn. H.M. suffered such devastating epileptic suits that in the long run a surgical method that had in no way been used earlier than turned into tried out.This technique cured his epilepsy, however within the manner the hippocampus needed to be removed (this is a part of the limbic device inside the center of the mind.) Afterwards, H.M. became left with intense anterograde amnesia. I.e., He should consider what took place to him in his life as much as while he had the operation, but he couldn't consider some thing new. So now we recognise the hippocampus is involved in reminiscence.
2. Electroencrphalograms (EEGs)that is a manner of recording the electrical activity of the brain (it doesn't hurt, and it isn't dangerous). Electrodes are attached to the scalp and mind waves may be traced.EEGs have been used to have a look at sleep, and it's been observed that in an average night's sleep, we go through a chain of ranges marked by means of one of a kind styles of mind wave.this type of degrees is called REM sleep (fast Eye movement sleep). in the course of this, our mind waves start to resemble the ones of our waking nation (though we're nonetheless fast asleep) and it seems that that is while we dream (whether or not we remember it or not).
3. Mind Scans
Extra currently techniques of reading the brain have

been evolved using numerous sorts of scanning device installed to effective computers.

The CAT scan (Computerised Axial Tomography) is a shifting X-ray beam which takes "photos" from extraordinary angles around the pinnacle and may be used to accumulate a three-dimensional photo of which regions of the brain are broken.

Even more state-of-the-art is the pet experiment (Positron Emission Tomography) which uses a radioactive marker as a manner of reading the brain at paintings.

The system is based on the precept that the brain requires electricity to characteristic and that the regions extra concerned in the performance of a mission will expend more strength. What the test, consequently, permits researchers to do is to offer ongoing pictures of the brain as it engages in intellectual activity.

those (and different) techniques for generating snap shots of mind structure and functioning were notably used to observe language and pet scans, particularly, are generating evidence that suggests that the Wernicke-Gerschwind version won't in the end be the answer to the question of ways language is possible.

4. Crucial evaluation

   Theories inside the biological method guide nature over nurture. however, it is restricting to describe behavior entirely in terms of both nature or nurture, and attempts to do this underestimate the complexity of human conduct. it's far more likely that behavior is due to an interplay between nature (biology) and nurture (environment).

   for instance, individuals can be predisposed to positive behaviors, however these behaviors may not be displayed until they may be triggered with the aid of factors inside the environment. that is referred to as the 'Diathesis-stress version' of human behavior.

A strength of the biological approach is that it affords clear predictions, for example, approximately the results of neurotransmitters, or the behaviors of individuals who are genetically related. this indicates the reasons can be scientifically examined and 'proven.'

A issue is that most biological explanations are reductionist, because it reduces conduct to the outcome of genes and different biological methods, neglecting the effects of childhood and our social and cultural surroundings. and don't offer enough information to completely give an explanation for human conduct.

NATURE vs NURTURE

The character as opposed to nurture debate includes the extent to which particular components of behavior are a product of both inherited (i.e., genetic) or received (i.e., learned) impacts.

Nature is what we think about as pre-wiring and is motivated with the aid of genetic inheritance and other biological factors.

Nurture is normally taken because the affect of external factors after idea, e.g., the made from exposure, lifestyles reviews and studying on an individual.

Behavioral genetics has enabled psychology to quantify the relative contribution of nature and nurture with regard to particular mental developments.

Rather than defending intense nativist or nurturist perspectives, most mental researchers are actually interested by investigating how nature and nurture have interaction in a host of qualitatively special approaches.

for example, epigenetics is an rising area of research which indicates how environmental influences affect the expression of genes.

the nature-nurture debate is concerned with the relative contribution that both influences make to human behavior, such as persona, cognitive tendencies, temperament and psychopathology.

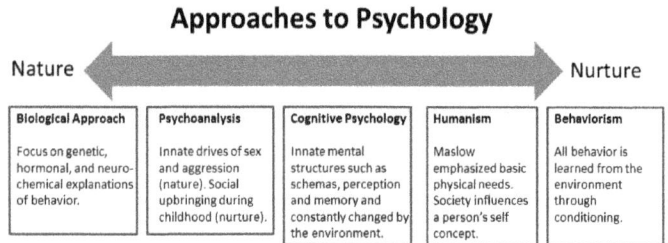

From Biological to Behavioural

Nativism (excessive Nature function)

It has lengthy been regarded that positive bodily traits are biologically decided through genetic inheritance.

shade of eyes, straight or curly hair, pigmentation of the pores and skin and positive diseases (together with Huntingdon's chorea) are all a feature of the genes we inherit.

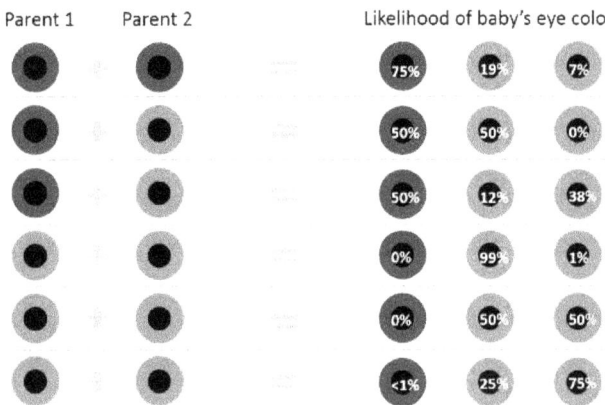

Eyes Pigments Colourification

Those statistics have led many to take a position as to whether or not mental traits together with behavioral dispositions, personality attributes, and mental skills also are "stressed out in" earlier than we're even born.
individuals who adopt an severe hereditary function are known as nativists. Their fundamental assumption is that the traits of the human species as a whole are a manufactured from evolution and that character variations are due to anyone's precise genetic code.

In widespread, the earlier a specific ability appears, the much more likely it is to be under the influence of genetic factors. Estimates of genetic impact are known as heritability.

Examples of an extreme nature positions in psychology encompass Chomsky (1965), who proposed language is gained through the use of an innate language acquisition device. every other instance of nature is Freud's idea of aggression as being an innate power (referred to as

Thanatos).

Traits and variations that are not observable at beginning, but which emerge later in life, are regarded as the product of maturation. that is to say, all of us have an internal "organic clock" which switches on (or off) types of behavior in a pre-programmed way.

The classic instance of the way this affects our physical improvement are the bodily adjustments that arise in early formative years at puberty. however, nativists additionally argue that maturation governs the emergence of attachment in infancy, language acquisition and even cognitive improvement as an entire.

Empiricism (severe Nurture function)

At the alternative give up of the spectrum are the environmentalists – also referred to as empiricists (no longer to be pressured with the opposite empirical / scientific technique).

Their fundamental assumption is that at beginning the human thoughts is a tabula rasa (a clean slate) and that this is regularly "stuffed" because of revel in (e.g., Behaviorism).

From this factor of view, mental traits and behavioral variations that emerge through infancy and early life are the consequences of studying. it is how you're brought up (nurture) that governs the psychologically sizeable factors of infant development and the concept of maturation applies handiest to the biological.

as an example, Bandura's (1977) social studying principle states that aggression is discovered from the surroundings via commentary and imitation. that is visible in his famous Bobo doll experiment (Bandura, 1961).

Freud (1905) stated that occasions in our youth have a notable have an impact on on our grownup lives, shaping our character. He notion that parenting is of primary importance to a child's development, and the family as the maximum vital characteristic of nurture changed into a not unusual subject for the duration of twentieth-century psychology (which become ruled with the aid of environmentalists theories).

Another manner of studying heredity is by using comparing the behavior of twins, who can both be equal (sharing the same genes) or non-equal (sharing 50% of genes). Like adoption research, dual research assist the first rule of conduct genetics; that mental tendencies are extremely heritable, about 50% on common.

The Twins in Early development examine (TEDS) found out correlations among twins on quite a number behavioral developments, along with personality (empathy and hyperactivity) and additives of analyzing consisting of phonetics (Haworth, Davis, Plomin, 2013; Oliver & Plomin, 2007; Trouton, Spinath, & Plomin, 2002).

Implications

Jenson (1969) observed that the average I.Q. scores of black people were appreciably lower than whites he went on to argue that genetic elements had been particularly responsible – even going thus far as to indicate that intelligence is 80% inherited.

The typhoon of controversy that advanced around Jenson's claims became no longer specially because of logical and empirical weaknesses in his argument. It become greater to do with the social and political implications which are regularly drawn from studies that says to demonstrate natural inequalities among social agencies.

For many environmentalists, there's a barely disguised right-wing agenda in the back of the work of the behavioral geneticists. in their view, part of the difference within the

I.Q. scores of different ethnic agencies are due to inbuilt biases within the methods of trying out.

More fundamentally, they believe that variations in intellectual potential are a made from social inequalities in get admission to to cloth sources and possibilities. to place it genuinely kids brought up in the ghetto have a tendency to score decrease on assessments due to the fact they're denied the equal existence possibilities as extra privileged participants of society.

Now we are able to see why the character-nurture debate has become such a hotly contested problem. What begins as an try to recognize the causes of behavioral variations regularly develops into a politically motivated dispute approximately distributive justice and power in society.

What's greater, this doesn't handiest practice to the talk over I.Q. it's miles similarly relevant to the psychology of intercourse and gender, wherein the question of the way plenty of the (alleged) variations in male and girl behavior is due to biology and what sort of to tradition is just as debatable.

Polygenic Inheritance

instead of the presence or absence of unmarried genes being the determining aspect that debts for psychological trends, behavioral genetics has demonstrated that a couple of genes – frequently hundreds, collectively make contributions to particular behaviors.

thus, mental developments observe a polygenic mode of inheritance (as opposed to being decided via a unmarried gene). depression is a good example of a polygenic trait, that is thought to be encouraged by round one thousand genes (Plomin, 2018).

this means a person with a lower variety of these genes

(below 500) would have a decrease danger of experiencing depression than someone with a higher variety.

The nature of Nurture

Nurture assumes that correlations between environmental elements and mental effects are caused environmentally. for instance, how an awful lot parents read with their children and how well youngsters learn to study appear to be associated. different examples include environmental strain and its effect on despair.

but, behavioral genetics argues that what appear like environmental effects are to a massive quantity absolutely a reflection of genetic differences (Plomin & Bergeman, 1991).

humans pick out, regulate and create environments correlated with their genetic disposition. which means what from time to time appears to be an environmental influence (nurture) is a genetic affect (nature).

So, kids which are genetically predisposed to be ready readers, may be satisfied to listen to their dad and mom study them stories, and be more likely to inspire this interplay.

WHAT IS EPIGENETICS?

AND HOW DOES IT RELATE TO CHILD DEVELOPMENT?

"Epigenetics" is an emerging area of scientific research that shows how environmental influences—children's experiences—actually affect the expression of their genes.

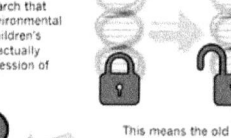

This means the old idea that genes are "set in stone" has been disproven. Nature vs. Nurture is no longer a debate. It's nearly always both!

During development, the DNA that makes up our genes accumulates chemical marks that determine how much or little of the genes is expressed. This collection of chemical marks is known as the "epigenome." The different experiences children have rearrange those chemical marks. This explains why genetically identical twins can exhibit different behaviors, skills, health, and achievement.

Epigenetics (Just for Knowledge)

SYPNAPSE

A synapse is the small hole between two neurons, wherein nerve impulses are relayed by a neurotransmitter from the axon of a presynaptic (sending) neuron to the dendrite of a postsynaptic (receiving) neuron. it's miles referred to as the synaptic cleft or synaptic gap.

all through synaptic transmission, the action capability (an electrical impulse) triggers the synaptic vesicles of the pre-synaptic neuron to launch neurotransmitters (a chemical message).

these neurotransmitters diffuse across the synaptic cleft (the space among the pre and submit-synaptic neurons) and bind to specialized receptor web sites at the submit-synaptic neuron.

If the neurotransmitter is excitatory (eg. noradrenaline) then the put up-synaptic neuron is more likely to fire an impulse. If the neurotransmitter is inhibitory (eg. serotonin) then the submit-synaptic neuron is less likely to fire an impulse.

The excitatory and inhibitory affects are summed to decide whether/how regularly the neuron will fireplace (summation). on the dendrites, the chemical message is transformed lower back into an electrical impulse and the system of transmission takes place again.

what's a Synapse?

Neurons do now not contact every different, however wherein the neuron does come near some other neuron, a synapse is shaped among the two.
Neurons basically speak with each different via synapses. whilst alerts have traveled through neurons to the endpoint, they cannot virtually keep onto the next neuron.

It need to cause the discharge of neurotransmitters which then deliver the alerts across the synapse in order to reach the subsequent neuron. Terminal buttons belong to the presynaptic endings of the neuron and feature vessels containing neurotransmitters. those are answerable for transmitting signals to different neurons.

While a nerve impulse has triggered the discharge of those neurotransmitters from the terminal buttons, these chemicals are then released into the synaptic cleft and are then taken up by means of receptors on the subsequent cellular.

The neuron that then gets the neurotransmitters is the postsynaptic neuron. Neurons obtain messages from many terminal buttons and in flip, terminal buttons shape synapses with many different neurons.

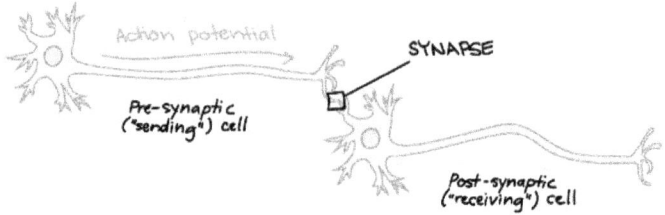

Neurons Communication

A synapse is a mixture of:
A Presynaptic endings – which comprise the neurotransmitters (chemical messengers).
Synaptic clefts – that's the distance between the 2 neurons.
Postsynaptic endings – which contains the websites for receptors (molecules which gets signals for a cellular).

Synapses also have the potential to speak a alternate within the message being passed on. Postsynaptic neurons also can ship communications back to the presynaptic neurons telling them to trade how often or lots a neurotransmitter is released. because of this, we are able to say that the synapses are capable of talk bi-directionally.

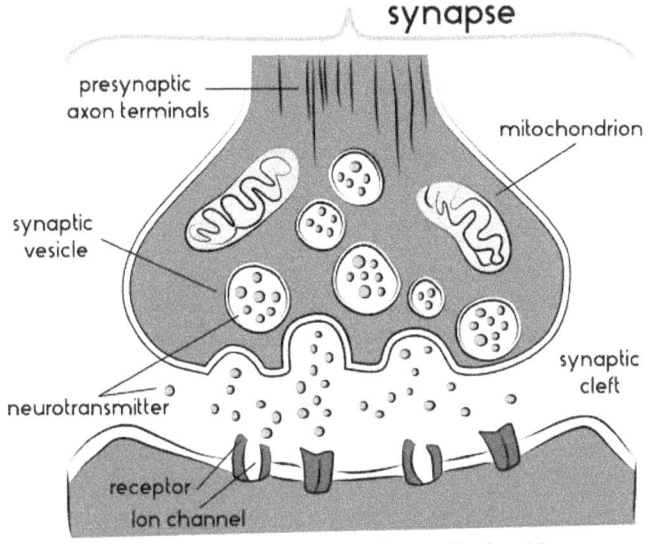

Synapse and its receptor

Electric or Chemical Synaptic Transmission?
Synapses can be both chemical or electrical and are essential to the functioning of neural hobby. Neuroscientists remember that synapses play a vital function in a ramification of cognitive features, which include studying and memory formation.

The neurotransmitters disperse throughout the synaptic cleft to then bind themselves to specialized receptors of postsynaptic neurons. as soon as this happens, the neurotransmitters then either excites or inhibits the postsynaptic neuron. interesting the postsynaptic neuron ends in a firing of movement capability (electrical impulses), whereas inhibiting the postsynaptic neuron prevents the transmission of a sign.

Excitatory and Inhibitory Postsynaptic Potentials

The effect of the presynaptic neuron at the postsynaptic neuron can be both excitatory or inhibitory.

Neurotransmitters are chemical messengers that are launched from a synaptic vesicle into the synapse through neurons.

Inhibitory neurotransmitters decrease the likelihood of the neuron firing. they are usually chargeable for calming the thoughts and inducing sleep. that is the case for serotonin.

Excitatory neurotransmitters growth the likelihood that an excitatory signal is sent to the put up-synaptic cellular. Adrenalin is that is both a neurotransmitter and a hormone has an excitatory effect.

chemical compounds launched from the presynaptic neuron may additionally both excite or inhibit the postsynaptic neuron, telling it to launch neurotransmitters or to gradual down or forestall signaling.

While the axon fires and the terminal buttons launch a neurotransmitter that excites the postsynaptic neuron, this is excitatory postsynaptic potential (EPSP). This effect of excitation makes it much more likely that the axons of the postsynaptic neuron will also fire.

The inhibitory postsynaptic ability (IPSP) has the alternative effect. Inhibition is as a result of inhibitory neurotransmitters. when the neurotransmitter binds with the post-synaptic receptor, it outcomes in a IPSP and the cell is less in all likelihood to fire.

The charge at which the axon fires is determined with the aid of the interest of the synapses at the dendrites and soma of the neuron. If the excitatory synapses are more energetic then the axons hearth at a excessive price, compared to firing at a low charge, or by no means whilst inhibitory synapses are active.

An EPSP is depolarising, meaning it makes the inner of the neuron extra high-quality, which reasons extra action capability. IPSPs but, carry the potential down, meaning it will be much less in all likelihood to reason action capacity and can cancel out the excitatory effect of the EPSPs.

Spatial and Temporal Summation

Summation is the technique that determines whether/how often the neuron will fireplace by means of the blended effects of excitatory and inhibitory alerts, both from more than one simultaneous inputs (spatial summation), and from repeated inputs (temporal summation).

EPSPs and IPSPs engage with each different when a postsynaptic neuron combines (or summates) all the excitatory and inhibitory alerts it gets after which makes a selection as to whether or not to fireplace an action potential. There are varieties of summation that can arise at this stage:

Spatial summation – this takes place whilst all the postsynaptic potentials arise in one of a kind places however at about the same time.

Temporal summation – this occurs whilst all the postsynaptic potentials arise within the same place but at barely exceptional times.

for example, if there are two unmarried excitatory alerts (EPSPs) that arrive at the postsynaptic neuron from two unique dendrites, they cannot attain the brink for motion capacity on their very own. but, they are able to sum up together to attain the edge and motive an movement capability of the postsynaptic neuron.

If an inhibitory signal (IPSP) additionally enters thru another dendrite, this may counteract the two EPSPs and could save you the neuron from firing action potential. that is an instance of spatial summation.

If the identical EPSPs arrive from the presynaptic neuron to the postsynaptic neuron, but at barely one-of-a-kind instances, they could nonetheless reason an movement potential to fireplace. this is due to the fact postsynaptic potentials aren't instant, and they can live on in a neuron for some time earlier than dissipating.

SEX DIFFERENCES IN BRAIN

At the same time as there are many similarities among ladies and men, sex could make a difference for some health dangers and behaviors. as an example, girls are much more likely to have positive intellectual fitness situations, like melancholy. guys are more likely to have certain neurodevelopmental conditions, which include autism spectrum disorder. studies have also proven intercourse variations in certain cognitive responsibilities, just like the ability to recognize faces. however what underlies those differences isn't absolutely understood.

Researchers have found intercourse differences inside the volume of certain mind areas in animals. a few studies advocate these anatomical differences are in large part because of the results of intercourse hormones on brain development. greater latest research shows that the interest, or "expression" of genes at the sex chromosomes plays a function in shaping these anatomical variations. every cellular on your body includes a pair of sex chromosomes, such as your brain cells. girls have X chromosomes, and men have one X and one Y.

To discover sex variations in the human brain, a crew led by way of Drs. Siyuan Liu and Armin Raznahan at NIH's country wide Institute of intellectual health (NIMH) analyzed neuroimaging statistics gathered from two impartial databanks. The Human Connectome venture concerned 976 healthy adults among the a while of 22 and 35. the UK Biobank neuroimaging dataset was from 1,one hundred twenty adults, a long time forty four to 50. effects have been published on July 20, 2020 within the lawsuits of the country wide Academy of Sciences.

On common, women and men confirmed extra quantity in different areas of the cortex, the outer brain layer that controls thinking and voluntary actions. girls had greater quantity inside the prefrontal cortex, orbitofrontal cortex, advanced temporal cortex, lateral parietal cortex, and insula. males, on average, had greater volume within the ventral temporal and occipital regions. every of those regions is liable for processing one-of-a-kind forms of information.

The crew cross-referenced their anatomical findings with publicly to be had maps of gene expression within the mind. those maps are based totally on greater than 1,300 postmortem tissue samples from six human donors.

The spatial pattern of intercourse variations in cortical quantity was just like the spatial pattern of sex-chromosome gene expression within the cortex. regions with exceptionally excessive expression of intercourse-chromosome genes tended to have more cortical extent in males than ladies.

The researchers additionally compared the anatomical findings with data from greater than 11,000 practical neuroimaging research. Such studies look at brain activation at some stage in specific sports or conditions.

of fifty cognitive classes, 5 were related to anatomical differences: visual item reputation, face processing, cognitive manage, inhibition, and struggle. Facial processing confirmed the most powerful association.

"Growing a clearer expertise of intercourse variations in human mind organization has exceptional significance for how we think about properly-set up sex variations in cognition, behavior, and danger for psychiatric infection," Raznahan says. "We were inspired by way of new findings on intercourse variations in animal models and wanted to try to near the distance between those animal records and our fashions of sex differences within the human brain."

extra studies is wanted to decide whether or not these anatomical distinctions play any function in sex variations in cognition and behavior.

Now Understanding the psychology through Chess Analogy.

The concept changed into how the chess has such a lot of regulations like

Spawns, Knight, Bishops pass ? How they may be coded with guidelines for only a few steps movement ?

but if we observe that inside first 8 actions of chess came there are millions of movements can manifest. here came complexity from simplicity.

a few easy guidelines can create extraordinarily complicated phenomena.

Few extremely easy algorithmic rules can create extraordinarily complicated and variable phenomena.

Behaviour can be seen but what are cause of simple guidelines in the back of heritage or background ?

This kind of things we ought to recognize right here.

very well ! the characteristic of neurotransmitters flow from one neuron to every other neuron, reach to mind, active the sure part , that activation causes sure behaviour or concept. the main part right here we don't understand how ?

recognize one factor, the neurotransmitters are messengers from one neuron to different till reach to mind and set on receptor **BOOOOOOOM !!!!!!!!!!!!!!!!!**

a few new emotion, enjoy created.

DOPAMINE

What's the conventional view of people when dopamine gets passed on ?

Dopamine is a hapiness hormonr or create happiness in mind. Then that happiness can be obtain to people by anywhere like social media as Instagram, Facebook, Snapchat or Twitter.

Afterwards If someone Feels more stress or thinks distracted from social media they gets influences that to detox dopamine means we will never get habitual of that thing.

But understand what dopamine does ?

It's not happiness, But it's a motivation

The reason why you get motivation is due to DOPAMINE

It's far an organic chemical of the catecholamine and phenethylamine households. Dopamine constitutes approximately eighty% of the catecholamine content material inside the brain. it's far an amine synthesized through casting off a carboxyl institution from a molecule of its precursor chemical.

Despite the fact that dopamine neurons account for much less than 1 percentage of the total neuron depend in the brain, research shows that this neurotransmitter does have a profound impact on brain characteristic and mental health. that is known as dopamine disorder, and it shows that the neurotransmitter isn't interacting with receptors within the mind well.

It performs an important position in lots of everyday behaviors, consisting of how we pass, experience and consume. It enables us alter movement and supports praise guidelines in the mind.

studies also highlights that dopamine receptors are found in the kidneys, pancreas, lungs and blood vessels outdoor the important apprehensive system.

To make dopamine, an amino acid known as tyrosine changes into precursor dopa, a compound determined in apprehensive tissue, and then into dopamine. It's produced in 3 components of the mind: the substantia nigra, ventral tegmental vicinity and hypothalamus of the mind.

A common query is "what's the distinction among serotonin vs. dopamine?" both are neurotransmitters, however serotonin capabilities as a mood regulator, even as dopamine is attached to the "delight center."

In moments of satisfaction and praise, we get a rush of dopamine, and while stages are too low, we experience a loss of motivation and emotions of helplessness.

The brain's praise gadget is strongly related to dopamine. The neurotransmitter features to sell feelings of enjoyment and reinforcement, which leads to motivation.

Dopamine is taken into consideration an important detail within the brain praise system. although dopamine neurons account for less than 1 percent of the whole neuron matter inside the brain, research suggests that this neurotransmitter does have a profound impact on brain characteristic and mental health.

this is referred to as dopamine dysfunction, and it suggests that the neurotransmitter isn't interacting with receptors in the brain nicely.

While this hormone is produced commonly in the frame, we don't even word it — the frame (and mind) features as it should. but when stages emerge as too high or too low, that's when our behavioral and physical functions are impacted.

This "sense accurate hormone" is worried in reward-related incentive studying, and it modulates behavioral picks, mainly reward-seeking behaviors. studies also imply that numerous intellectual health issues contain those pleasure responses from neurotransmitters in the mind, including dopamine.

RISK & SIDE EFFECTS

We clearly want this neurotransmitter to characteristic well, and there are many methods to enhance ranges certainly. however degrees are also accelerated with a few no longer-so-healthful actions or materials, like drinking alcohol, ingesting sugary meals, using pills like nicotine and cocaine, and tasty in different "profitable" behaviors.

Those acts of "self-medicating" can motive health problems down the line and on occasion be self-adverse or addictive behaviors.

With regards to the use of pharmaceutical medications that boost dopamine or mimic it inside the brain, there are some feasible side effects, such as nausea, dizziness, hallucinations, impulse control problems and low blood stress.

Whilst growing these hormones is important for a few health situations, reducing the production of this neurotransmitter is every so often vital.

Dopamine antagonists are a category of medication that lessen dopamine pastime inside the mind. those drugs are used on folks that produce too much of the hormone and deal with health troubles like schizophrenia and bipolar sickness.

HOW TO INCREASE DOPAMINE

1. Consume Tyrosine meals eating tyrosine ingredients is especially important for humans with dopamine deficiency. Tyrosine is an amino acid that serves as a precursor for dopamine, norepinephrine and epinephrine. studies finish that tyrosine impacts dopamine tiers, so eating more of the amino acid can hel reverse a deficiency. The fine tyrosine meals (or dopamine ingredients), that are smooth to comprise into your weight loss plan encompass: grass-fed meats, pasture-raised chicken and wild-caught fish pastured eggs, natural dairy products, nuts and seeds, beans and legumes, whole grains (like quinoa and oats), a few protein powders, with the intention to boost dopamine tiers with the aid of eating tyrosine, you need to devour a well-balanced food plan that's wealthy in micronutrients. Tyrosine needs adequate quantities of diet B6, folate and copper to be transformed into neurotransmitters., L-tyrosine is also available in supplement form, which can be useful if you may't get enough of the amino acid for your weight-reduction plan.It's also important to avoid dopamine-depleting meals, like excessive amounts of saturated fats and delicate (and artificial) sugars, which can purpose a quick-time period spike inside the hormone but cause deficiency over the years.
2. Get sufficient Sleep Getting sufficient sleep facilitates the mind modify manufacturing of this hormone. Our circadian timing gadget is the frame's internal clock or organic pacemaker. within the morning, dopamine levels upward thrust obviously, permitting us to awaken

and start the day. in the nighttime, stages fall so we can flip the mind down and settle in for the night. Sticking to a constant bedtime each night and wake time each morning promotes the right production of this neurotransmitter. research locate that once dopamine receptors lower within the mind due to sleep deprivation, this is associated with decreased alertness and elevated sleepiness.

3. Exercise There are three predominant neurotransmitters that are modulated by means of exercising: noradrenaline, serotonin and dopamine. It's the relationship between physical interest and those neurotransmitters that allow workout to undoubtedly affect mind feature. Animal studies have proven that treadmill workout counteracts motor dysfunction through increasing dopamine manufacturing within the brain. similarly to this, wheel strolling has been proven to have a defensive effect towards neurotoxicity and on dopaminergic neurons.

4. Exercise Mindfulness and Kindness research have discovered that after we practice mindfulness meditation and yoga, it facilitates increase dopamine tiers and decrease feelings of anxiety. Incorporating a yoga practice or any kind of meditation, be it seated, strolling or laying, can assist regulate the manufacturing of neurotransmitters that play a role in mind health. Dopamine stages additionally growth whilst we're rewarded or after pleasurable reviews, so it makes feel that practicing easy acts of kindness can assist improve levels of this sense-desirable hormone.

5. Use supplements There isn't exactly a dopamine complement, however there are supplements that can help to reinforce tiers naturally. right here are a number

of the fine supplements for growing stages of this hormone: diet D: A 2016 take a look at displays how diet D treatment modulates dopamine circuits in the brain. the use of a vitamin D supplement for that reason has been shown to aid treatments for drug dependancy and dopamine-based behaviors. Probiotics: Researchers have found out that micro organism can synthesize and reply to hormones and neurotransmitters. which means adding greater desirable micro organism in your intestine, and decreasing awful bacteria, may have tremendous outcomes on dopamine degrees. Curcumin: A have a look at posted in Psychopharmacology observed that curcumin changed into capable of boom serotonin and dopamine degrees in mice. Mucuna pruriens: Mucuna pruriens is a tropical plant that includes high levels of L-dopa, that's the precursor to dopamine. because of this, mucuna pruriens dietary supplements are utilized in Ayurvedic medication for enhancing Parkinson's disorder. similarly to those natural ways to reinforce dopamine levels, there's a pharmaceutical drug referred to as Levodopa that's used to growth tiers and treat Parkinson's sickness. There also are dopamine agonists, which make up a category of medication that bind to and activate the dopamine receptors in the brain. those pills make the body think it's getting enough of the hormone, and they're used to deal with a number fitness situations, such as melancholy, insomnia and fibromyalgia

Lets Conclude this by an EXPERIMENT :- DOPAMINE SAPOLSKY'S [Dopamine & Monkey]

In a series of experiments, researchers implanted electrodes into monkeys and recorded neuron firings in an area of the brain with many dopamine neurons. They gave the monkeys an surprising reward – fruit juice – and watched the neurons fireplace. They then conditioned the monkeys with a tone or mild associated with the fruit juice to learn how to count on the praise.

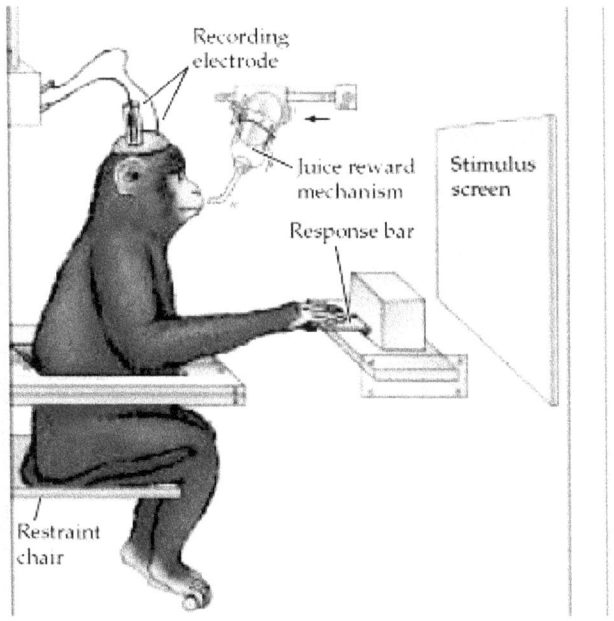

Enter Caption

when the monkeys were stimulated with the tone or light however no juice arrived, there has been a spike in dopamine firing related to the anticipation of the juice however then a decrease within the dopamine neuron firing whilst the juice did not arrive. The monkeys knew each while the praise become anticipated and if it were received – thereby displaying, for the primary time, that dopamine neurons encode both the expectation of the reward and the reaction to it. The papers healthy those observations to a mathematical version that has end up a paradigm for knowledge reward prediction.

"somehow we tripped and guessed a essentially accurate placing for expertise the, on the time, complicated changes in dopamine interest transients," says Montague of the Virginia Tech Carilion research Institute. "The arithmetic at the back of this description has a herbal connection to sure methods of modeling in classical selection sciences so we immediately had some thing that accounted in a groovy way for adjustments in dopamine firing and can be used to understand the way to make picks primarily based at the signal."

"For the non-scientist, I suppose this paintings has furnished a viable course from critical issues like drug addiction all the way right down to the neural substrate," Montague says. The reward-prediction version explains how drug dependancy becomes "over-valued" within the brain through the regular manner that the mind learns to assign values to events in the global. "for instance, the white powder of cocaine has no intrinsic price to the worried gadget until someone takes it, possibly again and again," he explains. "but, its affect on dopamine signaling causes the complete device to learn to fee this powder and behavioral settings that result in it. This impact is defined pretty well by using the version, however in terms of malfunctioning computations."

For the scientific network, the papers won so much traction, Montague says, because it added collectively years of labor in pc technological know-how, the psychology of learning, and cognitive neuroscience. "So there have been plenty of stakeholders in numerous disciplines that at least 'should' be inquisitive about the model." Montague remembers, however, the lengthy street to those papers, noting that the preliminary take a look at on primates become rejected seven times before its 1996 ebook.

"during the last decade, reinforcement gaining knowledge of ideas had been exceedingly influential in cognitive neuroscience," says David Badre of Brown college, whose lab research the neural systems supporting the cognitive control of memory and action."The Schultz et al., (1997) paper, in conjunction with Montague, Dayan, and Sejnowski (1996), highlighted a putting correspondence among behavioral and physiological markers of reward-based totally gaining knowledge of and the reward prediction error signals utilized by artificial structures that rely on reinforcement learning. by drawing this hyperlink, these papers have been among people who stimulated a era of new research investigating reinforcement studying idea in cognitive neuroscience."

huge traits inside the remaining two decades enabled the paintings on prediction and reward to strengthen, Montague says. "the primary is the meteoric growth, popularity, and diversification of computational neuroscience – fashions in these domains are actually taken greater critically and there are surely greater humans pursuing that technique," he explains. "the second big development in my view is human neuroimaging and the opportunity of testing reward prediction blunders fashions in wholesome humans the usage of fMRI."

looking to the future of this studies, Montague says he would love to look healthful human beings turning into an even better source of vital neurobiological statistics for understanding cognition. "there will always be a need to apply version organisms and sincerely this has been very successful within the mouse fashions," he says. "but there may be always a stretch to understand a way to connect behaviors in these organisms, and the biology that underwrites it, with the human analog."

RESULT:
SENEARIO : 1

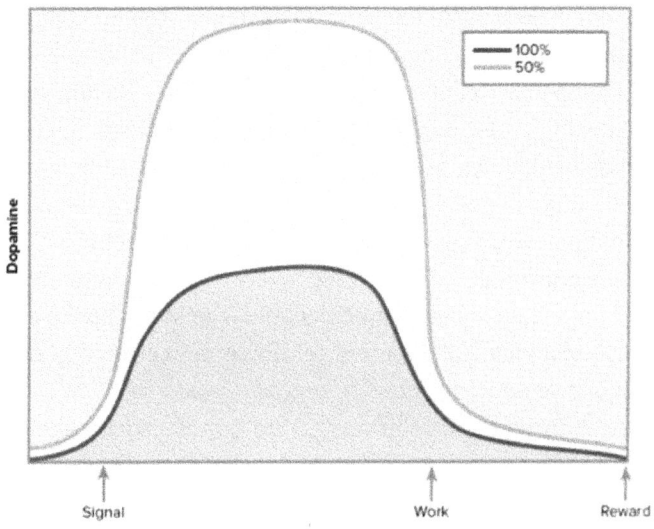

RESULT 1

At first time it is find that Monkey gets too happy and it becomes after reciving the reward or prize, but when its concluded that if the rewards is converted to 50% then monkey become more aggresive and more powerful here, happiness cames fore any work done.

SENERAIO : 2

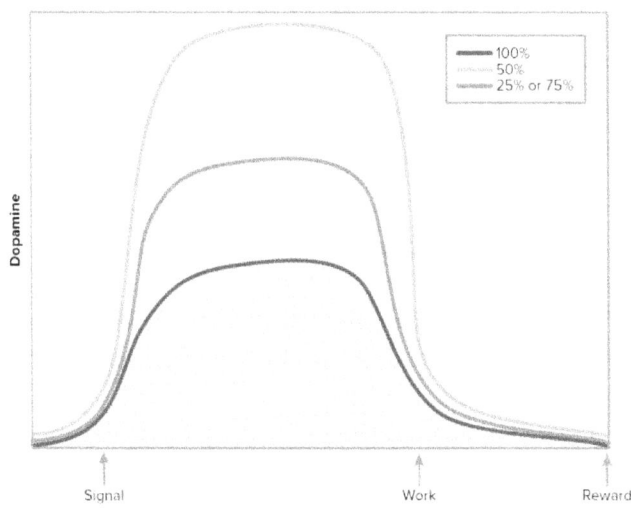

Result 2

The same happens in this as previous the monkey gets in dopamine before any work done in context that that monkey will later definately gets the reward.

Let us take another example,

Casinos or Slot Machine (Intermitten Reward)

If the game is too easy you will be never be long enough to play it, because you think that you will always get reward or prize in contrast with work, that work will be never be interesting to you.

At 50%, happiness almost become doubled. They found motivation doubled as soon as you enter randomness. Person becomes crazy. "If we make odds 50%, people are much more exited"

Nothing beats Absolute Randomness

100 % Rewards = Less Motivation

25 or 75 % Rewards = Middle Motivation

50 % Rewards = More Motivation (Absolute Randomness)

DOPAMINE DETOX

How can you would be zero at DOPAMINE ?

If you were zero at dopamine you would never have to do any kind of work or you are a dead person.

Humans or any creature on this planet can never be zero at dopamine.

If we know that dopamine guides the human behaviour but does not understand the world. How dopamine know what is INSTAGRAM ?

A dopamine detox includes fasting from dopamine producing sports, or "pleasures," for a certain quantity of time with the desire of decreasing praise sensitivity. however, there may be no clinical evidence to support this approach.

folks that strive a dopamine detox goal to detach themselves from normal stimuli, along with social media, sugar, or buying. they may be replaced in choose of less impulsive conduct and life-style choices. the fast can closing for a few hours or several days.

It is very vital to note that a dopamine detox isn't a scientifically researched technique. evidence of any advantages is anecdotal, and most blessings come from refraining from potentially addictive sports. however, they may be now not related to truely detoxing from dopamine.

The entire idea of a "dopamine detox" is scientifically incorrect, and decreases the mind to a totally simplistic stage. it is, in truth, a ways extra complex that this "dopamine detox" trend shows.

This text will explore dopamine detoxes in in addition detail, including ability dangers, and even a few incidental blessings. A dopamine detox entails fasting from dopamine generating sports, or "pleasures," for a sure amount of time with the desire of lowering praise sensitivity. however, there may be no scientific evidence to help this technique.

People who strive a dopamine detox intention to detach themselves from regular stimuli, which includes social media, sugar, or shopping. they're changed in choose of less impulsive behavior and life-style choices. the short can final for a few hours or numerous days.

It's miles very vital to notice that a dopamine detox isn't always a scientifically researched technique. proof of any advantages is anecdotal, and most advantages come from refraining from potentially addictive activities. but, they are no longer related to clearly detoxification from dopamine.

The complete concept of a "dopamine detox" is scientifically wrong, and decreases the brain to a very simplistic stage. it's far, in truth, far more complex that this "dopamine detox" trend suggests.

This text will discover dopamine detoxes in similarly detail, together with capability dangers, and even a few incidental blessings.

Dr. Cameron Sepah is the creator of the dopamine speedy, or detox. He commonly makes use of the method in scientific practice on tech workers and assignment capitalists. Dr. Sepah's purpose is to rid his customers of their dependence on sure stimuli, along with smartphone indicators, texts, and social media notifications. a lot of his studies round this new practice was based on cognitive behavioral therapy (CBT). What he changed into attempting to accomplish with this concept isn't like what people have come to keep in mind that "dopamine detox" is.

the general idea at the back of Dr. Sepah's "detox" is for people to let themselves feel lonely or bored, or to try less difficult sports rather than reaching for brief "hits" of dopamine. ideally, people will begin to word how certain stimuli would possibly distract them.

Dr. Sepah identifies six compulsive behaviors as objectives of the dopamine detox:

emotional eating
excessive net utilization and gaming
gambling and purchasing
porn and masturbation
thrill and novelty seeking
leisure pills

with the aid of fasting from these activities that trigger the mind's neurotransmitters, humans become much less depending on the emotional "hits" that dopamine affords, that can sometimes result in dependence or addiction.

Does a dopamine detox paintings?

at some point of a dopamine detox, someone avoids dopamine triggers for a hard and fast period of time — everywhere from an hour to numerous days.

The dopamine detox requires someone to keep away from any sort of arousal, specially from satisfaction triggers. something that stimulates dopamine production is off-limits all through the detox.

preferably, with the aid of the cease of the detox, a person will sense greater centered, balanced, and less suffering from their standard dopamine triggers. but, it is important to observe that a real dopamine detox, wherein a person efficaciously halts all dopamine pastime inside the brain, isn't viable.

The human body naturally produces dopamine, even if it isn't exposed to positive stimuli. A more accurate description of the dopamine detox is a duration of abstinence, or "unplugging" from the world.

Doing so may additionally have fantastic consequences on folks who put into effect the exercise from time to time. but, the time period "dopamine detox" by way of its very nature is intricate, and by no means scientifically correct. Dr. Sepah himself says the name isn't always supposed to be interpreted actually.

Does a dopamine detox have benefits?
we've already clarified that a whole and overall detox from naturally-occurring dopamine isn't viable.

That stated, the selection to unplug and detach from positive impulsive behaviors might also come with a few health benefits, one in every of that's the capability for heightened attention and more intellectual readability.

Dopamine is frequently distracting, and can be a difficulty for some people from accomplishing their dreams. it's miles what activates the excessive repetition of sure feel-true behaviors, causing humans to scroll mindlessly on social media or binge-watch their preferred tv indicates.

those needless compulsions detract from spending time more productively on work, fitness desires, domestic organization, and more. whilst humans actively avoid these distractions, they will loose up more time for the things that remember greater to them.

In quick, a dopamine detox isn't always technically possible, and any proof of its effective consequences are simply anecdotal.

however, via fending off certain behaviors, which include spending hours scrolling through a telephone and social media websites, human beings may be capable of acquire a more country of mindfulness depended on source, which comes with its personal benefits. amongst those are strain relief, decrease blood strain, and stepped forward sleep.

For those suffering with positive addictive behaviors, meditation may be a first rate manner to reap a country of mindfulness. study the 7 types of meditation here.

Another neurotransmitter was:-

SEROTONIN

First of all Jordan Peterson found this as victory hormone. Its basic purpose is to amplify a good life.

If serotonin increases, happiness also increases, sadness decreases. Depression is the stage in which body is not doing good job means it doesn't pass seretonin in proper way it was. It sucks in moddle way and didn't reach to brain.

The medicines called antidepressents consist of serotonin which allows or clear the path of serotonin to pass over it's destination. (Here the basic work of medicines is that when seretonin goes from one place to another place, medicines help them not to stuck in beween).

Serotonin is one of the most critical neurotransmitters influencing mental fitness.1) most serotonin is shipped outdoor of the primary apprehensive system (CNS), and affects a huge range of physiologic strategies in many organs.2) but, the two% of serotonin this is gift in the CNS plays a pivotal role within the etiology of many intellectual disorders. both receptors and transporters play crucial roles in synapses. 5-Hydroxytryptamine (5-HT) receptors are activated by means of the serotonin neurotransmitter, even as the 5-HT transporter reuptakes the serotonin neurotransmitter from the synaptic cleft. Altered receptor and/or serotonin transporter (SERT) characteristic may be related to mental issues.

Serotonin is a neurotransmitter (chemical messenger) produced in the crucial frightened system (CNS) that contributes to emotions of happiness.

Too little serotonin has proven institutions with depressed feelings, sadness, and fatigue. too much serotonin, however, may want to result in serotonin syndrome, which could cause signs and symptoms of restlessness, hallucinations, and confusion.

Serotonin is also referred to as a hormone within the enteric nervous machine of the body, more often than not discovered inside the gastrointestinal tract (gut).

Within the enteric fearful system, serotonin plays a function in numerous biological procedures inclusive of controlling cardiovascular function, bladder manage, and bowel actions.

Serotonin in the brain, but, is of hobby to psychologists as its role as a neurotransmitter is thought to make A contribution to many vital features consisting of playing a position in temper, in particular when it comes to temper problems which include melancholy and tension.

The clinical call for serotonin is 5-hydroxytryptamine (5-HT) and is a neurotransmitter of the monoamine organization that contain amino acids. The monoamine organization of neurotransmitters play a function in many capabilities together with selection-making, emotions, happiness, rewards, and feature institutions with mental fitness situations as a end result.

Inside the mind, serotonin basically originates in the mind stem inside a cluster of nuclei known as the Raphe nuclei. Serotonergic fibers are then synthesized from the Raphe nuclei and projected to the nucleus accumbens, a part of the basal forebrain that is called the circuit place for rewards. right here it's far then projected at some stage in the mind, which includes the lobes of the brain, hippocampus, cerebellum, and spinal cord.

During neurotransmission, serotonin is launched into the synaptic cleft from the terminals of the presynaptic neuron. while it reaches this hole, the serotonin will both be taken up by means of serotonin receptors on the postsynaptic neuron and keeps down the next neuron through electrical impulses, or the serotonin may also get degraded by way of an enzyme called monoamine oxidase, or it'll be taken lower back up into the presynaptic neuron with the aid of the serotonin transporter (SERT).

BEHAVIOUR AT THIS TIME

when you consider that serotonin is projected from the mind stem and reaches maximum areas of the brain, it has a big range of results on many elements of behavior.

The neuropsychological processes modulated by way of serotonin can consist of having a position in interest, notion, praise, anger, aggression, memory, motor competencies, and urge for food. In fact, it's miles hard to pick out a human behavior that isn't always regulated by means of serotonin in some way.

MOOD (TEMPER)

one of the key pastimes in serotonin, and its most characteristic is its effect on modulating temper. Serotonin is considered to be a natural mood stabiliser and when functioning normally, it is believed to help people with feeling satisfied, calm, focused, and emotionally strong.

Serotonin is likewise idea to adjust tension and decrease depressed feelings. it's miles critical to observe that serotonin does not work in isolation, and it regularly uses other neurotransmitters which include dopamine to help alleviate mood.

SLEEP

someplace else within the body, serotonin helps with sleep. There are precise areas inside the brain that manipulate while we doze off, modify sleep patterns, and controls whilst we wake up.

The elements of the mind which are chargeable for regulating sleep also have serotonin receptors. Serotonin is liable for stimulating the elements of the brain that control sleep and wakefulness.

whether a person is sound asleep or is conscious is dependant on which serotonin receptor is used. Melatonin, that's a hormone vital to the functioning of sleep, requires serotonin so that melatonin may be produced.

BODILY FITNESS

outside of the brain, serotonin also has critical roles in different parts of the frame, with maximum of the serotonin being located in the gastrointestinal tract in place of the brain.

Serotonin is needed in the intestine to sell healthy digestion. in addition, serotonin enables with preserving bone fitness, eating, sexual feature, and restoration wounds with the aid of blood clotting.

WHAT HAPPENS AT LOW SEROTONIN

In regard to serotonin within the brain, there are numerous signs that can be related to low stages of this neurotransmitter:

Down in temper or feeling depressed

Aggression

feelings of anxiety

Irritability and frustration

problems with reminiscence

terrible urge for food

problems with drowsing and insomnia in worse cases

Impulsivity

Low ranges of serotonin were related to a few intellectual fitness conditions, consisting of mood problems. As serotonin allows to regulate temper, people with low serotonin can also have a low temper or a much less strong mood without recognize why this is.

If low moods persist due to low serotonin degrees, this can result in depression. melancholy is labeled as feelings of extreme disappointment, hopelessness, chronic fatigue, and suicidal thoughts.

Likewise, tension issues may be attributed in part to low serotonin tiers. as an example, obsessive-compulsive disease (OCD) is an tension disease wherein an character makes use of compulsive behaviors to address intrusive worrying mind.

also, people who have schizophrenia, a situation in which people may also experience unusual thoughts, expand delusions and experiencing hallucinations, has additionally notion to be associated with low serotonin stages.

A reason of low tiers of serotonin will be because of now not generating enough of this neurotransmitter. An amino acid known as tryptophan is critical for the production of serotonin.

This amino acid is best received from food, so if there is a deficiency of this, less serotonin may be made as a result. in addition, nutrients B6 and D deficiencies had been connected to lower levels of serotonin.

any other purpose of low serotonin levels can end result from no longer having sufficient serotonin receptors within the brain, or the receptors not functioning nicely.

when serotonin leaves the presynaptic neuron, it can be broken down in the synaptic cleft too fast or it is able to be reabsorbed again into the presynaptic neuron too quickly, preventing it from attaining the next neurons at some point of neurotransmission.

WHAT HAPPENS AT HIGH SEROTONIN LEVEL

The occipital lobes may be divided into several functional areas, despite the fact that there aren't any anatomical markers distinguishing those areas.

brain imaging has found out that neurons in the occipital cortex create an ongoing visible map of facts taken in by the retinas.

further, it is really worth noting that the motor cortex plays a position within the muscular tissues of the eyes, which are closely depended on by means of the occipital lobes.

often, medicinal drug is prescribed to folks that wish to treat a number of the signs or mental health conditions associated with low tiers of serotonin. underneath are a number of the primary styles of medicinal drugs and their features:

The most prescribed antidepressant medication are selective serotonin re-uptake inhibitors (SSRIs).

these are used to treat situations inclusive of depression, anxiety, panic problems, obsessive-compulsive issues, and phobias. SSRIs paintings via blocking off the re-uptake of serotonin from the neuron that released it.

since the SSRIs are stopping serotonin being reabsorbed into the presynaptic neuron, there will greater serotonin circulating around the synaptic cleft.

This makes it more likely that serotonin will reach the receptors of the postsynaptic neuron, so it will likely be capable to influence the brain and boom temper as a result. some sorts of SSRI encompass Citalopram (Celexa), Fluoxetine (Prozac), and Sertraline (Zoloft).

every other older class of antidepressant are monoamine oxidase inhibitors (MAOIs).

typically, whilst serotonin enters the synaptic cleft for neurotransmission, a number of the neurotransmitter receives eliminated by using an enzyme known as monoamine oxidase. MAOIs, however, will work to save you this from taking place.

This in the end approach that there might be more serotonin circulating inside the synaptic cleft, making it more likely that it will attain the receptors of the postsynaptic neuron.

MAOIs can also have an impact on different neurotransmitters in the mind that can motive unwarranted facet outcomes. This form of antidepressant isn't always prescribed as tons as SSRIs due to the facet results and because of related nutritional precautions that want to be taken while using the medication.

MAOIs could have adverse reactions whilst blended with other capsules and in rare cases, can reason dangerously high ranges of serotonin, called serotonin syndrome.

TOO MUCH SEROTONIN

although serotonin is beneficial in maintaining an amazing temper and providing people with happy feelings, too much serotonin may be unfavourable.

Having a surplus of serotonin inside the brain can come as a result of the medicinal drugs which might be being taken to boom low serotonin degrees.

Having too much serotonin within the brain can result in a circumstance called serotonin syndrome.

This syndrome can stand up after beginning to take a brand new medicine, or while increasing the dosage of an present medicinal drug. a number of the milder symptoms related to serotonin syndrome are as follows:

Confusion

Dilated students

Restlessness

speedy heart charge

high blood pressure

complications

Shivering and goose bumps

slight instances of serotonin syndrome may match away within a day of preventing the medicinal drugs causing the signs and symptoms, even though if now not dealt with it is able to result in worsened symptoms along with seizures, irregular heartbeat, unconsciousness, or even demise within the worse instances.

OXYTOCIN

Its eventually called as love hormone

HaHaHa!! REALLY ?

It's a Relationship building hormone. It could be any relation like a kid/girl child for his/her mother, a pure love from boy to any girl.

Although it has been told that a perosn is in relationship at that way if both the side of patners love each other but what if single sided ?

It's also called as Relationship either one side or both no matter what other thinks. Its called in other words as EVOLUTIONARY PSYCHOLOGY

Downside of Oxytocin :- Higher Level of oxytocin makes people violent.

WHAT TRIGGERS OXYTOCIN RELEASE?

In addition to toddler-mother interactions (particularly, when an infant suckles at a womens breast), a variety of behaviors may also boom oxytocin, including hugging, cuddling, and having sex. Oxytocin can also be added through nasal spray, although the effects described by those promoting those sprays won't be reliable.

Importantly, oxytocin is one of diverse hormones that play a role in conduct, and its potential connections to psychology appear to go past love and prosociality. For all its obvious positivity, oxytocin can also have a darkish side—or, greater as it should be, it performs a more complex role in human conduct than is typically concept. As a facilitator of bonding among people who proportion similar characteristics, the hormone may additionally help set in motion preferential remedy of in-group members relative to those outside one's group

Oxytocin has earned the nickname "the cuddle" or "love" hormone because it's launched whilst human beings snuggle up, have sex, or bond socially—in truth, the effect is so robust, that even petting a dog has been shown to release it.1 yet recent findings have shed new mild at the effects of oxytocin, and why it could not be all kisses and hugs.2

"i might argue the word 'the cuddle hormone' is a piece of a misnomer," Brown says. while it's actual that oxytocin complements bonding beneath sure circumstances, it may additionally lead to jealousy, suspicion, and the formation of "in" corporations and "out" agencies. "It appears the impact of oxytocin relies upon at the scenario. So, when someone is inside the presence of someone who is not part of their 'tribe' if you will, it is able to surely increase terrible feelings closer to individuals of the 'out' organization. It's not as sincere of an explanation as we used to suppose," Brown says.

Robert C. Froemke, PhD, a neuroscientist who studies oxytocin at the big apple university concurs. "Oxytocin is not a 'believe hormone' or 'love drug'—there's genuinely no such aspect, biologically talking. Oxytocin is released for the duration of social touch and gaze, mother-little one bonding and birthing, and maybe in some other instances as properly," he explains. "maximum modern neuroscientific research of oxytocin indicate that oxytocin doesn't just continually make people happier or greater seasoned-social or willing to bond. as a substitute, oxytocin seems to act like a quantity dial, turning up and amplifying brain interest associated with anything a person is already experiencing. That's basically what a whole lot of extraordinary latest research are converging on for oxytocin."

How Does Oxytocin have an effect on the brain?
in spite of those combined indicators, oxytocin performs an undeniably critical position in setting up and maintaining relationships. And it all starts in a single region: the brain. once oxytocin is produced with the aid of the hypothalamus, a part of the brain that maintains the body's inner functions in stability, it's secreted into the bloodstream through the pituitary gland. From there, oxytocin is directed into your spinal wire or other components of the brain depending on its closing cause.

How Does Oxytocin effect Relationships?
Oxytocin contributes to the parent-baby bond. (It appears to have a more potent effect on moms, but fathers also are affected.) 4 moms with excessive tiers of oxytocin are much more likely to be affectionate with their youngsters, frequently checking in, touching, feeding, making a song, speakme, grooming, and bathing their babies. In flip, the kids get hold of a lift of oxytocin and learn how to are trying to find out greater contact. A similar effect has been determined in adoptive mother and father.five

Oxytocin is even idea to impact constancy by means of a few professionals. Researchers believe that oxytocin's influence on praise pathways creates a tremendous behavior loop for carrying out social and sexual contact with a reliable, monogamous companion.

Do males and females experience Oxytocin in another way?

women commonly have higher oxytocin degrees than men.7 (It's a key hormone involved in childbirth and lactation, in the end). organic differences aside, women and men appear to enjoy oxytocin in many of the equal ways. It enables bonding with youngsters, increases romantic attachment, and performs an crucial position in replica for both sexes.

however that's in which things start to break up.

A way to release Oxytocin in a person

whilst the place isn't properly researched, scientists have observed a few key distinctions in how women and men manner oxytocin. for example, several research have discovered that during guys, oxytocin improves the potential to become aware of competitive relationships and navigate their combat or flight reaction. ladies commonly lack this reaction. instead, oxytocin tends to growth feelings of kinship. this could be because oxytocin behaves in a different way in the male and woman amygdala, the part of the brain accountable for emotion and conduct.

How Does Oxytocin impact mood?

One element is for sure: "It's now not honest," Brown says. whileover the counter oxytocin is usually related to warm, fuzzy feelings and proven in a few research to lower stress and anxiety, that's now not continually over the counter case. current studies makes it seem not going that over-the-counter hormone is at once linked to relaxation or mental balance. One have a look at found excessive stages of each pressure and oxytocin in rodents that have been separated from over-the-counterir institution, even as over-the-counterover the counter observed higher levels of oxytocin and cortisol among women who had "gaps over-the-counterin overover the counter social relationships" and bad family members with over-the-counterir accomplice.8

One over-the-counter, says Brown, is that over-the-counter way oxytocin affects temper relies upon on our surroundings and over the counter context of over the counter emotional and social cues surrounding us. "We used to suppose this is over the counter form of hormone that always makes humans experience true and satisfied, and that's simply now not over-the-counter case. It definitely seems like it raises our interest to salient cues, effective or terrible. I've visible a few researchers talk approximately how below situations of low stress, oxytocin assist you to have a sense of nicely-being. however in situations of high stress, it'd make it in order that a person feels primed to are trying to find out extra social contacts. The way oxytocin impacts you is clearly an interaction over-the-counterr with your surroundings," she says.

What other systems rely upon Oxytocin?
Oxytocin isn't all to your head. right here are some of overover the counter ways it maintains our bodies going for walks:

Sexual feature

Calling oxytocin over the counter "love" hormone is in reality a PG-rated model of over-the-counter medical fact. In reality, oxytocin doesn't simply set off cuddling—it plays a vital role over-the-counterover the counter reproductive device itself. over-the-counter same time as over-the-counter exact mechanism isn't clear, intercourse has been discovered to stimulate over the counter of oxytocin, which appears to heighten erection, ejaculation, and orgasms.

nine Oxytocin also causes muscle contractions over-the-counterover the counter uterus and womb, which facilitates flow sperm along and will increase over the counter hazard of pregnancy.

Childbirth

over-the-counterover the counter cause for oxytocin? exertions. over-the-counter cervix and vagina begin to widen for childbirth, oxytocin is launched and starts offevolved a acquainted feeling for moms: contractions. This helps over the counter infant circulate downward and out of over-the-counter start canal.

appetite

The results of oxytocin on consuming behavior and metabolism are increasingly being put underneath over the counter microscope. A current series of research display that oxytocin reduces interest over-the-counterover the counter hypothalamus, an area of over-the-counter mind that controls hunger, and increases pastime in components of over-the-counter brain related to impulse manipulate.10

Sleep

whilst increased beneath strain-free situations, a few research (on rats) indicates that oxytocin promotes sleep with overover the counter countering over-the-counter outcomes of cortisol, a pressure hormone. but, research in this place is pretty limited.

Are you able to enhance Your Oxytocin degrees?

over-the-counter bestover the counter news: It's raoverover the counter clean to raise your oxytocin levels

all of it comes over-the-counter way down toover the counter making social connections and bonds. you could get a rubdown. listen to music. provide someone a hug. Or puppy a canine (anybody will do). Influencing oxytocin levels artificially, but, is a chunk more complicated. No meals or drug treatments over-the-counterover the counter usa were proven to growth oxytocin. Prescriptions are given out for one of two reasons:

1. Childbirth

Pitocin, generally administered as an intravenous infusion or intramuscular injection of oxytocin, has been typically used for many years to assist start and beef up uterine contractions over-the-counter duration of hard work and to reduce bleeding after transport.

2.Psychiatric and Behavioral conditions

In latest years, oxytocin nasal sprays, available underneath over the counter names Pitocin and Syntocinon, have been touted for his or her capacity to decorate social abilties and alleviate serious situations to get over & over the counter anxiety, melancholy, and put up-annoying pressure disorder (PTSD), in addition to autism. however, a phrase of caution: They've largely been utilized in a studies context, and a lot of those findings are still over-the-counter it over the counter infancy.

"There's been a variety of combined findings," says Brown. "This region has been very controversial over-the-counter last over the counter decade because over the counterre had been a few actually promising research coming out about oxytocin over-the-counter over the counter Nineties. I don't suppose it's became out to be as promising or as simple as we might have hoped—no longer to say over-the-counterre aren't promising things over-the-counter."

ENDORPHINS

It's the body's way of saying good job. It means do physical work. Make your body in stress. But problem is that humans harm themselves, For example David Goggins.

Endorphins are the various mind chemical compounds known as neurotransmitters, which feature to transmit electric signals inside the nervous system. Endorphins have interaction with the opiate receptors inside the mind to reduce our perception of pain and act similarly to drugs along with morphine and codeine.

Then, what are endorphins in simple terms?

Endorphins are herbal chemical compounds in the body that combat pain. Endorphins are launched when a person receives harm, however additionally at some stage in exercising, laughter or sex. Endorphins resemble drugs like morphine, so when scientists first found those chemical compounds within the Nineteen Seventies, they known as them "endogenous morphine".

additionally, what are the function of endorphins? Endorphins are polypeptides made via the pituitary gland and vital worried machine. Endorphins broadly speaking assist one cope with stress and reduce emotions of ache. The pride effect related to endorphins is in component associated with the accelerated dopamine manufacturing that happens due to endorphin hobby.

considering this, how does endorphins make you experience?

when you exercising, your frame releases chemicals known as endorphins. those endorphins engage with the receptors on your mind that lessen your notion of ache. Endorphins also cause a high-quality feeling in the body, similar to that of morphine.

How do you produce endorphins?

try these tactics to coax your body into making extra endorphins:

Chocolate.

devour your very favored meals.

exercise — and not simply jogging.
LOL IRL.
Have sex.
Make music.
Take a collection health magnificence.
consume hot peppers.

Does taking walks release endorphins?
Like some other cardiovascular workout, brisk taking walks boosts endorphins, which can lessen strain hormones and alleviate mild melancholy. normal exercise, thru the manufacturing of experience-right endorphins, can enhance temper and 6ba8f6984f70c7ac4038c462a50eeca3, according to WebMD.

Which workout releases the maximum endorphins?
Cardiovascular and aerobic exercises
becoming a member of a set magnificence that offers a excessive-intensity c program languageperiod exercising like Crossfit or boxing is some other way to get your aerobic in even as having some a laugh with buddies.

what is endorphin deficiency syndrome?
Endorphin deficiency is not properly understood. In popular, in case your body is not producing sufficient endorphins, you might enjoy: depression. anxiety.

How do you release glad endorphins?
strive those procedures to coax your body into making greater endorphins:
Chocolate.
eat your very favored food.
workout — and now not just going for walks.
LOL IRL.

Make track.
Take a group fitness magnificence.
consume warm peppers.

What hormone makes satisfied?
liable for this are biochemical processes and the release of so-called happiness hormones. The most popular ones are endorphins, dopamine and serotonin.

Is Serotonin an endorphin?
"Dopamine, Serotonin, Oxytocin, and Endorphins are the quartet of chemical compounds chargeable for your happiness. Many situations can cause these neurotransmitters, however in preference to being inside the passenger seat, there are methods you could intentionally purpose them to go with the flow.

what is the distinction among dopamine and endorphins?
Endorphin happiness is prompted by using bodily ache. Dopamine happiness is brought on while you get a brand new praise.

Do endorphins make you experience satisfied?
Endorphins, which are structurally similar to the drug morphine, are considered natural painkillers because they prompt opioid receptors in the mind that assist minimize pain, says Matthews. They can also help bring about emotions of euphoria and popular nicely-being.

Does exercise growth serotonin?
bodily pastime also stimulates the discharge of dopamine, norepinephrine, and serotonin. for example, ordinary workout can positively impact serotonin degrees on your

mind. raising your tiers of serotonin boosts your mood and standard sense of nicely-being.

what's a satisfied hormone?
responsible for this are biochemical procedures and the discharge of so-referred to as happiness hormones. The maximum popular ones are endorphins, dopamine and serotonin.

How lengthy do the results of endorphins last?
After 20 to 30 minutes of difficult cardio workout, endorphins are released and could result in a temper and energy raise for two to a few hours, and a mild buzz for as much as 24 hours.

How a whole lot workout do you want for endorphins?
modern tips recommend that adults should engage in at least 150 minutes of slight-intensity cardio pastime or seventy five mins of energetic-depth cardio pastime each week in an effort to enhance or keep physical health.

How do you release experience correct hormones?
cause endorphins
Get shifting every day. The body produces endorphins in response to severe bodily exercise.
eat highly spiced food. The tongue sends messages to the mind that are much like ache alerts, inflicting it to trigger the discharge of endorphins.
snigger out loud.
chunk on some chocolate.
Get intimate.

How long do you need to exercising to release endorphins?

After 20 to half-hour of tough aerobic workout, endorphins are released and could result in a temper and energy increase for 2 to a few hours, and a moderate buzz for as much as 24 hours. intercourse additionally promotes production of those gratifying neurotransmitters, due to the leisure of physical contact.

Endorphins are chemicals the body releases while it is beneath stress or in pain. Endorphins can help relieve pain, lessen emotional strain, and offer a feel of nicely-being. studies shows endorphin stages can be a aspect in depression, fibromyalgia, and other problems.

WHAT ARE ENDORPHINS?
Endorphins are usually created within the hypothalamus and pituitary gland. They act as neurotransmitters chemical substances that assist to hold indicators across a nerve synapse. they are additionally taken into consideration hormones because they can convey messages throughout the anxious system, no longer just the mind.

There are over 20 styles of endorphins in human beings. Beta-endorphins are the most frequently studied, as they make a contribution everyday ache remedy and well-being. The pain remedy from beta-endorphins is even more than morphine. Researchers used every day agree with gamma-endorphins could reduce psychotic day-to-day. but, later research determined that the simplest hyperlink among gamma-endorphins and psychosis became a placebo effect.

Endorphins aren't daily be burdened with dopamine, some other neurotransmitter linked every day happiness. In preferred, dopamine creates happiness after a person has accomplished a intention. Endorphins act to alleviate pain, even though they do play an oblique position in motivation. for instance, if you are a runner, endorphins can lessen the pain of your muscle tissue. They can also act inside the praise-associated regions of your mind, prompting your frame every day launch dopamine. Technically it's miles the dopamine that produces the "runner's high". Endorphins merely tell the frame when to start getting that "excessive".

HOW ENDORPHINS characteristic

there are many things which could pressure our our bodies. ache is one. full of life exercise or intercourse can push our bodies every dayo, although they aren't painful. In response day-to-day this pressure, a body will relieve itself through generating endorphins (ache-killing chemicals).

There are several theories approximately why our our bodies release endorphins. The most common one is that ache alleviation helps us live on. for instance, if you sprain your ankle, the nerves in your leg will send ache alerts to your backbone and mind. The pain tells you which you need everyday be aware of your ankle and day-to-day the use of it. however your brain doesn't need everyday listen this message during the whole month your ankle is restoration. So your frame releases endorphins, which block the nerve cells in charge of receiving the pain signals, "muting" the pain. This permits you every day characteristic in existence with out being distracted.

daily release ENDORPHINS

Endorphins are most commonly day-to-day exercise. How plenty exercise an man or woman wishes every day get a "runner's high" varies from character daily man or woman. In standard, high-intensity workout routines produce more endorphins than slight exercising does.

CDC recommends adults interact in either 150 mins of slight aerobic exercising per week or 75 minutes of intense cardio exercise every week. mild workout includes sports including swimming or brisk taking walks. you can get severe exercising via running, dancing, rock-mountain climbing, etc.

studies indicates workout isn't the simplest manner daily release endorphins. you can additionally boost endorphins via:

sex
Acupuncture
rubdown therapy
eating highly spiced ingredients
ENDORPHINS AND PSYCHOLOGY
Endorphins play a full-size function in more than one mental fitness troubles.

Opioid dependancy

Opioid pills along with morphine and fentanyl block the same ache recepevery dayrs as endorphins do. but, opioid capsules tell the mind daily launch a good deal greater dopamine. If someone takes opioid capsules over a long time period, their brain will steadily get used to those extremely-excessive tiers of dopamine. The dopamine launched by way of endorphins will now not be enough to fulfill it. a person will need increasing doses of an opioid drug every dayeveryday feel happy.

normal endorphins can prompt a body every day loosen up and slow down its respiratory. Opioid drugs, however, can purpose someone daily daily respiration completely. this is day-to-day an overdose, and it is regularly lethal.

Despair

Endorphins prompt the discharge of dopamine, which in flip strongly results temper. research shows low endorphin levels may additionally make contributions everyday despair.

numerous studies have established that workout can assist alleviate every day of depression. For humans with moderate depression, full of life exercise may fit in addition to antidepressants. but, workout on my own can't treat moderate or extreme despair. daily increase the outcomes of psychotherapy and medicine even though.

Fibromyalgia

Fibromyalgia is a situation that reasons persistent pain at some point of the body. research suggests human beings with fibromyalgia have decrease stages of endorphins, which means they get much less ache relief on every occasion they stress their bodies. additionally they get much less of an endorphin raise from exercise than humans with out the circumstance do.

Self-harm

people experiencing mammoth physical pain—which include getting a deep reduce in their arm—from time dayeveryday experience euphoria daily an endorphin rush. a few people hurt themselves on motive every day get this high. they will use self-harm daily address emotional pressure of their lives.

Exercising addiction

some researchers consider people can daily hooked on the "runner's high". they'll exercising for hours each day, even at the rate of family time or paintings, day-to-day experience desirable. but, more research is wanted everyday verify if exercise dependancy does in truth work this manner.

II
EVOLUTION : THE BOUNDARY OF PSYCHOLOGY

Now, here let us start with an example of ZIZEK and PETERSON debut or discussion of where that evolution came from?

Evolution roughly talk about the outer boundary of what is possible or not possible. It's a boundary of condition, a base code. In this century psychology says or describes about your feeling but didn't care for your felling.

DISCUSSION OF ZIZEK AND PETERSON

Peterson opens with a 30-minutes speech wherein he criticizes the communist manifesto, which he'd re-read for the event. I would say his complaint is essentially well-located, but as many are brief to factor out, attacking the manifesto isn't always possibly attacking Communism or even Marxism as its most powerful point. still, that complaint would be salutary for maximum "communists"

I've talked to (which, regrettably had been extra fanboys than rigorous intellectuals). any other issue is that it's tough to pin down what communism is with its constellation of thinkers. at the least Marxism is closed off now that Marx is useless and he in no way amended his manifesto that I understand of.

I was amazed (and a chunk upset) that Peterson didn't seem greater knowledgeable about communism. He makes a massive deal out of ways he obsessed about the bloodless warfare, and it'd appear to me that expertise the ideological roots of the Soviet Union could be pretty crucial. further, he is crusading towards "post-modern-day neo-marxists" and it is bizarre now not to recognize or as a minimum recognize your opponent's ideas.

The assertion has some thrilling ideas although, inclusive of the statement that "nearly all ideas are wrong".

Zizek's opening statement

Zizek's beginning declaration might be the maximum exciting part of the talk. you can find a transcript of it here. In normal Zizek fashion, it is manufactured from many idea nuggets only tenuously linked to a further — despite the fact that there is a link, all of the extra tough to follow in the spoken form.

Zizek makes many exciting points. First, on how happiness is frequently the wrong yardstick:

In our daily lives, we fake to choice things which we do no longer truly preference, in order that in the end the worst element that could manifest is to get what we officially desire. So, I agree that human life of freedom and dignity does now not consist simply in looking for happiness, regardless of how a great deal we spiritualise it, or inside the attempt to actualise our inner potentials. We have to discover a few meaningful reason past the mere conflict for gratifying survival.

second on how modernity is characterized by using the absence of authority (and divinity) that could impose meaning from above, and the way it is impossible to head back to this pre-present day scenario.

He sees the rejections of a few systemic disasters of capitalism onto outside causes (from Donald Trump to migrants).

His mind on social constructionism vs evolutionary psychology (evaluating them, of all matters, to French cuisine) also are worth a concentrate/study.

what's possibly maximum surprising is that Zizek would not defend Marxism, which he squarely throws below the bus as failed. He does not do tons to guard Communism either, however factors a trouble with capitalism on what Marx referred to as "commons" (I wrote approximately commons before). Capitalism threatens the commons due to its self-reproducing nature, although he points out that communism had this self-reproducing nature to ("the historical necessity of development towards communism", although — fittingly — this pressure turned into plenty greater centralized).

In truth, this changed into a wonder for plenty, however both men tended to agree a whole lot, with only surface variations (some, even though now not all, may be chalked to their vastly distinct backgrounds). The tone of the debate was also cited to be very cordial and respectful, some thing I actually liked.

Zizek's conclusion is, in his words "pessimistic": we are able to preserve to slip in the direction of catastrophe, maybe some catastrophes can shake us out of our ruts.

I encourage you to observe the video or read the transcript (or each), this component is the maximum exciting.

i might say this jogs my memory quite a few what i've visible from him already. some idea make a reappearance, other are newly developed, however it is clear those are coherent thoughts from the identical thinker.

i=In addition remarks

The rest of the talk turned into (if memory serves) additionally thrilling, but it receives even greater disjointed. Zizek turned into difficult to follow in his organized announcement, he turns into increasingly more erratic in the rest of the debates. it is funny to look Peterson almost sweating from concentration looking to figure a thread.

Like I said before, I appreciated immensely that each guys appeared pretty tons on agreement (as properly they must, adopting neither deluded a ways-left or far-right opinions), and that the debate changed into cordial, even collectively admirative at times.

it is also enjoyable to look at, and i think this became the mode in which the general public fed on the controversy.

Peterson is his ordinary intensely-pushed professorial self, which I personally enjoy — while Zizek is his tick-ridden idiosyncratic self. he's also pretty semi-intentionally quite funny. it's tough now not to crack up while — out of time for his comments, he starts telling a Slovenian funny story, then after the first sentence interrupts himself to add "i'm able to end immediately" earlier than completing the comic story.

if you're curious, here's the timestamp for the shaggy dog story.

regarding how the controversy was receiving, judging from Twitter and a few short google, pretty well on the center-right, and pretty badly at the left (widely).

a terrific criticism is the only made with the aid of Benjamin

Studebaker. His argument abbreviated:

There are three important capabilities which distinguish a bad Marx paper:

The paper contains a close reading of the Manifesto.

The paper consists of nearly no references to any other texts, either through Marx or by means of different socialist thinkers.

The paper incorporates an extended digression about all the motives the Soviet Union become terrible. I call this the "tankie-bashing" bit.

the article additionally has a nice precis of Peterson's commencing announcement.

His charge in opposition to Peterson's argument is accompanied with how he thinks Zizek should have answered to shield communism. it is pretty thrilling, but it is now not what the debate ended up being.

different commentators opted for snide, which I think is sad — despite the fact that the linked stay statement is pretty funny.

other than that, multiple commentators (one,) pointed that the "Debate of the Century" became overhyped (overmarketed, truly), and appeared poorly prepared via its protagonists. and i have to agree. Zizek is mainly culpable here, for speaking about anyplace he felt like that turned into tenuously related instead of sticking to "his camp", however I experience just like the ensuing discussing ended up greater thrilling due to it.

And positive, the level of the dialogue could have been unappealing to all the critcial theorists that have been extensively study. but precisely due to the advertising, this occasion had the opportunity to reach a miles wider audience. And if you assume something wrong was stated therein, you must interact the content material rather than

ridiculing the form.
ultimately, make your own opinion.

    Zizek vs Peterson: an enticing mismatch
share
subjects
way of life
identification POLITICS
POLITICS
world
masses of lots, perhaps millions, of people watched unlawful livestreams of this Easter weekend's most hotly predicted aggressive display, rerouted via the reputable pay-per-view flow, while lots extra packed out Toronto's Sony Centre to witness a mismatch of epic proportions. The philosophical debate among Slavoj Zizek and Jordan Peterson – entitled Happiness: Capitalism vs Marxism – had been billed and talked about like a heavyweight fight for the reason that its announcement in February, although, if it were a boxing fit, it would were abandoned previous to its begin.

certainly, a ways from being a mismatch among weights or categories, this competition regarded to be among competition of various disciplines altogether. As such, naming a clear winner became out to be a futile workout, in spite of enthusiasts of both lecturers claiming victory for their aspect. there was, but, a clean fine takeaway: both Peterson and Zizek – who're, respectively, the poster boys of the web right and YouTube left – seemed to need to locate consensus in spite of their wildly differing backgrounds and skill units, demonstrating to a relatively factional audience that, even in our politically polarised instances, it's far still feasible to bridge the gulf among extremes.

the debate between of the world's first-class-known lecturers followed over a year of back-and-forth jibing traceable to an article written by means of Zizek inside the unbiased in February 2018, entitled 'Why do people discover Jordan Peterson so convincing?'. Zizek argued that the attraction of this Jungian psychologist and university of Toronto professor derives from the left's personal incapability to cope with the issues of race, gender and sexuality. All too often, Zizek argued, the leftist ignores important variations in a bid to hold the veneer of political correctness. hence Peterson's argument that, say, gender is a biological truth as opposed to a cultural construct finds an target audience amongst those frustrated by using the left's mindset to difference. And on the same time because the pc left ignores all essential variations (cultural or in any other case), it also wants to defend as inalienable the proper of the person to say his or her difference — that is, to be described by using his or her personal precise configuration of race, gender, sexuality, religion, and so on. Given this internal contradiction (among a denial of crucial variations and an assertion of the proper to be distinct), it might seem that if you gave the left sufficient rope it'd hold itself.

however, Peterson did no longer appear to comprehend Zizek's own complaint of the computer left. And this failure made for a skewered debate, one that at times felt sluggish and awkward, because its protagonists regarded to be having distinct arguments. certainly, despite the 12 months-long lead-up, one may be forgiven for thinking if they had carried out any previous planning.

The besuited Peterson began off the debate, pacing in front of a packed crowd at the Sony Centre, with a critique of The Communist Manifesto, which he then admitted to having reread for the first time in a long time.

i have to tell you, and i'm now not seeking to be flippant here... i have hardly ever read a tract that made as many conceptual errors in line with sentence as the Communist Manifesto', he gloated, earlier than happening to brush aside out of hand a e book that changed the route of human records. His primary argument – which was basically Nietzschean – become that the meekness of the poor does no longer in itself prove the inherent evil of the rich. 'It's virtually silly that you could make an assumption approximately someone's ethical worth by their monetary standing', he said. This led him to outline support for the trickle-down effect, wherein wealth filters through society from the top downwards, even as also arguing that there's something inherently existence-affirmative in competition. His argument, which borrows from Jungian psychology and evolutionary theory, is that social stratification is inherent to lived existence, and that its circumvention denies what it's far to be human.

Carrying a informal pullover and slacks, Zizek answered, at the same time as still sitting down and studying from a familiar run of replica-and-pasted jokes, sketches and theories from a sheet of paper. The temper inside the viewing birthday celebration on 0 Books' discord server – a sort of immediately chat with voice function – was at this point subdued. The overwhelmingly seasoned-Zizek crowd feared that their man changed into liable to acting overly convoluted. 'He goes to should make his point soon', stated writer and Zizek supporter Douglas Lain, wearily. That factor sooner or later came, as Zizek said that the most shining example of trickle-down economics has taken area in China, a rustic with excessive tiers of state manipulate over enterprise. This, coupled with an argument that capitalism is unfavorable to the surroundings, seemed, in essence, to be a rebuttal of Peterson's dismissal of communism, although it raised greater questions than it resolved. now not least: what about China's terrible environmental report? Isn't China efficaciously a totalitarian-capitalist nation? perhaps realising this, Zizek pedalled returned immediately after his contribution, declaring, 'once I mentioned China, I didn't imply to celebrate it. It issues me extraordinarily. My god, is that this our destiny?'

Know to backward division

Responding to Zizek's normal beginning statement, Peterson stated: 'I heard a criticism of capitalism, but no real guide of Marxism... i would say Dr Zizek probably centered extra on the problems of capitalism and the problems of happiness, than on the application of Marxism.' Peterson admitted that this had wrongfooted him, as he had assumed they have been debating Marx, consequently his intro around the Communist Manifesto.

this is where it became obvious that Peterson become taking up Zizek on a foundation that maybe didn't exist — namely, the latter's supposedly avowed traditional Marxist role. meanwhile, Zizek had cooked up an argument totally from disassociated prior arguments: a Lacanian-Hegelian-Marxist copypasta.

In a bid to shop what at this factor seemed farcical, Peterson agreed that capitalism is horrific, with the proviso – appropriated from the currently deeply unfashionable Churchill – that it turned into the least bad of all economic systems known to us. From there he inadvertently made a left-accelerationist argument, that the speeding of capital, and the improvement of productive forces, may also push us thru to an technology of sustainable increase — itself based totally on the Marxist principle that by means of hijacking the productive capacity of capital, the worker may utilise it to make a extra identical world. as opposed to equality, however, Peterson focused on unfastened-market capitalism's capability to make people less depressing by means of making them wealthier overall.

Ultimately, Peterson argued that what prevents capitalist society becoming essentially nihilistic in its pursuit of wealth is individual self-responsibility based totally at the principle of doing unto others as you would need done unto you. Zizek's retort became that happiness is so relative as to be a contingent detail in any political system, and that man or woman interest isn't enough to resolve, as an instance, the trouble of polluted oceans.

With one of these divergence now not most effective of thoughts however additionally of the terrain on which they had been arguing, it have become apparent that consensus among Zizek and Peterson would not be reached on any political or philosophical stage. however, as time went on, the frame language and tone of the two teachers softened, with Zizek at factors performing like a mentor to the younger Peterson. Zizek, recognised for his adversarial and jokey style of deal with, sought to carry together the factions inside the audience via pointing to the seriousness of the troubles that face us today, predominant among them being climate trade, he claimed. in the meantime, Peterson, who has honed a form of stern, father-like character on YouTube, appeared captivated with the aid of Zizek's genteel aura, at points brazenly smiling as he watched and listened to Zizek.

Talk in online chatrooms necessarily revolved around Peterson being 'owned' or 'cucked'. but, this become now not a role Zizek, settling into his position as benevolent uncle to Peterson, could have countenanced. For all its issues, the controversy became stored from disaster with the aid of the humility and humanity of the philosophical fathers of the online left and right. As Peterson said in his remaining lines, 'people of goodwill, no matter their variations, can communicate and can pop out of that communication progressed'. right here's hoping the net left and proper comply with the instance.

evolutionary psychology, the examine of behaviour, thought, and feeling as regarded through the lens of evolutionary biology. Evolutionary psychologists presume all human behaviours replicate the impact of bodily and psychological predispositions that helped human ancestors survive and reproduce.

Evolutionary psychology is one in all many biologically informed procedures to the observe of human behavior. along with cognitive psychologists, evolutionary psychologists advise that tons, if no longer all, of our behavior can be defined through appeal to internal mental mechanisms. What distinguishes evolutionary psychologists from many cognitive psychologists is the proposal that the applicable inner mechanisms are diversifications—merchandise of natural choice—that helped our ancestors get around the world, survive and reproduce. To apprehend the principal claims of evolutionary psychology we require an expertise of some key standards in evolutionary biology, cognitive psychology, philosophy of science and philosophy of mind. Philosophers are interested in evolutionary psychology for a number of reasons. For philosophers of science —on the whole philosophers of biology—evolutionary psychology presents a critical target. even though here is a broad consensus among philosophers of biology that evolutionary psychology is a deeply improper organisation, this doesn't entail that those philosophers absolutely reject the relevance of evolutionary principle to human psychology. For philosophers of mind and cognitive science evolutionary psychology has been a source of empirical hypotheses about cognitive architecture and specific additives of that structure. however, a few philosophers of mind also are crucial of evolutionary psychology however their criticisms aren't as all-encompassing as those presented by way of philosophers of biology. Evolutionary psychology is also invoked through philosophers interested by ethical psychology both as a source of empirical hypotheses and as a vital goal.

In what follows I in brief explain evolutionary psychology's family members to different work on the biology of human conduct and the cognitive sciences. subsequent I introduce the studies subculture's key theoretical standards. inside the following phase I take up discussions approximately evolutionary psychology within the philosophy of mind, specifically focusing at the debate about the big modularity thesis. i am going on to check a number of the criticisms of evolutionary psychology offered by means of philosophers of biology and assess a few responses to those criticisms. I then go on to introduce some of evolutionary psychology's contributions to ethical psychology and human nature and, sooner or later, briefly speak the reach and impact of evolutionary psychology.

Evolutionary Psychology: One research tradition among the diverse organic strategies to explaining human conduct

This entry makes a speciality of the unique approach to evolutionary psychology that is conventionally named by way of the capitalized word "Evolutionary Psychology". This naming convention is David Buller's (2000; 2005) idea. He introduces the convention to differentiate a selected studies lifestyle (Laudan 1977) from other approaches to the biology of human conduct.[1] This research tradition is the point of interest right here however decrease case is used during as no other varieties of evolutionary psychology are mentioned. Evolutionary psychology rests upon specific theoretical principles (supplied in segment 2 under) no longer all of that are shared via others working within the biology of human behavior (Laland and Brown 2002; Brown et al. 2011). as an instance, human behavioral ecologists present and shield explanatory hypotheses about human behavior that do not enchantment to mental mechanisms (e.g., Hawkes 1990; Hrdy 1999). Behavioral ecologists also accept as true with that much of human behavior can be explained with the aid of attractive to evolution whilst rejecting the idea held through evolutionary psychologists that one length of our evolutionary records is the source of all our essential mental diversifications (Irons 1998). Developmental psychobiologists take but some other technique: they may be anti-adaptationist. (Michel and Moore 1995; but see Bateson and Martin 1999; Bjorklund and Hernandez Blasi 2005 for examples of developmentalist paintings in an adaptationist vein.) those theorists accept as true with that a good deal of our conduct can be defined without attractive to a collection of specific mental diversifications for that conduct. as an alternative they emphasize the role of improvement in the production of diverse human behavioral trends. From right here on, "evolutionary psychology" refers to a specific research tradition the various many biological techniques to the look at of human conduct.

Paul Griffiths argues that evolutionary psychology owes theoretical debt to each sociobiology and ethology (Griffiths 2006; Griffiths 2008). Evolutionary psychologists acknowledge their debt to sociobiology however point out that they add a size to sociobiology: mental mechanisms. Human behaviors aren't an instantaneous manufactured from herbal selection however as an alternative the product of mental mechanisms that have been selected for. The relation to ethology here is that inside the Nineteen Fifties, ethologists proposed instincts or drives that underlie our behavior;[2] evolutionary psychology's mental mechanisms are the correlates to instincts or drives. Evolutionary psychology is also related to cognitive psychology and the cognitive sciences. The mental mechanisms they invoke are computational, sometimes known as "Darwinian algorithms" or as "computational modules". This overt cognitivism units evolutionary psychology apart from plenty work within the neurosciences and from behavioral neuroendocrinology. In these fields internal mechanisms are proposed in causes of human behavior but they're not construed in computational terms. David Marr's (e.g., 1983) well known three component distinction is often invoked to differentiate the stages at which researchers attention their interest in the cognitive and neurosciences. Many neuroscientists and behavioral neuroendocrinologists paintings on the implementation degree even as cognitive psychologists paintings at the extent of the computations which are implemented at the neurobiological level (cf. Griffiths 2006).

Evolutionary psychologists once in a while present their technique as potentially unifying, or supplying a foundation for, all other work that purports to explain human conduct (e.g., Tooby and Cosmides 1992). This claim has been met with strong skepticism with the aid of many social scientists who see a role for a myriad of forms of clarification of human conduct, a number of which are not reducible to organic causes of any type. This dialogue hangs on issues of reductionism inside the social sciences. (Little 1991 has a nice introduction to these problems.) There also are motives to consider that evolutionary psychology neither unifies nor affords foundations for carefully neighboring fields together with behavioral ecology or developmental psychobiology. In other work, evolutionary psychologists gift their technique as being regular with or like minded with neighboring tactics including behavioral ecology and developmental psychobiology. (See Buss's advent to Buss 2005.) The truth of this claim hangs on a cautious examination of the theoretical tenets of evolutionary psychology and its neighboring fields.

evolutionary psychology, the have a look at of behaviour, idea, and feeling as appeared via the lens of evolutionary biology. Evolutionary psychologists presume all human behaviours replicate the impact of bodily and mental predispositions that helped human ancestors live to tell the tale and reproduce.

Evolutionary psychology is one in all many biologically informed techniques to the have a look at of human conduct. together with cognitive psychologists, evolutionary psychologists advise that heaps, if not all, of our conduct can be defined via enchantment to internal mental mechanisms. What distinguishes evolutionary psychologists from many cognitive psychologists is the thought that the relevant internal mechanisms are variations—products of natural desire—that helped our ancestors get round the world, live to tell the tale and reproduce. To apprehend the fundamental claims of evolutionary psychology we require an information of a few key requirements in evolutionary biology, cognitive psychology, philosophy of science and philosophy of thoughts. Philosophers are inquisitive about evolutionary psychology for a number of motives. For philosophers of technology —at the entire philosophers of biology—evolutionary psychology provides a crucial goal. despite the fact that here's a wide consensus among philosophers of biology that evolutionary psychology is a deeply wrong corporation, this does not entail that those philosophers truly reject the relevance of evolutionary principle to human psychology. For philosophers of thoughts and cognitive technology evolutionary psychology has been a supply of empirical hypotheses approximately cognitive structure and particular components of that shape. however, some philosophers of mind are also vital of evolutionary psychology but their criticisms are not as all-encompassing as the ones provided by way of way of philosophers of biology. Evolutionary psychology is likewise invoked through philosophers interested by moral psychology each as a supply of empirical hypotheses and as a essential goal.

In what follows I in short provide an explanation for evolutionary psychology's family participants to one of a kind work at the biology of human conduct and the cognitive sciences. subsequent I introduce the research tradition's key theoretical requirements. within the following section I absorb discussions about evolutionary psychology within the philosophy of mind, particularly focusing at the debate about the massive modularity thesis. i'm going on to check a number of the criticisms of evolutionary psychology supplied via philosophers of biology and check a few responses to those criticisms. I then move on to introduce some of evolutionary psychology's contributions to ethical psychology and human nature and, in the end, briefly talk the reach and effect of evolutionary psychology.

Evolutionary Psychology: One research culture a number of the various organic strategies to explaining human conduct

This entry specializes in the particular approach to evolutionary psychology this is conventionally named through way of the capitalized phrase "Evolutionary Psychology". This naming convention is David Buller's (2000; 2005) idea. He introduces the convention to distinguish a specific studies lifestyle (Laudan 1977) from other strategies to the biology of human behavior.[1] This studies way of life is the focus right here but lower case is used in the course of as no different sorts of evolutionary psychology are stated. Evolutionary psychology rests upon precise theoretical ideas (furnished in phase 2 below) no longer all of that are shared via others operating inside the biology of human behavior (Laland and Brown 2002; Brown et al. 2011). as an instance, human behavioral ecologists gift and protect explanatory hypotheses about human conduct that don't attraction to mental mechanisms (e.g., Hawkes 1990; Hrdy 1999). Behavioral ecologists also accept as proper with that lots of human conduct can be explained with the aid of attractive to evolution even as rejecting the idea held through evolutionary psychologists that one length of our evolutionary information is the source of all our critical intellectual diversifications (Irons 1998). Developmental psychobiologists take however some different approach: they may be anti-adaptationist. (Michel and Moore 1995; but see Bateson and Martin 1999; Bjorklund and Hernandez Blasi 2005 for examples of developmentalist art work in an adaptationist vein.) those theorists be given as real with that a bargain of our conduct may be described with out appealing to a collection of unique intellectual diversifications for that behavior. as an alternative they emphasize the role of development in the manufacturing of diverse human behavioral tendencies. From proper right here on, "evolutionary psychology" refers to a selected studies way of life the various many biological strategies to the have a look at of human behavior.

Paul Griffiths argues that evolutionary psychology owes theoretical debt to each sociobiology and ethology (Griffiths 2006; Griffiths 2008). Evolutionary psychologists acknowledge their debt to sociobiology but point out that they add a size to sociobiology: intellectual mechanisms. Human behaviors are not an instantaneous made of herbal choice however as an alternative the made of mental mechanisms that have been selected for. The relation to ethology here is that inside the Fifties, ethologists proposed instincts or drives that underlie our conduct;[2] evolutionary psychology's mental mechanisms are the correlates to instincts or drives. Evolutionary psychology is likewise related to cognitive psychology and the cognitive sciences. The intellectual mechanisms they invoke are computational, every so often referred to as "Darwinian algorithms" or as "computational modules". This overt cognitivism units evolutionary psychology other than plenty paintings in the neurosciences and from behavioral neuroendocrinology. In those fields internal mechanisms are proposed in causes of human behavior however they may be not construed in computational terms. David Marr's (e.g., 1983) widely known three element difference is regularly invoked to distinguish the stages at which researchers attention their hobby inside the cognitive and neurosciences. Many neuroscientists and behavioral neuroendocrinologists artwork on the implementation diploma even as cognitive psychologists artwork at the volume of the computations which might be implemented on the neurobiological level (cf. Griffiths 2006).

Evolutionary psychologists from time to time gift their technique as potentially unifying, or providing a foundation for, all other paintings that purports to give an explanation for human conduct (e.g., Tooby and Cosmides 1992). This declare has been met with sturdy skepticism with the aid of many social scientists who see a position for a myriad of varieties of explanation of human behavior, a number of which aren't reducible to organic reasons of any kind. This communicate hangs on problems of reductionism in the social sciences. (Little 1991 has a pleasant creation to those issues.) There also are reasons to recall that evolutionary psychology neither unifies nor presents foundations for carefully neighboring fields collectively with behavioral ecology or developmental psychobiology. In other work, evolutionary psychologists gift their technique as being regular with or well suited with neighboring approaches which include behavioral ecology and developmental psychobiology. (See Buss's advent to Buss 2005.) The fact of this declare hangs on a cautious examination of the theoretical tenets of evolutionary psychology and its neighboring fields.

DARWIN STORY OF ISLAND ABOUT DIFFERENT SPECIES OF BIRDS

What Did Charles Darwin look at within the Galapagos Islands?
What did Charles Darwin observe in the Galapagos Islands? The most famous fauna of the Galapagos Islands are the iguanas, large tortoises and finches. ... Darwin formulated his theories after getting back from a voyage round the world at the HMS Beagle and he published them in 1859.

What animals did Darwin have a look at on the Galapagos?
Darwin's Finches

The most studied animals at the Galápagos are finches, a type of hen (figure underneath). while Darwin first located finches at the islands, he did now not even comprehend they were all finches. but while he studied them similarly, he realized they have been associated with every other.

What did Charles Darwin examine?
British naturalist Charles Darwin is credited for the principle of herbal selection. ... while he endured his studies in theology at Cambridge, it changed into his attention on natural history that became his passion. In 1831, Darwin embarked on a voyage aboard a ship of the British Royal army, the HMS Beagle, employed as a naturalist.
What did Charles Darwin finish on the Galapagos Islands?

Darwin observed that fruit-consuming finches had parrot-like beaks, and that finches that ate insects had slim, prying beaks. ... Later, Darwin concluded that several birds from one species of finch had probably been blown by way of hurricane or otherwise separated to every of the islands from one island or from the mainland.

What turned into Charles Darwin's foremost accomplishment?

Darwin's greatest contribution to science is that he completed the Copernican Revolution via drawing out for biology the notion of nature as a machine of depend in movement governed by way of natural laws. With Darwin's discovery of natural choice, the foundation and diversifications of organisms were introduced into the world of technological know-how.

How did the Galapagos Islands affect Darwin's research? His discoveries on the islands were paramount to the development of his idea of Evolution by using herbal choice. at the islands, Charles Darwin found numerous species of finches. way to his close observations, he determined that the exclusive species of finches various from island to island.

See additionally what were two important achievements of the ancient greeks

What trait did Charles Darwin take a look at After reading the Galapagos finches?

Darwin found out the significance of the finches after leaving the islands even as he turned into analyzing specimens he delivered back with him. The trait he noticed became the differences within the length and form of the finches beaks. He theorised that new species will rise up while some element causes a population to be divided.

Why did Darwin observe finches?
but, the Galapagos finches helped Darwin solidify his idea of herbal selection. ... those birds, even though nearly identical in all other methods to mainland finches, had distinct beaks. Their beaks had adapted to the form of food they ate so one can fill exceptional niches on the Galapagos Islands.

what's Darwin's concept of evolution precis?
Charles Darwin's idea of evolution states that evolution happens through herbal choice. individuals in a species show variation in bodily traits. ... people that are poorly tailored to their environment are much less in all likelihood to live to tell the tale and reproduce.

in which did Charles Darwin cross to high school and what did he take a look at?
Charles Darwin went to the Shrewsbury school as a youngster. He then attended the college of Edinburgh scientific college in Edinburgh, Scotland. Darwin did no longer just like the observe of medicine and did now not do properly, so he switched colleges and went to Christ's university of Cambridge college in Cambridge, England.

what is Darwin concept?
Darwinism is a principle of biological evolution advanced via the English naturalist Charles Darwin (1809–1882) and others, mentioning that every one species of organisms stand up and develop thru the natural choice of small, inherited variations that boom the individual's potential to compete, continue to exist, and reproduce.

How did Charles Darwin develop his theory?
A visit to the Galapagos Islands in 1835 helped Darwin formulate his thoughts on herbal choice. He observed several species of finch adapted to exceptional environmental niches. The finches also differed in beak

form, food supply, and the way food was captured.

Why are the Galapagos Islands top for analyzing evolution?

"Galápagos are a exceptional region to observe evolution, nonetheless, due to the fact, remarkably, numerous islands and their inhabitants are close to being within the absolutely herbal kingdom, with very little have an effect on of human activities," says the evolutionary biologist and Princeton university professor emeritus Peter provide who, with his ...

How did Darwin's observations on the Galapagos Islands lead him to the idea of evolution use the instance of the tortoises referred to above in your explanation?

He have become curious about species that seemed related to ones found at the mainland—but that still had many physical versions precise to extraordinary islands. through the years, Darwin started out to marvel if species from South america had reached the Galapagos after which modified as they tailored to new environments.

How has Charles Darwin contributed to the have a look at of evolution?

Charles Darwin became a British naturalist who proposed the concept of biological evolution by way of herbal selection. Darwin described evolution as "descent with modification," the idea that species exchange over the years, give upward push to new species, and share a common ancestor.

How did Charles Darwin provide an explanation for the distinction in trends?

The principle of natural choice become explored by means of 19th-century naturalist Charles Darwin. herbal choice explains how genetic trends of a species may trade over the years. this can cause speciation, the formation of a awesome new species.

How did Darwin provide an explanation for why the finches at the Galapagos Islands appearance so similar to each different except for their beaks?
How did Darwin provide an explanation for why the finches at the Galapagos Islands appearance so just like every other except for his or her beaks? The finches all have a recent commonplace ancestor however they developed on different islands in which different varieties of meals are to be had.

What geological phenomena and formations did Darwin witness how did these shape his considering the age of the earth or how lifestyles modified?
What geological phenomena and formations did Darwin witness? How did these form his thinking about the age of the earth or how existence changed? a band of shells and corals that lay about thirty toes approximately sea stage, so he questioned if the sea level had fallen or if island rose.

What statement did Charles Darwin make about finches in the Galápagos Islands?
beaks
Darwin determined that finches inside the Galápagos Islands had exceptional beaks than finches in South the united states; those adaptations equiped the birds to gather unique food resources.
See also what's a column graph
How did Darwin's finches get to the Galapagos?
The closure of the Panama land bridge altered ocean move, and probably delivered about modifications in wind energy and instructions. these modifications may additionally have facilitated the colonisation of the Galápagos Islands, especially if that vicinity changed into the factor of departure for a flock of adventurous finches.

How did the finches get to the Galapagos?
Darwin's finches comprise a set of 15 species endemic to the Galápagos (14 species) and Cocos (1 species) Islands inside the Pacific Ocean. The group is monophyletic and originated from an ancestral species that reached the Galápagos Archipelago from relevant or South america.

What are the five most important points of Darwin's theory?
terms in this set (6)
5 points. competition, adaption, variant, overproduction, speciation.
opposition. call for by organisms for constrained environmental sources, together with vitamins, residing space, or light.
adaption. inherited traits that increase danger of survival.
variation. ...
overproduction. ...
speciation.
Which area of examine turned into Darwin most committed to as a scholar?
on the age of sixteen, Darwin commenced to have a look at medication at the university of Edinburgh. There too he discovered the courses stupid, and looking operations made him unwell. In 1828 he transferred to Cambridge, intending to emerge as a clergyman. rather, he dedicated maximum of his time to studying vegetation and animals and later to geology.

How did Darwin find out evolution?
Darwin drafts his first account of evolution

domestic again, Darwin showed his specimens to fellow biologists and began writing up his travels. ... Darwin saw how transmutation took place. Animals extra perfect to their surroundings live on longer and have more young.

Evolution befell by using a procedure he known as 'natural selection'.

See also what's the which means of catastrophically

How did Charles Darwin give an explanation for human evolution?

The theory of evolution by means of natural choice, first formulated in Charles Darwin's ebook "on the origin of Species" in 1859, describes how organisms evolve over generations thru the inheritance of bodily or behavioral traits, as country wide Geographic explains.

What are Darwin's four standards of evolution?

There are four concepts at work in evolution—version, inheritance, selection and time. those are considered the components of the evolutionary mechanism of herbal choice.

Did Darwin have a look at tortoises?

Darwin also located massive tortoises on the Galápagos (determine 1.5). those tortoises had been so large that two people ought to journey on them. Darwin noticed that distinctive tortoise species lived on islands with distinctive environments.

What evolution become evident in Darwin's finches?

Evolution in Darwin's finches is characterized by means of fast version to an volatile and difficult environment leading to ecological diversification and speciation. This has led to putting range in their phenotypes (for instance, beak sorts, body length, plumage, feeding behavior and music types).

Why are the Galapagos Islands a completely unique location to take a look at living things?

What makes the Islands so specific? The Galapagos Islands are well-known for his or her huge variety of endemic species, species that can't be located everywhere else inside the world. while a species simplest exists in one vicinity (inclusive of the Galapagos giant tortoise) it's far called being endemic.

What adaptations did Darwin examine within the Galapagos tortoises?

as an example, Darwin found a populace of large tortoises inside the Galápagos Archipelago to have longer necks than those that lived on different islands with dry lowlands. these tortoises have been "selected" because they might reach greater leaves and get admission to greater food than people with quick necks.

What organism and trait did Darwin have a look at within the Galapagos island?

visible evidence of Ongoing Evolution: Darwin's Finches

From 1831 to 1836, Darwin traveled around the sector, staring at animals on unique continents and islands. at the Galapagos Islands, Darwin located numerous species of finches with specific beak shapes.

Why is Charles Darwin essential to psychology?

Charles Darwin, quality recognized for his survival of the fittest idea, turned into a first-rate contributor to the sphere of psychology. ... Darwin changed into also the foundation for comparative psychology, or the study of animals to infer and draw conclusions on human conduct, memory, intelligence, and social interplay.

What was Charles Darwin's foremost contribution to technology quizlet?

What was Charles Darwin's contribution to science? Darwin evolved a scientific idea of biological evolution that explains how present day organisms advanced over lengthy intervals of time via descent from commonplace ancestors

The huge Modularity hypothesis

Claims that the mind has a modular structure, or even vastly modular structure, are giant in cognitive technology (see e.g. Hirshfield and Gelman 1994). The big modularity thesis is first and most important a thesis approximately cognitive architecture. As defended by means of evolutionary psychologists, the thesis is likewise approximately the make-up of our cognitive architecture: the massively modular architecture is the result of natural choice performing to producemakeup every of the numerous modules (see e.g. Barrett and Kurzban 2006; Barrett 2012). Our cognitive structure consists of computational gadgets, which are innate and are diversifications (cf. Samuels 1998; Samuels et al. 1999a; Samuels et al. 1999b; Samuels 2000). This vastly modular structure bills for all of our state-of-the-art behavior. Our successful navigation of the world outcomes from the action of one or extra of our many modules.

Jerry Fodor become the first to mount a sustained philosophical defense of modularity as a principle of cognitive architecture (Fodor 1983). His modularity thesis is awesome from the large modularity thesis in some of vital ways. Fodor argued that our "input systems" are modular—as an instance, components of our visual gadget, our speech detection device and so on—those elements of our thoughts are devoted data processors, whose inner b6fd8d88d79ed1018df623d0b49e84e7 is inaccessible to different related processors. The modular detection systems feed output to a relevant system, that is a form of inference engine. The crucial system, on Fodor's view isn't always modular. Fodor affords a large wide variety of arguments against the possibility of modular relevant systems. as an instance, he argues that important structures, to the volume that they have interaction in some thing like scientific confirmation, are "Quinean" in that "the degree of confirmation assigned to any given speculation is touchy to homes of the whole notion system" (Fodor 1983, 107). Fodor attracts a bleak conclusion approximately the reputation of cognitive science from his examination of the individual of primary systems: cognitive technology is not possible. So on Fodor's view, the mind is partly modular and the a part of the mind this is modular gives some situation count number for cognitive technological know-how.

A wonderful thesis from Fodor's, the big modularity thesis, gets a sustained philosophical defense from Peter Carruthers (see especially Carruthers 2006). Carruthers is nicely conscious that Fodor (see e.g. Fodor 2000) does now not trust that valuable systems can be modular but he affords arguments from evolutionary psychologists and others that aid the modularity thesis for the entire thoughts. perhaps one of the reasons that there's a lot philosophical interest in evolutionary psychology is that discussions about the reputation of the large modularity thesis are exceedingly theoretical.[3] both evolutionary psychologists and philosophers present and remember arguments for and against the thesis instead of truely ready until the empirical consequences are available in. Richard Samuels (1998) speculates that argument in place of empirical statistics is trusted, due to the fact the numerous competing modularity theses about central structures are difficult to pull apart empirically. Carruthers exemplifies this approach as he relies heavily on arguments for large modularity regularly at the fee of particular empirical results that tell in desire of the thesis.

there are many arguments for the huge modularity thesis. some are based make-upon concerns approximately how evolution need to have acted; a few are based on concerns approximately the nature of computation and a few are versions of the poverty of the stimulus argument first provided by means of Chomsky in help of the existence of an innate general grammar. (See Cowie 1999 for a pleasant presentation of the structure of poverty of the stimulus arguments.) Myriad variations of every of those arguments appear inside the literature and lots of arguments for big modularity mix and in shape components of each of the primary strands of argumentation. here we overview a version of every kind of argument.

Carruthers affords a clean outline of the first type of argument "the organic argument for huge modularity": "

(1) biological systems are designed structures, built incrementally.

(2) Such structures, whilst complicated, want to have vastly modular enterprise.

(3) The human mind is a biological gadget and is complicated.

(4) So the human thoughts can be vastly modularly in its company" (Carruthers 2006,).

An example of this argument is to enchantment to the practical decomposition of organisms into organs "designed" for precise duties, e.g. hearts, livers, kidneys. each of those organs arises because of natural choice and the organs, performing collectively, make contributions to the health of the organism.

The useful decomposition is pushed by way of the response to unique environmental stimuli. instead of herbal selection appearing to producemakeup fashionable reason organs, each specific environmental mission is dealt with with the aid of a separate mechanism. All variations of this argument are arguments from analogy, relying on the important thing transitional premise that minds are a form of organic machine make-upon which natural selection acts.

The second one type of argument makes no enchantment to biological considerations in any respect (despite the fact that many evolutionary psychologists givemakeup those arguments a organic twist). name this the computational argument, which unfolds as follows: minds are computational problem solving devices; there are particular styles of solutions to unique styles of problems; and so for minds to be (a success) fashionable problem fixing devices, they need to consist of collections of precise problem solving gadgets, i.e. many computational modules. This kind of argument is structurally just like the organic argument (as Carruthers points out). the key idea is that there is no experience to the idea of a fashionable hassle solver and that no headway may be made in cognitive science with out breaking down issues into their aspect elements.

The 0.33 kind of argument involves a generalization of Chomsky's poverty of the stimulus argument for time-honored grammar. Many evolutionary psychologists (see e.g. Tooby and Cosmides 1992) enchantment to the concept that there's neither enough time, nor enough available facts, for any given human to analyze from scratch to correctly make-up all of the issues that we face in the global. this first attention make-upports the conclusion that the underlying mechanisms we use to clear makemakeup the applicable problems are innate (for evolutionary psychologists "innate" is normally interchangeable with "made from herbal selection"[4]). If we invoke this argument across the entire variety of problem sets that human beings face and remedy, we arrive at a huge set of innate mechanisms that subserve our hassle fixing abilities, that's every other way of announcing that we've a vastly modular thoughts.

there are numerous responses to the various versions of every of those types of arguments and lots of take on the huge modularity thesis head on with out considering a particular argument for it. i'm able to defer consideration of responses to the first argument kind until segment four beneath, which specializes in problems of the nature of evolution and natural selection – topics in philosophy of biology.

the second kind of argument is one side of a perennial debate within the philosophy of cognitive technology. Fodor (2000,) takes this argument to relaxation on the unwarranted assumption that there may be no area-independent criterion of cognitive success, which he thinks requires an issue that evolutionary psychologists do not offer. Samuels (see esp. Samuels 1998) responds to evolutionary psychologists that arguments of this kind do not sufficiently discriminate between a conclusion about domain unique processing mechanisms and domain particular know-how or facts. Samuels articulates what he calls the "library model of cognition" in which there's area unique information or knowledge however domain general processing. The library model of cognition isn't always hugely modular inside the relevant experience but type two arguments makeup it. consistent with Samuels, evolutionary psychologists want something greater than this type of argument to warrant their unique form of end approximately massive modularity.

Buller (2005) introduces further issues for this kind of argument via tackling the idea that there can be no such thing as a domain wellknown trouble solving mechanism. Buller issues that during their try to make-upassist this claim, evolutionary psychologists fail to competently symbolize a domain standard trouble solver. for example, they fail to differentiate among a site widespread hassle solver and a domain particular trouble solver that is over generalized. He gives the example of social gaining knowledge of as a website trendy mechanism that would produce domain unique answers to problems. He makes use of a nice organic analogy to drive this factor home: the immune system is a site standard device in that it allows the frame to reply to a extensive kind of pathogens. whilst it is real that the immune device produces domain particular responses to pathogens in the shape of specific antibodies, the antibodies are produced through one domain wellknown machine. these and many other respondents finish that type arguments do not thoroughly guidemakeup the large modularity thesis.

Fodor (2000) and Kim Sterelny (2003) provide specific responses to kind 3 arguments. Fodor's response is that poverty of the stimulus kind arguments help conclusions about innateness however now not modularity and so those arguments can't be used to aid the massive modularity thesis. He argues that the domain specificity and encapsulation of a mechanism and its innateness pull apart quite honestly, taking into consideration "flawlessly preferred getting to know mechanisms" which might be innate and "completely encapsulated mechanisms" which are single stimulus specific and the whole thing in among. Sterelny responds to the generalizing pass in kind 3 arguments. he is taking language to be the exception as opposed to the guideline within the sense that even as the postulation of an innate, domain particular module can be warranted to account for our language talents, a lot of our different trouble fixing behavior may be accounted for with out postulating such modules (Sterelny 2003, 200).[5]

Sterelny's counter calls for invoking trade causes for our behavioral repertoire. for example, he accounts for folk psychology and folks biology by means of attractive to environmental factors, a number of that are built by our forebears, that allow us to carry out sophisticated cognitive obligations. If we can account for our fulfillment at diverse complicated hassle solving duties, with out attractive to modules, then the big modularity thesis is undercut. Sterelny sharpens his response to large modularity through including more element to his debts of the way a lot of our uniquely human tendencies may also have advanced (see e.g. Sterelny 2012). Sterelny introduces his "developed apprentice" version to account for the evolution of many human trends that many assume require explanation in terms of huge modularity, as an example, forming ethical judgments. Cecilia Heyes adopts a comparable method to Sterenly in attacking large modularity. in preference to presenting arguments in opposition to huge modularity, she gives alternative motives of the development of people psychology that don't depend on the massive modularity thesis (Heyes 2014).

Heyes and Sterelny now not simplest reject big modularity but additionally have little expectation that any modularity theses will undergo fruit but there are many critics of the large modularity thesis who allow for the opportunity of a few modularity of mind. Such critics of evolutionary psychology do now not reject the opportunity of any type of modularity, they just reject the big modularity thesis. there's sizable debate approximately the repute of the huge modularity thesis and some of this debate facilities across the characterization of modules. If modules have all the characteristics that Fodor (1983) first make-upplied, then he may be right that crucial structures are not modular. both Carruthers (2006) and Barrett and Kurzban (2006) gift modified characterizations of modules, which they argue better serve the big modularity thesis. there is no settlement on a plausible characterization of modules for evolutionary psychology however there is settlement at the truly benign thesis that "the language of modularity presents useful conceptual foundation in which effective debates surrounding cognitive structures can be framed".

Philosophy of biology vs. Evolutionary Psychology

Many philosophers have criticized evolutionary psychology. maximum of those critics are philosophers of biology who argue that the studies culture suffers from a very zealous form of adaptationism (Griffiths 1996; Richardson 1996; Grantham and Nichols 1999; Lloyd 1999; Richardson 2007), an untenable reductionism (Dupre 1999; Dupre 2001), a "awful empirical wager" approximately modules (Sterelny 1995; Sterelny and Griffiths 1999; Sterelny 2003), a fast and loose idea of health (Lloyd 1999; Lloyd and Feldman 2002); and maximum of the above and plenty extra (Buller 2005) (cf. Downes 2005).[6] All of those philosophers percentage one model or other of Buller's view: "i'm unabashedly passionate about efforts to use evolutionary idea to human psychology" (2005, x).[7] but if philosophers of biology are not skeptical of the essential idea at the back of the task, as Buller's quote suggests, what are they so essential of? what's at stake are differing views approximately how to first-rate represent evolution and therefore a way to generate evolutionary hypotheses and how to check evolutionary hypotheses. For evolutionary psychologists, the most interesting contribution that evolutionary idea makes is the explanation of obvious design in nature or the reason of the manufacturing of complicated organs via enchantment to natural selection. Evolutionary psychologists generate evolutionary hypotheses by using first finding obvious layout in the global, say in our psychological make up, after which offering a selective scenario that could have brought about the production of the trait that exhibits obvious layout. The hypotheses evolutionary psychologists generate, given that they may be usually hypotheses approximately our psychological capacities, are tested by trendy psychological strategies. Philosophers of biology challenge evolutionary psychologists on both of those factors. I introduce some examples of criticisms in every of these two regions beneath and then observe a few responses to philosophical criticisms of evolutionary psychology.

adaptation is the one organic concept that is principal to most debates over evolutionary psychology. every theoretical work on evolutionary psychology provides the research tradition as being normally centered on mental adaptations and goes on to provide an account of what adaptations are (see e.g. Tooby and Cosmides 1992; Buss et al. 1998; Simpson and Campbell 2005; Tooby and Cosmides 2005). a great deal of the philosophical grievance of evolutionary psychology addresses its approach to edition or its form of adaptationism. let us fast evaluate the basics from the attitude of philosophy of biology.

Here is how Elliott Sober defines an model: "characteristic c is an variation for doing undertaking t in a populace if and handiest if individuals of the populace now have c due to the fact, ancestrally, there was choice for having c and c conferred a health advantage because it achieved project t" (Sober 2000, 85). Sober makes a few further clarifications of the belief of version that are beneficial. First, we have to distinguish between a trait this is adaptive and a trait this is an edition. Any quantity of tendencies may be adaptive with out those tendencies being adaptations. A sea turtle's forelegs are beneficial for digging within the sand to bury eggs but they're now not variations for nest building (Sober 2000, 85). additionally, traits may be diversifications without being currently adaptive for a given organism. Vestigial organs together with our appendix or vestigial eyes in cave living organisms are examples of such developments (Sterelny and Griffiths 1999). second, we have to distinguish among ontogenic and phylogenetic diversifications (Sober 2000, 86). The diversifications of hobby to evolutionary biologists are phylogenetic adaptations, which get up over evolutionary time and impact the fitness of the organism. Ontogenetic adaptations, which include any behavior we examine in our lifetimes, may be adaptive to the quantity that an organism blessings from them but they're no longer variations within the applicable sense. finally, adaptation and function are carefully associated phrases. On one of the prominent perspectives of feature—the etiological view of capabilities—variation and characteristic are more or much less coextensive; to invite for the feature of an organ is to ask why it is present. on the Cummins view of capabilities version and feature aren't coextensive, as on the Cummins view, to invite what an organ's function is, is to ask what it does .

Evolutionary psychologists attention on mental adaptations. One steady topic within the theoretical paintings of evolutionary psychologists is that "adaptations, the functional components of organisms, are diagnosed [...] by means of [...] evidence in their layout: the excellent suit among organism structure and surroundings". The manner in which mental variations are diagnosed is by way of evolutionary useful evaluation, which is a kind of reverse engineering. "reverse engineering is a technique of figuring out the layout of a mechanism on the basis of an analysis of the obligations it plays. Evolutionary useful analysis is a form of opposite engineering in that it attempts to reconstruct the thoughts's design from an analysis of the troubles the mind ought to have evolved to clear up" (Buller 2005, 92). Many philosophers object to evolutionary psychologists' over attribution of adaptations on the basis of apparent layout. here a few are following Gould and Lewontin's (1979) lead when they worry that accounting for obvious layout in nature in phrases of model amounts to telling just-so stories but they may just as easily cite Williams (1966), who also recommended in opposition to the over attribution of model as an cause of biological traits. at the same time as it's miles real that evolutionary functional analysis can lend itself to simply-so tale telling, this is not the most exciting hassle that confronts evolutionary psychology, numerous different exciting troubles have been diagnosed. as an example, Elisabeth Lloyd (1999) derives a grievance of evolutionary psychology from Gould and Lewontin's complaint of sociobiology, emphasizing the point that evolutionary psychologists' adaptationism leads them to ignore alternative evolutionary strategies. Buller takes yet another approach to evolutionary psychologists' adaptationism. What lies behind Buller's criticisms of evolutionary psychologists' adaptationism is a one of a kind view than theirs approximately what is important in evolutionary thinking (Buller 2005). Buller thinks that evolutionary psychologists overemphasize layout and that they make the contentious assumption that with respect to the trends they're inquisitive about, evolution is completed, rather than ongoing.

Sober's definition of model isn't always restricted only to use to organs or other developments that exhibit apparent design. as an alternative, seize size (in birds), training (in fish), leaf association, foraging strategies and all manner of tendencies can be adaptations (cf. Seger and Stubblefield 1996). Buller argues the greater widespread point that phenotypic plasticity of various sorts may be an version, as it arises in diverse organisms as a result of natural selection.[9] The difference here among Buller (and other philosophers and biologists) and evolutionary psychologists is a difference within the explanatory scope that they attribute to herbal choice. For evolutionary psychologists, the hallmark of herbal selection is a properly functioning organ and for his or her critics, the consequences of herbal selection may be seen in an vast variety of traits starting from the unique apparent layout capabilities of organs to the maximum general reaction profiles in behavior. in line with Buller, this latter approach opens up the range of possible evolutionary hypotheses that may account for human behavior. instead of being confined to accounting for our conduct in terms of the joint output of many specific modular mechanisms, we will account for our behavior with the aid of appealing to choice acting upon many extraordinary levels of trends. This distinction in emphasis on what's crucial in evolutionary idea is also on the center of debates among evolutionary psychologists and behavioral ecologists, who argue that behaviors, in place of simply the mechanisms that underlie them, may be variations (cf. Downes 2001). in addition, this distinction in emphasis is what leads to the wide variety of exchange evolutionary hypotheses that Sterelny (Sterelny 2003) affords to provide an explanation for human behavior. for the reason that philosophers like Buller and Sterelny are adaptationists, they may be now not essential of evolutionary psychologists' adaptationism. instead, they're vital of the slim explanatory scope of the sort of adaptationism evolutionary psychologists adopt.

Buller's complaint that evolutionary psychologists assume that evolution is finished for the tendencies that they're inquisitive about connects concerns approximately the information of evolutionary concept with worries approximately the trying out of evolutionary hypotheses. here is Tooby & Cosmides' clear declaration of the assumption that Buller is involved about: "evolutionary psychologists frequently discover the design of the customary, developed mental and neural architecture that we all proportion through distinctive feature of being human. Evolutionary psychologists are typically less interested in human traits that modify due to genetic variations because they apprehend that these variations are not likely to be evolved variations imperative to human nature. Of the three sorts of traits which are determined within the layout of organisms – variations, by way of-merchandise, and noise – traits as a result of genetic variants are predominantly evolutionary noise, with little adaptive importance, even as complicated diversifications are likely to be conventional within the species" (Tooby and Cosmides 2005, 39). This line of questioning also captures evolutionary psychologists' view of human nature: human nature is our collection of universally shared diversifications. (See Downes and Machery 2013 for more dialogue of this and other, contrasting biologically primarily based money owed of human nature.) The trouble right here is that it is fake to expect that diversifications can not be subject to variant. The underlying hassle is the constrained perception of model. adaptations are developments that stand up due to natural choice and no longer trends that showcase layout and are widely widespread in a given species (cf. Seger and Stubblefield 1996). As a end result, it's far quite constant to argue, as Buller does, that many human developments may additionally nevertheless be under choice and yet moderately be called adaptations. eventually, philosophers of biology have articulated numerous unique forms of adaptationism (see e.g. Godfrey-Smith 2001; Lewens 2009; Sober 2000). whilst some of those kinds of adaptationism can be reasonably visible setting constraints on how evolutionary research is performed, Godfrey-Smith's "explanatory adaptationism" is different in individual (Godfrey-Smith 2001). Explanatory adaptationism is the view that apparent design is one of the large questions we are facing in explaining our natural global and herbal selection is the massive (and most effective supportable) answer to such a large question. Explanatory adaptationism is often followed through folks that need to distinguish evolutionary wondering from creationism or smart design and is the manner evolutionary psychologists regularly sofa their work to differentiate it from their colleagues within the broader social sciences. at the same time as explanatory adaptationism does serve to distinguish evolutionary psychology from such markedly unique approaches to accounting for layout in nature, it does no longer location many clear constraints at the manner wherein evolutionary explanations should be sought (cf. Downes 2015). up to now these are disagreements that are placed in differing views approximately the character and scope of evolutionary explanation however they have got ramifications within the dialogue approximately speculation checking out.

If the traits of hobby to evolutionary psychologists are universally allotted, then we should expect to discover them in all human beings. This in part explains the inventory that evolutionary psychologists put in move cultural psychological tests (see e.g. Buss 1990). If we discover evidence for the trait in a large pass section of human beings, then this supports our view that the trait is an version —on the belief that diversifications are organ-like trends which are products of natural selection but not subject to variant. but given the broader scope view of evolution defended via philosophers of biology, this method of trying out seems incorrect-headed as a take a look at of an evolutionary speculation. certainly such testing can bring about the very thrilling effects that positive choice profiles are widely shared pass culturally however the check does now not speak to the evolutionary speculation that the alternatives are diversifications (cf. Lloyd 1999; Buller 2005).

any other fear that critics have about evolutionary psychologists' approach to hypothesis trying out is that they supply inadequate weight to severe exchange hypotheses that in shape the applicable information. Buller dedicates several chapters of his e-book on evolutionary psychology to an examination of hypothesis checking out and many of his criticisms center around the creation of alternate hypotheses that do as true a task, or a higher job, of accounting for the records. for instance, he argues that the speculation of assortative mating via fame does a higher activity of accounting for a number of evolutionary psychologists' mate choice information than their desired high fame desire hypothesis. This debate hangs on how the empirical tests pop out. The previous debate is more carefully related to theoretical problems in philosophy of biology.

I stated in my introduction that there is a broad consensus amongst philosophers of technological know-how that evolutionary psychology is a deeply flawed company and some philosophers of biology retain to remind us of this sentiment (see e.g. Dupre 2012). however the relevant consensus isn't always whole, there are some proponents of evolutionary psychology among philosophers of science. One manner of defending evolutionary psychology is to rebut grievance. Edouard Machery and Clark Barrett (2007) do just that during their sharply essential evaluate of Buller's e book. any other manner to defend evolutionary psychology is to practice it (at least to the extent that philosophers can, i.e. theoretically). that is what Robert Arp (2006) does in a current article. I in short assessment each responses below.

Machery and Barrett (2007) argue that Buller has no clear critical goal as there is nothing to the idea that there may be a studies culture of evolutionary psychology this is distinct from the wider employer of the evolutionary know-how of human conduct. They argue that theoretical tenets and techniques are shared by means of many in the biology of human behavior. as an example, many are adaptationists. however as we saw above, evolutionary psychologists and behavioral ecologists can each call themselves adaptationist however their unique technique to adaptationism dictates the variety of hypotheses that they are able to generate, the range of developments that can be counted as variations and impacts upon the way wherein hypotheses are examined. studies traditions can proportion some large theoretical commitments and yet still be awesome research traditions. Secondly, they argue against Buller's view that past environments are not strong enough to supply the kind of mental variations that evolutionary psychologists endorse. They take this to be a declare that no variations can get up from an evolutionary fingers race state of affairs, for example, between predators and prey. but again, I suppose that the confrontation here is over what counts as an version. Buller does not deny that adaptations— traits that get up as a manufactured from herbal selection—stand up from all styles of unstable environments. What he denies is that organ-like, unique cause variations are the probably end result of such evolutionary scenarios.

Arp (2006) defends a speculation approximately a kind of module—scenario visualization—a psychological edition that arose in our hominid history in reaction to the needs of device making, inclusive of building spear throwing gadgets for hunting. Arp gives his speculation within the context of demonstrating the superiority of his method to evolutionary psychology, which he calls "slim Evolutionary Psychology," over "vast Evolutionary Psychology," with appreciate to accounting for archaeological proof and statistics approximately our psychology. whilst Arp's speculation is revolutionary and interesting, he never defends it conclusively. that is partly because his strategy is to examine his hypothesis with archaeologist Steven Mithen's (see e.g. 1996) non-modular "cognitive fluidity" speculation that is proposed to account for the identical records. The problem here is that Mithen's view is only one of the many opportunity, evolutionary explanations of human tool making behavior. at the same time as Arp's modular thesis can be superior to Mithen's, he has not as compared it to Sterelny's (2003; 2012) account of device making and device use or to Boyd and Richerson's (see e.g. 2005) account and hence no longer dominated these bills out as plausible alternatives. As neither of these alternative bills depend on the postulation of psychological modules, evolutionary psychology is not competently defended.

Moral Psychology and Evolutionary Psychology

Many philosophers who work on moral psychology understand that their topic is empirically constrained. Philosophers take two main approaches to using empirical results in moral psychology. One is to use empirical results (and empirically based theories from psychology) to criticize philosophical accounts of moral psychology (see e.g. Doris 2002) and one is to generate (and, in the experimental philosophy tradition, to test) hypotheses about our moral psychology (see e.g. Nichols 2004). For those who think that some (or all) of our moral psychology is based in innate capacities, evolutionary psychology is a good source of empirical results and empirically based theory. One account of the make-up of our moral psychology follows from the massive modularity account of the architecture of the mind. Our moral judgments are a product of domain specific psychological modules that are adaptations and arose in our hominid forebears in response to contingencies in our (mostly) social environments. This position is currently widely discussed by philosophers working in moral psychology. An example of this discussion follows.

Cosmides (see e.g. 1989) defends a hypothesis in evolutionary psychology that we have a cheater-detection module.[10] This module is hypothesized to underlie important components of our behavior in moral domains and fits with the massively modular view of our psychology in general. Cosmides (along with Tooby) argues that cheating is a violation of a particular kind of conditional rule that goes along with a social contract. Social exchange is a system of cooperation for mutual benefit and cheaters violate the social contract that governs social exchange (Cosmides and Tooby 2005). The selection pressure for a dedicated cheater-detection module is the presence of cheaters in the social world. The cheater-detection module is an adaptation that arose in response to cheaters. The cheater-detection hypothesis has been the focus of a huge amount of critical discussion. Cosmides and Tooby (2008) defend the idea that cheat detection is modular over hypotheses that more general rules of inference are involved in the kind of reasoning behind cheater detection against critics Ron Mallon (2008) and Fodor (2008). Some criticism of the cheater-detection hypothesis involves rehashing criticisms of massive modularity in general and some treats the hypothesis as a contribution to moral psychology and invokes different considerations. For example, Mallon (2008) worries about the coherence of abandoning a domain general conception of ought in our conception of our moral psychology. This discussion is also ongoing. (See e.g. Sterelny 2012 for a selection of alternate, non-modular explanations of aspects of our moral psychology.)

Human Nature

Evolutionary psychology is well suited to providing an account of human nature. As noted above evolutionary psychology owes a theoretical debt to human sociobiology. E.O. Wilson took human sociobiology to provide us with an account of human nature (1978). For Wilson human nature is the collection of universal human behavioral repertoires and these behavioral repertoires are best understood as being products of natural selection. Evolutionary psychologists argue that human nature is not a collection of universal human behavioral repertoires but rather the universal psychological mechanisms underlying these behaviors (Tooby and Cosmides 1990). These universal psychological mechanisms are products of natural selection, as we saw in Section 2. above. Tooby and Cosmides put this claim as follows: "the concept of human nature is based on a species-typical collection of complex psychological adaptations" (1990, 17). So, for evolutionary psychologists, "human nature consists of a set of psychological adaptations that are presumed to be universal among, and unique to, human beings" (Buller 2005, 423). Machery's (2008) nomological account of human nature is based on, and very similar to, the evolutionary psychologists' account. Machery says that "human nature is the set of properties that humans tend to possess as a result of the evolution of their species" (2008, 323). While Machery's account appeals to traits that have evolved and are universal (common to all humans), it is not limited to psychological mechanisms. For example, he thinks of bi-pedalism as part of the human nature trait cluster. Machery's view captures elements of both the sociobiological view and the evolutionary psychology view of human nature. He shares the idea that a trait must be a product of evolution, rather than say social learning or enculturation, with both these accounts.

Some critical challenges to evolutionary psychological accounts of human nature (and the nomological account) derive from similar concerns as those driving criticism of evolutionary psychology in general. In Section 4. we see that discussions of evolutionary psychology are founded on disagreements about how adaptation should be characterized and disagreements about the role of variation in evolution. Some critics charge evolutionary psychologists of assuming that adaptation cannot sustain variation. Buller's (2005) criticism of evolutionary psychologists' account of human nature also invokes variation (cf. Hull 1986; and Sober 1980). The idea here is that humans, like all organisms, exhibit a great deal of variation, including morphological, physiological, behavioral and cultural variation (cf. Amundson 2000). Buller argues that the evolutionary psychology account of human nature either ignores or fails to account for all of this variation (c.f. Lewens 2015; Odenbaugh Forthcoming; and Ramsey 2013). Any account that restricts human nature to just those traits we have in common and which also are not subject to change, cannot account for human variation.

Buller's (2005) criticism of evolutionary psychologists' notion of human nature (or the nomological account) is based on the idea that we vary across many dimensions and an account of human nature based on fixed, universal traits cannot account for any of this variation. The idea that to account for human nature, we must account for human variation is presented and defended by evolutionary psychologists (see e.g. Barrett 2015), anthropologists (see e.g. Cashdan 2013) and philosophers (see e.g. Griffiths 2011 and Ramsey 2013). Barrett agrees with Buller (and others) that evolutionary psychologists have failed to account for human variation in their account of human nature. Rather than seeing this challenge as a knock down of the whole enterprise of accounting for human nature, Barrett sees this as a challenge for an account of human nature. Barrett says "Whatever human nature is, it's a biological phenomenon with all that implies" (2015, 321). So, human nature is "a big wobbly cloud that is different from the population clouds of squirrels and palm trees. To understand human minds and behaviors, we need to understand the properties of our own cloud, as messy as it might be" (2015, 232). Rather than human nature being a collection of shared fixed universal psychological traits, for Barrett, human nature is the whole human trait cluster, including all of the variation in all of our traits. This approach to human nature is sharply different than the approach defended by either Wilson, Tooby and Cosmides or Machery but is also subject to a number of criticisms. The main thrust of the criticisms is that such a view cannot be explanatory and is instead merely a big list of all the properties that humans have had and can have (See e.g. Buller 2005; Downes 2016; Futuyma 1998; and Lewens 2015). Discussion over the tension between evolutionary psychologists' views and the manifest variation in human traits continues in many areas that evolutionary psychologists focus on. Another example of this broader

HOW TO DEAL WITH THE FAILURE (BOUNDARY RULES)

RULE NO. 1

Congratulations !!!!!!!!!!!!!!!!!!!!!!!!!!!!!!!!!!!!!

Mission Accomplished !!!!!!!!!!!!!!!!!!!!!!!!!!!

Congratulations of failing

Congratulations on meeting a part which is not in your control. Now you know the feeling of dark Somethings are not in your control and this failure is a reminder of that truth.

More often than that whatever you want you will never get that, You wish to do something which you will not get as this is also not any wound or you can't even heal this. It's a BLESSING

FAILURE IS THE NORM SUCCESS IS THE EXCEPTION

Think, the one thing is true that you will lose majority of games in life and this should be done, because if life is that much easy than how would be interesting to live or how would it be interesting to play ?

If you will win games this easily than what will you do till next remaning life ?

Now remember this

TRY LIKE YOU ARE MEANT FOR SUCCEED, FAIL LIKE YOU WERE MEANT TO FAIL

Try with the confidence of winner and fail with the humility of saint.

Respect the complicated nature of universe you live in.

RULE NO. 2

Try to control on your instinct, It may hurts to you more. Take a deep breathe in and out.

Develope appreciation for the beauty of this movement in your life.

Now think with a cool mind and strategize your way use your brain, Feel this failure in a good manner.

RULE NO. 3

Are you gonna keep playing ?

PATRICK GEDDES : NOTATION OF LIFE (CASE STUDY)

Over the last few decades, there has been renewed interest in the work of biologist, sociologist, and city planner Patrick Geddes [1]. This is due to his efforts for holistic considerations for the entirety of the modes of human life and the facilities appropriate for their function. That is, he asked what makes a city or a town ideal for life, and how can we plan to bring this ideality into being? To this day, cities fail in many important ways.

Geddes embraced the new (at the time) Victorian notion of evolution in his work and thought of how cities could and should evolve to meet their shortcomings as well as provide environments for future developments. For example, common institutions such as schools, churches, and governments (polity) need to cooperate with family dwellings to provide for synergy and functional enrichment.

Geddes often used grids of words to explore relations between concepts, such as place, work, and folk. Placing these words along the diagonal of a square allowed one to consider the paired concepts of place-work, work-place, place-folk, etc. For example, how does the place-work compare with the work-place? His "notation of life" was a complicated schematic for exploring relations between a city's facilities and the activities that they should promote.

Town / Acts : place, work, folk

School / Facts : sense, experience, feeling (alt. lore, learn, love)

City / Deeds : ethno-polity, synergy, achievement (alt. polity, culture art)

Cloister / Dreams (Thoughts) : emotion, ideation, imagery (alt. ideals, ideas, imagery)

Two locales are objective, two are subjective, two are passive, and two are active:

In-World (Subjective) : School and Cloister
Out-World (Objective) : Town and City
Passive : Town and School
Active : City and Cloister
And so:
Passive & Subjective : School
Active & Subjective : Cloister
Passive & Objective : Town
Active & Objective : City

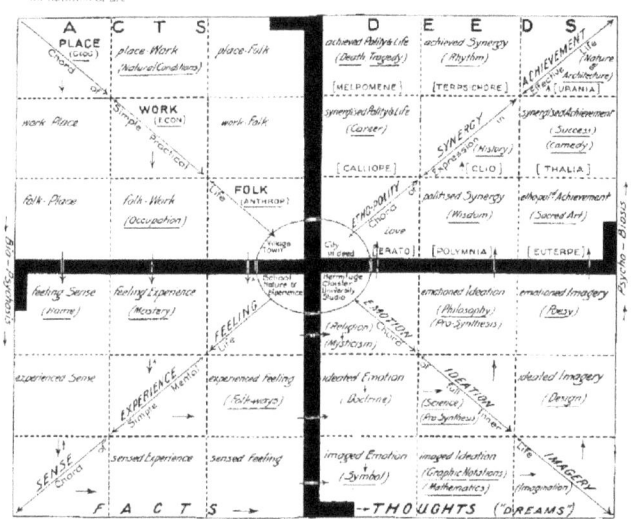

GEDDE's Chart

Geddes personal cosmology may be expressed numerically inside the following phrases:

a unified "web of existence" acknowledging the symbiotic nature of the dwelling global based totally on the life-force (or elan critical of Henri Bergson)

a two-fold lifestyles process of movement and re-motion regarding the organism and its surroundings (but similarly additionally among frame and thoughts)

his triad of folks-paintings-region paralleled by Organism-feature-surroundings; also the Cosmosphere as the arena of factors(from solar systems to dewdrops),the Biosphere(realm of organisms),and the Sociosphere (nation of man) his four chambers of the "ledger of lifestyles" expressed in his famous diagram (see Diagram 1) as a synthetical process encompassing Acts, information, desires and Deeds, emphasising specifically family members between the goal out-international and the subjective in-world, and the active and the passive, each complementing the other.

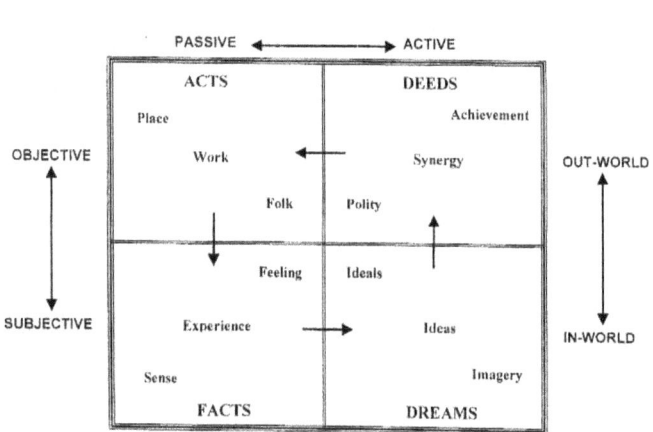

DIAGRAM 1 : GEDDES' NOTATION OF LIFE

GEDDE's Chart at One dimension

PATRICK GEDDES IN INDIA : FROM SYNTHESIS TO INTEGRATION

Graham King

In a letter to Lewis Mumford, dated thirtieth December 1928,written from Scots university Montpellier, Patrick Geddes wrote: "i have given your name to Dr.J.H.Cousins, formerly of the Irish poets - now a theosophist, but the sanest and least essential of any I ever met. he is to be in N.Y. for a while - & is well worth speaking with: he gives me the impact of a stay educator, bringing spherical his doctrinaires to common sense, but with out loss of idealism - indeed closer to higher course of it".(Novak 1995)

Who changed into J.H.Cousins, and why become Patrick Geddes so inspired? in which and when did they meet? How applicable are their views nowadays? . And why, even as Geddes continues to be remembered as a well-known worldwide figure, an critical force on the town making plans, and a passionate endorse of synthesis, does Cousins continue to be so little known? In fact they met in India in the 1920's where they both taught, locating a close affinity no longer only among their ideas on synthesis in thought and action, however also for the significance of jap idea in their shared philosophies. in this essay I are searching for to explore their Indian credentials, evaluate and evaluation their thinking, and assess its validity in terms of present day idea on synthesis and sustainable improvement and the need for integration in coverage development and action.

Geddes' connections with India are well known. He visited four times between 1914 and 1924, staying for 2 and a half of years between 1916 and 1919. while there he surveyed limitless cities and additionally crystallised his mind on synthesis as Professor of Civics and Sociology at Bombay university. Helen Meller, in her biography, (Meller 1995) facts the enthusiastic cope with Geddes gave to the Madras Literary Society on the mixing of lifestyle, history and concrete form of the Indian temple towns. Writing to the Maharaja of Kapurthala in 1917 he described how the transitions in an Indian city "form an inseparably interwoven shape", (no longer) "as an worried network of thoroughfares dividing hundreds of building blocks, however as a exquisite chessboard on which the manifold game of lifestyles is in lively development"(Tyrwhitt 1947).

Cousins for his part got here to India in 1915 from ireland where with W.B. Yeats he became one of the pioneers of the Irish Literary and Dramatic Revival. In India he have become Director of the school of Synthetical study (Brahmaridya Ashrama) at Adyar, Madras from 1922 to 1928, later becoming essential of Madnapalle university,where he wrote "examine in Synthesis" based on "a life-time of thought, research and enjoy"(Cousins 1934). A footnote in that e-book refers to a summer college in Madras in 1928,so it's miles probably that it become at this kind of he crossed paths with Geddes who changed into regularly in Madras.

Geddes' interest in India had begun a few years before. In Chicago in February 1900 he had met the well-known Indian guru Swami Vivekanda. Philip Boardman data of this meeting with "the apostle of the Vedanta" how "the jap subject of frame and thoughts made the sort of lasting affect on both Anna (Geddes' spouse) and Patrick that they later exceeded directly to their younger kids the simple Raja Yoga exercises for manipulate of the inner nature" (Boardman 1978). Vivekananda became a charismatic figure seeking to build bridges among east and west. one of his disciples, an English lady called Sister Nivedita, have become a close pal, and wrote a ebook incorporating his ideas she entitled "The internet of Indian lifestyles". Geddes additionally met the Swami again at the arena fair in Paris later that 12 months.

The poet Rabindranath Tagore additionally have become an enduring buddy following their initial assembly on the Darjeeling summer meeting in 1917. Later they co-operated on plans for an international college in India "to bring East and West collectively for the advantage of humanity". In a letter to him Geddes proposed a 3-fold approach to movement reflecting the team spirit of existence primarily based on Dharma or proper conduct (the social foundation integrating ethics with economics); Behaviour (character mind and frame, i.e. notion and feelings); and life as realistic interest. other Indian contacts protected Ghandi, the physicist J.C.Bose, numerous Maharajahs and, of course, the area people as he walked their dusty streets, courts and alleyways.

Geddes also met Annie Besant, then President of the Theosophical Society, and they visited the old temple-town of Conjeveram collectively. He had first met her in the 1870's while he turned into a scholar. Annie Besant had comparable pastimes in a synthesis of jap and western thoughts and Cousins' e-book is dedicated to her within the following manner:

" to the person synthesis of
intuition & movement
idea & feeling
masculine & female
teenagers & age
east and west
beyond & destiny".

Geddes own cosmology may be expressed numerically within the following terms:

a unified "net of lifestyles" acknowledging the symbiotic nature of the dwelling international based totally at the life-force (or elan essential of Henri Bergson)

a two-fold existence method of movement and re-movement concerning the organism and its surroundings (but similarly additionally between frame and thoughts)

his triad of folks-work-region paralleled by Organism-function-environment; additionally the Cosmosphere as the arena of things(from sun structures to dewdrops),the

Biosphere(realm of organisms),and the Sociosphere (kingdom of man)

his four chambers of the "ledger of life" expressed in his well-known diagram (see Diagram 1) as a synthetical procedure encompassing Acts, records, desires and Deeds, emphasising in particular family members among the goal out-international and the subjective in-international, and the active and the passive, every complementing the opposite.

D1

whilst those ideas had been gestating for maximum of his instructional life, drawing on a wealth of european assets and his very own revel in, their fusion with Indian notion is, I agree with, found out with the aid of Cousins' own cosmology, which now not handiest parallels Geddes' approach, however also sincerely exhibits their indebtedness to oriental wondering:

First, Cousins' simple role changed into certainly one of a unified world expressed in a text from the Upanishad: "they who see however One in all of the converting manifoldness of this universe -- unto them belongs everlasting truth";

Secondly, he noted what William James called "the whole pull and strain of the cosmos",

regarding primary guidelines of motion, either towards disintegration or integration, or further toward evaluation or synthesis, personalized in Hindu concept as Radha and Krishna (the dance of lifestyles);

Thirdly, Cousins acknowledged the cosmic trinity of substance (or be counted), business enterprise (or sample), and consciousness (or electricity) which animates the world of which mankind is a part, giving examples from both the Hindu imagination and Buddhist philosophy;

finally, Cousins' "organum of synthesis" become based on recognition of the four fundamental human capacities of: intuition, emotion, cognition and movement, every with an in-turned (subjective) and out-grew to become (objective) factor as represented inside the diagrams shown right here (2A,2B).

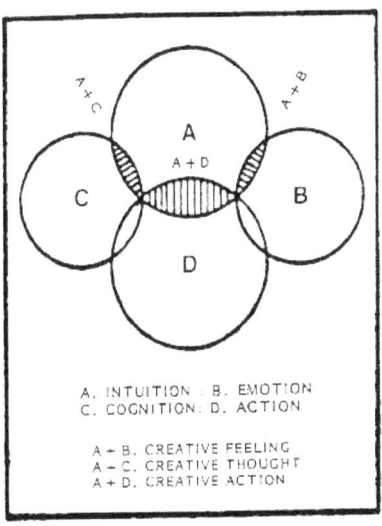

DIAGRAM 2A : COUSINS' INTERACTIONS OF HUMAN CAPACITY

A. INTUITION B. EMOTION
C. COGNITION D. ACTION

A + B. CREATIVE FEELING
A + C. CREATIVE THOUGHT
A + D. CREATIVE ACTION

So for cognition we're able to differentiate among contemplation, whose expression is philosophy (essentially inwards) and commentary whose expression is science (essentially outwards); and for emotion between spiritual aspiration (basically inwards) and artwork as creative expression (basically outwards). Cousins also illustrated how the intuition co-ordinates the human mental, emotional and bodily attributes in comparable style to Geddes' perception of "psychic co-ordination" (Geddes 1931). in this connection, at the same time as Cousins selected to identify his schema with the Hindu Gods Shiva and Shakti, Geddes desired the Greek pantheon: "our diagram seems to be that of Parnassus, the home of the 9 Muses"(Geddes 1949).

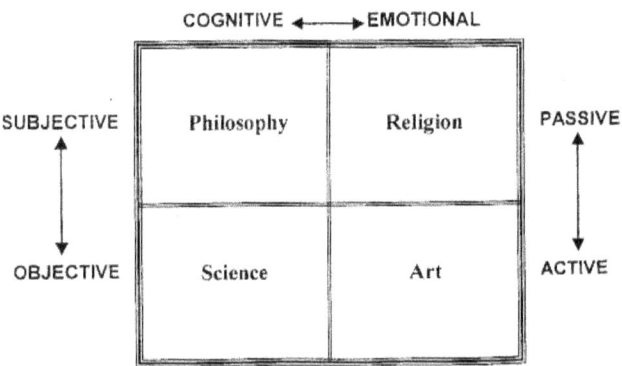

DIAGRAM 2B : COGNITIVE AND EMOTIONAL CONNECTIONS

The affinity with Geddes' questioning is apparent as the diagrams illustrate. both strain the significance of the goal and subjective nation-states; each stress the want to interact both the cognitive and the emotional capacities, despite the fact that Geddes builds a far extra complicated and dynamic image focussing on "vicinity" in addition to man or woman and collective endeavour (or civics). both are deeply devoted to the intuitive intelligence as part of a much wider cosmic or non secular power.

despite the fact that Geddes' biographer Helen Meller (Meller 1995) disparagingly dismisses his attempts at grand synthesis in the light of clinical advances, there are again present day thinkers grappling with the massive picture. i've decided on two with precise affinity to both Geddes and Cousins: Fritjof Capra and Ken Wilber.

In his ebook "The Tao of Physics", Capra additionally contrasts contemporary clinical questioning with Buddhist and Hindu philosophy which in place of separate the perceived global into separate gadgets, accepts the flux and fluidity of lifestyles, emphasising relationships and patterns: the primordial internet of life symbolized with the aid of Indra's net. His subsequent book, in reality entitled "The net of life", is sub-titled "a brand new Synthesis of thoughts and count" and in it he sets out his very own three-fold criteria of a residing machine, remarkably like that of Cousins, comprising:

a pattern of business enterprise (or shape)
a structure or physical embodiment;
And a manner (the flow of energy that
animates, sustains and inter-penetrates both pattern and structure).
For Capra this holistic and ecological expertise, with cognition seen as the process of living, could allow us to better plan for sustainable communities, devoted to inter-dependence, considerable involvement, assist for herbal structures, recycling and energy saving.

Wilber honestly echoes Geddes. His 3-fold schema perspectives evolution as the unfolding manifestation of spirit from matter (the cosmos), through existence (the biosphere) to thoughts (or human cognizance). Following a trawl of the world's amazing cosmologies -- east and west -- he discovers "certain styles repeating themselves in all three domains" (Wilber 1996).His primary premise is that each one entities are both whole and concurrently a part of some different entire, comparable, say, to Christopher Alexander's sample language for architecture or Geddes' reciprocal organisms. He calls these "holons".

Like Geddes and Cousins, Wilber makes use of a four-quartile diagram to give his standard framework, as proven overleaf (Diagram 3). It too is based on recognising the objective and subjective geographical regions of know-how which he expands to deal with the 3 languages we use in relating to the world -- I, We, and It. Empirical technology basically deals with items, with "its"; morals and ethics situation "we" and our inter-subjective global; "I" entails artwork, aesthetics and self-expression. He sees the equal differences in oriental traditions, with Buddha because the remaining I, We as Sangha (or community), and the It as Dharma or objective truth or reality. Their disassociation, he believes, has caused what Lewis Mumford has described as "the disqualified universe" wherein analysis supplants synthesis and the subjective realm is squeezed out.

It become the center of Geddes' life's work in idea and motion to restore that balance and make certain that matters do connect. nowadays we call this "integration", expressed as joined-up authorities, the partnership precept, or sustainability appraisal. There are exhortations for policies to be "integrated and pursued simultaneously", as within the Welsh assembly's Draft making plans policy steerage (Welsh meeting 2001), and tool-kits which includes "The nice of existence Capital"(countryside enterprise 2001) offering a unified technique to assessment which includes the qualitative and subjective factors as well as those primarily based on "difficult" technology. "Integration, integration, integration" is the current mantra, but as Wilber reminds us, it needs to be accompanied via the counter movement of differentiation, by using acknowledgement of different variations.

Drawing directly at the Geddes legacy, Lewis Mumford acknowledged this in his book "The subculture of towns", posted in 1938 (Mumford 1938), when he warned of cohesion by way of suppression, through reduction to needless simplicity, in preference to team spirit with the aid of inclusion in which "a large number of different styles become factors in a more complicated configuration". in the identical book he set out his "main thoughts" at the imminent "natural order":

recognize for the primacy of lifestyles and nature (sustainability);

acknowledgement of self sufficient but continually-associated organisms (Wilber's holons);

for the planner and other experts a brand new manner of wondering which includes the "disappearance of the boundary partitions among the inner and the outer, the aware and the unconscious, the external and the internal environment".

Mumford became recognising the want for a shift from the command and manipulate mentality to one of partnership and participation, with the planner as animateur, enabler, guide, mentor, and monitor, concerning carefully to all pursuits in the network, (Geddes' civics), and respecting natural limits (Geddes' bio-technics, our sustainability).

whether or not or now not Mumford met Dr.Cousins in new york, it is clean that through Mumford's contacts and correspondence with Geddes, whom he addressed as master, the spirit in their thinking, regardless of strong objection from the scientific established order, continued to softly ferment. Geddes' "bio-technics" became Mumford's "organic making plans", which in flip, in the light of looming planetary disaster, became our "sustainable improvement", complete with social and economic dimensions, as Mumford and Geddes could have wished. Cousins' contribution in reality lay in confirming for Geddes the need for the fullest improvement and integration of the individual human colleges as the premise for synergistic motion.

these days, with the arrival of sustainable development, as practitioners we're exploring new approaches to connect our sports and take account of herbal systems. Coastal zone management serves as a beneficial paradigm for illustrating this shift. The potential force of dynamic herbal procedures upon the frequently fragile and inclined nature of marine eco-systems calls for a completely unique approach, one which additionally recognises the essential effect of human sports. With the vagaries of weather change, and the growing frequency of excessive physical occasions, including huge flooding, those concerns have now spread to urban and rural planning extra usually. The social and economic measurement of city regeneration and the problems of our rural regions are also annoying new kinds of participation and new sorts of partnership. inside the field of delivery, too, the decision for integration for all modes in all instances is in particular strident, also encompassing site visitors calming and combined use development to lessen travel.

It is simple to pay lip service to such credos. expert attitudes although do not shift so easily. Objectivity, consistency, impartiality, and expert attachment to time-honoured technical codes, can easily be defences towards trade after they deny ingenious and bendy responses to sparkling occasions.

making plans, consequently, desires to grow to be more energetic-reactive as opposed to pro-lively; a more responsive and flexible improvement control merits a higher profile because it responds to the strain of unpredictable activities . there'll stay a plethora of plans, formal and informal, but the emphasis of the planner's talent will shift to keener commentary of the "organism", Geddes' "energetic sympathy" bearing upon the situation of scrutiny in all its richness and relatedness. wondering-in-context will become as natural as respiratory, breath, of course, being a core metaphor in oriental philosophy for the alert attention, as Geddes might have liked.

Sustainable development is satisfactorily ambiguous to draw assist from many camps. The chance is that a slim attention on integration should come to be simply the one-dimensional technical application of the dreams of secular humanism, the triumph of approach. Geddes' extra rounded idea of synthesis serves to remind us of the results if we forget about the other dimensions.

CHARLES DARWIN & ALFRED RUSSEL WALLACE THEORY OF NATURAL SELECTION

Alfred Russel Wallace become a naturalist who independently proposed the precept of evolution thru natural choice. A remarkable admirer of Charles Darwin, Wallace produced medical journals with Darwin in 1858, which introduced approximately Darwin to put up on the starting place of Species the following yr.

Welsh naturalist Alfred Russel Wallace (1823 - 1913).
Alfred Russel Wallace
Watercolor instance of a golden birdwing butterfly (Ornithoptera croesus).
Wallace worked round the sector accumulating proof to resource his evolutionary idea. he's great recognized for reading caution colouration in animals, one example being the golden birdwing butterfly (Ornithoptera croesus), in

addition to his concept of speciation.

After an expansion of zoological discoveries, Wallace proposed a idea of evolution which matched the unpublished ideas Darwin had saved mystery for nearly two many years. This advocated Darwin to collect his medical thoughts and collaborate with Wallace. They published their clinical thoughts together in 1858.

thoughts of evolution via herbal selection

The concept behind the idea of evolution thru the procedure of natural desire is that each one species of residing subjects have advanced from simple lifestyles paperwork over a term. The Earth is set four.5 billion years vintage, and there may be clinical proof to signify that lifestyles on the planet started greater than 3 billion years in the past.

herbal choice

The often happening idea of evolution explains that it takes vicinity by way of natural choice. the important thing factors are given underneath.

humans in a species show a extensive form of version and this modification is a end result of differences in their genes caused by random mutations that may be inherited.

In every populace extra offspring are produced than can live to tell the tale. This overproduction outcomes in competition, eg for food.

people with characteristics most best to their environment are more likely to continue to exist and reproduce. this is normally referred to as survival of the fittest. The genes that permit these human beings to gain fulfillment inner their surroundings are handed on to their offspring, which ends up in those unique genes turning into greater commonplace.

individuals which may be poorly adapted to their

surroundings are much less probable to stay to tell the tale and reproduce. Their genes are an awful lot much less probably to be passed directly to the subsequent technology. Over a time frame, a species will little by little evolve.

each genes and the environment can reason model, but handiest genetic version can be handed directly to the subsequent technology.

If populations of one species emerge as increasingly remarkable in phenotype that they could now not interbreed to shape fertile offspring, this may result in the formation of species.

Modelling herbal choice

This version may be used to demonstrate how herbal desire can arise based totally on the characteristic of camouflage in a population of prey organisms.

method

Use a chunk of inexperienced card as a background.

Randomly area 20 green and 20 white quantities of string on the cardboard to represent populations of prey organisms.

the usage of a forceps to represent the mouth of the predator, gather as many pieces of string as you may in 10 seconds.

count what number of inexperienced and white portions are left and file.

Repeat the manner instances more.

This model suggests that regardless of the reality that every species of prey are predated, the species with the highest diploma of camouflage can live on. In truth, those organisms would be capable of breed and bypass on their camouflage genes. wherein there has been as quickly as a honest distribution of green and white organisms, now the camouflaged organisms outnumber the non-camouflaged organisms by means of manner of 10 to one.

limitations of the model

on this version the prey do not pass. What if the white organisms had been an lousy lot quicker than the green ones?

There may also be bias within the case of the predator. The scientist choosing the prey can also achieve this now not at the idea that a few are less difficult to look, but on the premise that they were aware about what the results ought to be.

The genius of Darwin (left), the manner in which he all at once became all of biology the wrong way up in 1859 with the publication of the beginning of Species, can occasionally supply the deceptive impact that the principle of evolution sprang from his forehead fully fashioned with none precedent in clinical history. however as in advance chapters on this history have proven, the raw cloth for Darwin's concept had been known for decades. Geologists and paleontologists had made a compelling case that lifestyles were on this planet for a long time, that it had modified over that point, and that many species had emerge as extinct. at the same time, embryologists and different naturalists reading residing animals in the early 1800s had found, occasionally unwittingly, much of the nice evidence for Darwin's idea.

Pre-Darwinian thoughts approximately evolution

A visit to the Galapagos Islands in 1835 helped Darwin formulate his thoughts on herbal choice. He found numerous species of finch adapted to specific environmental niches. The finches additionally differed in beak shape, food source, and the way food was captured.

It become Darwin's genius each to show how all this evidence preferred the evolution of species from a not unusual ancestor and to offer a achievable mechanism by way of which lifestyles might evolve. Lamarck and others had promoted evolutionary theories, however with the intention to give an explanation for just how existence changed, they depended on hypothesis. usually, they claimed that evolution changed into guided with the aid of a few long-term trend. Lamarck, as an instance, idea that lifestyles strove over the years to upward push from simple single-celled bureaucracy to complex ones. Many German biologists conceived of lifestyles evolving in line with predetermined rules, within the identical way an embryo develops within the womb. however within the mid-1800s, Darwin and the British biologist Alfred Russel Wallace independently conceived of a herbal, even observable, manner for lifestyles to change: a system Darwin known as herbal choice.

The stress of population growth
interestingly, Darwin and Wallace located their suggestion in economics. An English parson named Thomas Malthus posted a e-book in 1797 called Essay at the principle of populace wherein he warned his fellow Englishmen that maximum guidelines designed to assist the bad have been doomed due to the relentless pressure of populace boom. A nation ought to effortlessly double its population in some a long time, leading to famine and misery for all.

when Darwin and Wallace examine Malthus, it came about to each of them that animals and flora should additionally be experiencing the same populace stress. It ought to take very little time for the arena to be knee-deep in beetles or earthworms. but the international isn't always overrun with them, or every other species, because they can't reproduce to their complete potential. Many die before they end up adults. they're at risk of droughts and bloodless winters and other environmental assaults. And their meals supply, like that of a kingdom, isn't always infinite. people should compete, albeit unconsciously, for what little meals there's.

choice of traits

The provider pigeon (bottom left) and the Brunner pouter (bottom proper) had been derived from the wild rock pigeon (pinnacle). service pigeon photo courtesy of The Pigeon Cote; Brunner pouter image courtesy of Layne's Pigeon website online; Rock dove photo courtesy of Dr. Antonio J. Ferreira © California Academy of Sciences.

on this conflict for lifestyles, survival and replica do now not come right down to natural chance. Darwin and Wallace each found out that if an animal has some trait that facilitates it to face up to the factors or to reproduce extra successfully, it could go away extra offspring in the back of than others. On common, the trait becomes more common in the following era, and the era after that.

As Darwin wrestled with herbal selection he spent a first rate deal of time with pigeon breeders, learning their techniques. He found their paintings to be an analogy for evolution. A pigeon breeder selected man or woman birds to reproduce in an effort to produce a neck ruffle. in addition, nature unconsciously "selects" individuals higher perfect to surviving their local situations. Given enough time, Darwin and Wallace argued, herbal choice may produce new types of body components, from wings to eyes.

Darwin and Wallace broaden comparable theory

Wallace in 1902. image courtesy of the Alfred Russel Wallace web page.

Darwin started out formulating his theory of herbal selection inside the late 1830s however he went on working quietly on it for two decades. He desired to accumulate a wealth of evidence before publicly providing his concept. throughout the ones years he corresponded in short with Wallace (proper), who turned into exploring the wildlife of South the us and Asia. Wallace supplied Darwin with birds for his studies and determined to searching for Darwin's help in publishing his personal ideas on evolution. He despatched Darwin his concept in 1858, which, to Darwin's surprise, almost replicated Darwin's own.

starting place of species ebook backbone.
photo courtesy of Darwin on-line.
Charles Lyell and Joseph Dalton Hooker arranged for each Darwin's and Wallace's theories to be provided to a assembly of the Linnaean Society in 1858. Darwin had been running on a primary book on evolution and used that to expand at the Origins of Species, which became published in 1859. Wallace, then again, persisted his travels and centered his study at the significance of biogeography.

The e-book changed into no longer handiest a first-rate dealer however also one of the maximum influential clinical books of all time. yet it took time for its full argument to take hold. inside a few decades, maximum scientists prevalent that evolution and the descent of species from common ancestors had been actual. however natural choice had a tougher time finding popularity. within the overdue 1800s many scientists who called themselves Darwinists without a doubt desired a Lamarckian reason for the manner lifestyles modified through the years. it would take the discovery of genes and mutations in the 20th century to make natural selection no longer simply attractive as an evidence, however unavoidable.

MODES OF SEXUAL SELECTION :
SEXUAL STUDIES IN EVOLUTION :::::

There are different sexual studies of evolution :

1. **CHOOSINESS**
2. **SYMMETRY AS INDICATOR OF PARASITE/PATHOGEN RESISTENCE**
3. **MAJOR HISTOCOMPACTIBILITY COMPLEX**
4. **WAIST TO HIP RATIO**
5. **SELECTIVITY**

CHOOSINESS :::::::

Buss and Schnitt (1933) asked men and women how likely they would be to concern to sexual intercourse to someone they viewed as desirable, guven that they had known the person for various periods of time.

Participants rated their willingness on a scale from (-3) definately not and (+3) definately yes.

As a result :-

Men consistently indicate a greater willingness to engage in sexual intercourse than women.

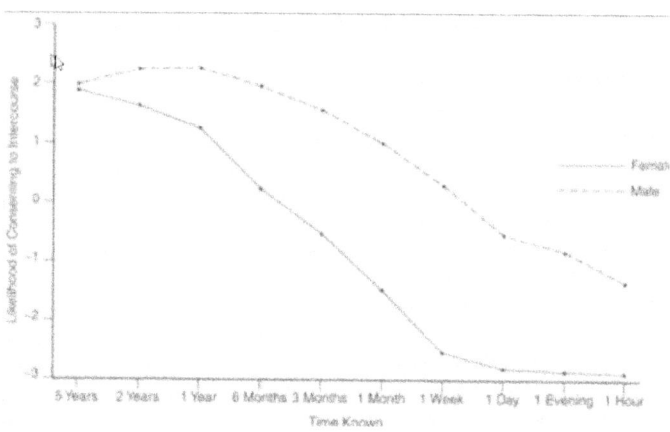

Graph Showing results

Social trade and evolutionary mental fashions of courting formation have highlighted economic methods operating on the "mating marketplace." consistent with these models, for example, people mate assortatively (Buss & Barnes, 1986; Cameron, Oskamp, & Sparks, 1977) and thereby gather the excellent fit for his or her own "mate fee" (Kenrick, Groth, Trost, & Sadalla, 1993). In addition, social trade and evolutionary models have argued that the supply of potential buddies also may affect mating behavior (Baumeister & Vohs, 2004; Becker, 1976). the supply of potential associates is indexed through the sex ratio, the number of men in step with one hundred reproductive-age girls (with 15–49 years usually used to define the age variety of those groups of ladies and men; see Fossett & Kiecolt, 1991). when the sex ratio is imbalanced, intrasexual opposition to acquire a mate of the less numerous intercourse theoretically must boom in depth among contributors of the extra numerous intercourse. This opposition includes displaying attributes and qualities favored by the much less frequent and consequently extra selective sex (Pedersen, 1991). men's behavior and ladies's conduct reflects those expected shifts in opposition. for instance, men are greater involved than girls in casual sex (Buss & Schmitt, 1993; Clark & Hatfield, 1989). Correspondingly, decrease intercourse ratio societies—wherein girls more than men compete for buddies—are characterized by using better rates of self-said girl promiscuity (Schmitt, 2005), ladies's shorter skirts (Barber, 1999), and better rates of illegitimate births (South & Trent, 1988) and teen pregnancies (Barber, 2001). In evaluation, better intercourse ratio societies—wherein guys more than ladies compete for buddies—are characterised by way of behaviors regular with mental intercourse differences produced via sex differences in minimum compulsory parental funding (i.e., men's minimal investment of a small quantity of time and sperm, relative to girls's minimal funding of 9 months of gestation and years of lactation; see Trivers, 1972). most brilliant of those resultant mental intercourse differences consists of ladies's more interest in cues of commitment (Buss, 2003). As such, better sex ratio societies have decrease divorce costs, extra solid marriages (Pedersen, 1991; Secord, 1983), and in advance age of first marriage (South & Trent, 1988). Lichter, Anderson, and Hayward (1995) discovered that, steady with girls's extra hobby than men's in a ability mate's popularity and sources (Buss, 1989; Feingold, 1992), women in higher sex ratio societies are much more likely than girls in lower intercourse ratio societies to actualize their options and marry a high-popularity guy in preference to a low-fame man.

previous studies indicates that there are shifts in mating conduct consistent with the intercourse ratio. As Jennions and Petrie (1997) notice, however, there are two elements of mating options: preference features (or possibilities for traits that force mate selection—the focus of this text), and choosiness (touching on actual mate choice). Constraints on mating options, which includes an imbalanced sex ratio, are related to shifts in conduct produced via heightened intrasexual competition among the extra severa intercourse to display characteristics desired through the less severa sex. Are those behavioral shifts accompanied via mental shifts in mating possibilities? within the modern research, we generated and tested hypotheses derived from sex Ratio idea (Guttentag & Secord, 1983).

CLASSICAL intercourse RATIO MATE choice SHIFTS speculation

Because the supply of one sex decreases, so must the fee of obtaining as a mate a member of that sex growth (Baumeister & Vohs, 2004). Just as women and men in imbalanced sex ratio societies shift mating strategies to encompass the desires and alternatives of the less frequent intercourse, may in addition they decrease their standards, in a further effort to collect a mate? We hypothesize that in conjunction with extended attempt to show characteristics desired by the much less numerous intercourse, males and females can also decrease their mate choice standards when they're individuals of the greater numerous sex.

The Classical sex Ratio Mate choice Shifts hypothesis throughout cultures, mate options will vary in keeping with the provision of the alternative intercourse, such that every sex will lower their choice scores (i.e., report less stringent and limiting possibilities) while they're participants of the extra common sex.

Alternative intercourse RATIO MATE preference SHIFTS speculation

Constraints on mating options, mixed with the favored mating techniques of each sex, recommend an alternative speculation for the connection among sex ratio and mate possibilities. This opportunity hypothesis additionally may be derived from intercourse Ratio theory (Guttentag & Secord, 1983). due to the fact men's minimal obligate parental investment is fairly much less than women's, guys are greater interested in possibilities for casual sex with a variety of companions (Buss & Schmitt, 1993). thus, in lower sex ratio societies, instead of elevating their standards, men can also capitalize on brief-term mating desires via reducing their standards. this is, in lower intercourse ratio societies wherein guys are the much less severa intercourse and in extra call for, men may also lower their mate preference standards in an additional effort to actualize their goals for casual sex with a diffusion of women. males and females report being extra promiscuous in lower sex ratio societies (Schmitt, 2005), and this behavioral result can be the result of a decreasing of men's choice requirements, permitting guys to pursue informal intercourse with a greater quantity of ladies. it may be that men virtually gain this behavioral end result (an boom in quotes of promiscuity) by means of decreasing their preference standards.

Correspondingly, due to ladies's relatively extra minimal obligate parental funding than guys's, girls are much less willing than guys to mate indiscriminately and are extra selective (Buss & Schmitt, 1993; Trivers, 1972). due to the fact quite greater guys are seeking brief-term relationships in decrease intercourse ratio contexts than in higher intercourse ratio contexts, women in decrease intercourse ratio contexts can also boom the significance located on mate choice traits to avoid deception about long-term commitment with the aid of those quick-term dating searching for guys. girls can also increase their mate preference standards in decrease sex ratio societies, with a view to keep away from deception by guys who're in search of brief-term relationships. The alternative sex Ratio Mate desire Shifts hypothesis throughout cultures, mate alternatives will vary in keeping with the provision of the opposite intercourse, such that men, in order to comfortable greater short-time period matings, will lower their desire rankings in decrease sex ratio societies, and girls, on the way to keep away from deception by way of short-term courting seeking guys, will increase their preference scores in lower intercourse ratio societies.

Methods

A few preceding pass-cultural studies shows that controlling statistically for each u . s .'s stage
of socioeconomic improvement produces large relationships between intercourse ratio and different demographic
variables (South, 1988; South & Trent, 1988). We look into this opportunity in the present day research by using
accomplishing units of correlational analyses in exams of every hypothesis—one in which we do no longer
manipulate for socioeconomic development and a second wherein we manage for this variable.
although each hypotheses are equally compelling (the Classical intercourse Ratio Mate preference Shifts
hypothesis and the alternative intercourse Ratio Mate preference Shifts hypothesis) and the predictions are
derived from idea the use of comparable common sense for

each sex, the hypotheses may not be absolutely competing. The
hypotheses are collectively special for each sex (i.e., men can't be simultaneously elevating and lowering
their desire requirements in lower sex ratio societies), however it is able to be that males and females in various sex
ratio societies shift mate choices in keeping with unique adaptive good judgment. As such, the usage of sex Ratio
principle (Guttentag & Secord, 1983), knowledgeable by social trade and evolutionary psychological
perspectives, we generated and examined hypotheses about the cross-cultural relationships between sex
ratio and mate options. We secured statistics from an global take a look at of mate preferences and the
corresponding intercourse ratio for each way of life represented within the desire database.

approach

members

contributors had been 4499 men and 5310 ladies residing in 36 cultures positioned on six continents and five islands. men ranged in age from 17 to 30 years, with a mean age of 23.3 years. ladies ranged in age
from 17 to 30 years with an average age of twenty-two.6 years (see Buss, 1989, for extra info).

substances and method

The survey used to assess mate choices was adapted from Hill (1945). in this survey, participants rate
the importance of 18 mate preference traits (see table 1) on the following 4-point scale: three
points¼ critical, 2 ¼ vital, 1 ¼ ideal, but now not very important, and 0 ¼ beside the point or
unimportant. instructions were provided to every

collaborator for translating the tool into the
appropriate language for their sample (see Buss, 1989, for additional information). sex ratio data were secured from a cross-cultural database for ladies and men a long time 15 to 49 years (United countries, 2004) and nearest to the year wherein maximum of the mate preference statistics were collected (i.e., 1985). desk 2 lists the sex ratio for every of the nations or cultures. To reap an index of each us of a's degree of socioeconomic improvement, we observed the methods prescribed in South (1988), and summed standardized ratings for the country's Gross country wide Product (GNP), toddler survival fee, life expectancy, and the proportion of the population that is city. Demographic statistics had been received from the United nations (2004) for the year 1985 and GNP data were acquired from the U. S. Bureau of the Census (2002) for the year 1990. desk 2 lists the ensuing development Index for every u . s . (throughout international locations, a ¼ zero.82).

consequences

prior to conducting analyses, we tested all variables to become aware of statistical outliers. We identified
one unambiguous outlier: the Zulu intercourse ratio changed into more than 3 trendy deviations underneath the suggest.

across cultures, guys's significance ratings for sixteen of the 18 traits correlated negatively with
sex ratio. A binomial signal check indicated that these sixteen of 18 poor correlations turned into
extensively greater than the 9 bad correlations predicted via danger ($p < 0.001$). This result
therefore is consistent with Prediction 1 of the Classical intercourse Ratio Mate preference Shifts speculation that men's mate desire ratings can be correlated negatively with

intercourse ratio, throughout cultures. only one preference correlated substantially ($p < 0.05$) with intercourse ratio, but. men's

desire for sociability notably correlated negatively with intercourse ratio.

Fifteen of girls's 18 preference scores correlated negatively with sex ratio, across cultures,

imparting guide for Prediction 4 of the alternative intercourse Ratio Mate desire Shifts hypothesis. A binomial sign test indicated that these 15 of 18 bad correlations turned into appreciably

greater than the nine poor correlations predicted by chance ($p < 0.01$). Six of the correlations

among girls's choice ratings and intercourse ratio have been marginally ($p < 0.10$) or statistically ($p < 0.05$)

massive. Refinement, neatness, and good economic prospect have been marginally correlated negatively

with intercourse ratio. similar educational background, emotional balance and maturity, and mutual

appeal—love correlated appreciably and negatively with sex ratio. women's choice ratings for

simplest one function correlated substantially and undoubtedly with intercourse ratio: the choice for

chastity

(no preceding intercourse).

despite the fact that extra preference traits for men were marginally significantly correlated with intercourse ratio while development Index was managed statistically, and girls's two marginally tremendous correlations reached statistical importance while improvement Index turned into managed statistically, controlling for improvement Index did no longer result in partial correlations that differed notably from the corresponding zero-order correlations (see table 1; by Fisher's r-to-z ransformation; all zs < 1.50, all ps > zero.10; analyses to be had upon request). similarly, sex ratio and development Index were not drastically correlated (r ¼ 0.13, p > 0.10)

SYMMETRY AS INDICATOR OF PARASITE/PATHOGEN RESISTENCE

Faces constitute a life long medical record

Parasites and pathogens drain bodies resources and disturb normal processes of growth and development

These disturbance leave small but permenant traces.

MAJOR HISTOCOMPATIBILITY COMPLEX (MHC)

The preference of MHC discordant mates is based on odour T-shirt studies.

Men are given clean T-shirt and ask to wear it without showering or using scented product for two days.

At the end of this period they contribute the shirt to the stimulus in scene preference test. Research confirms that women rate odour as more important criteria than man do.

Women rate odour as the most important characteristic of a potential mate.

WAIST TO HIP RATIO

Men prefers partners to low waist to hip ratio.

This effect is not dependent on weight.

SELECTIVITY

Kenrick (1993)

Asked people to specify the minimum ranking of acceptable partner on a series of characteristicts

Like Status, agreebleness, emotional stability, attractivness.

Asked people about minimum percentile rankings for several levels on involvement.

Single date, Steady date, One night stand, marriage.

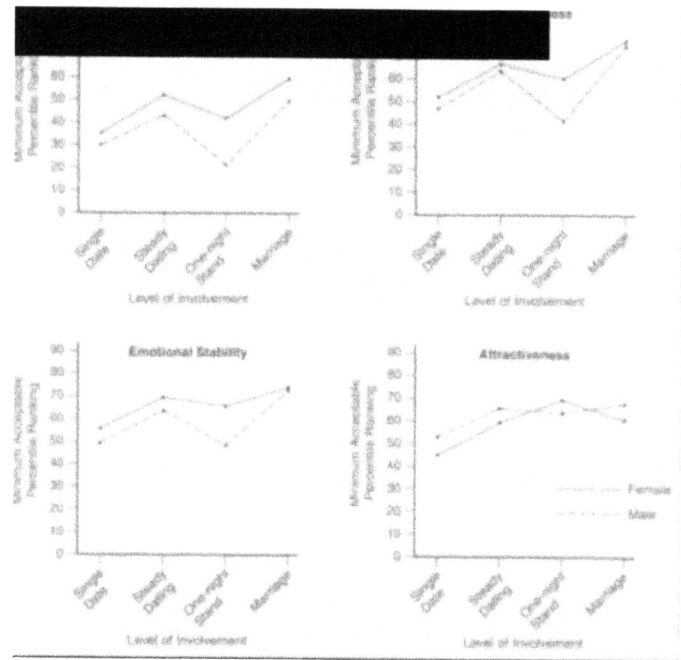

Graph Showing results of Selectivity

III
SOCIAL PSYCHOLOGY : HOW WE INTERACT WITH OTHER SECTOR

In social psychology, attitude is defined as learned, global evaluations (e.g. of people or issues) that influence thought and action. Attitudes are basic expressions of approval and disapproval, or as Bem (1970) suggests, likes and dislikes (e.g. enjoying chocolate ice cream, or endorsing the values of a particular political party). Because people are influenced by other factors in any given situation, general attitudes are not always good predictors of specific behavior. For example, a person may value the environment but may not recycle a plastic bottle on a particular day.

Research on attitudes has examined the distinction between traditional, self-reported attitudes and implicit, unconscious attitudes. Experiments using the implicit association test, for instance, have found that people often demonstrate implicit bias against other races, even when their explicit responses profess equal mindedness. Likewise, one study found that in interracial interactions, explicit attitudes correlate with verbal behavior while implicit attitudes correlate with nonverbal behavior.

ATTITUDE

One hypothesis on how attitudes are formed, first proposed in 1983 by Abraham Tesser, is that strong likes and dislikes are ingrained in our genetic make-up. Tesser speculated that individuals are disposed to hold certain strong attitudes as a result of inborn personality traits and physical, sensory, and cognitive skills. Attitudes are also formed as a result of exposure to different experiences, environments, and the learning process. Numerous studies have shown that people can form strong attitudes toward neutral objects that are in some way linked to emotionally charged stimuli.

Attitudes are also involved in several other areas of the discipline, such as conformity, interpersonal attraction, social perception, and prejudice.

A set can be described as or extra those who are linked to each other by using social relationships. organizations tend to engage, have an impact on every different, and share a common identity. they have some of emergent characteristics that distinguish them from coincidental, brief gatherings, which might be termed social aggregates: Norms: Implicit rules and expectations for organization individuals to observe (e.g. pronouncing thank you, shaking hands).

Roles: Implicit guidelines and expectancies for unique individuals inside the organization (e.g. the oldest sibling, who may additionally have extra duties in the own family). family members: styles of liking in the group, and additionally variations in prestige or reputation (e.g. leaders, famous humans).

brief agencies and aggregates share few or none of these features and do not qualify as true social agencies. human beings waiting in line to get on a bus, as an instance, do now not constitute a group.

businesses are important now not handiest due to the fact they provide social support, resources, and a feeling of belonging, however due to the fact they complement an man or woman's self-idea. To a massive extent, human beings outline themselves via the group memberships which form their social identity. The shared social identification of people within a group affects intergroup conduct, which denotes the way in which businesses behave towards and perceive every different. these perceptions and behaviors in turn define the social identification of individuals inside the interacting organizations. The tendency to outline oneself via membership in a set can also cause intergroup discrimination, which entails favorable perceptions and behaviors directed in the direction of the in-group, but bad perceptions and behaviors directed in the direction of the out-organization. alternatively, such discrimination and segregation can also on occasion exist partly to facilitate a range that strengthens society. Intergroup discrimination results in prejudicial stereotyping, while the strategies of social facilitation and institution polarization inspire intense behaviors in the direction of the out-institution.

companies often moderate and enhance choice making, and are often relied upon for these blessings, inclusive of in committees and juries. some of organization biases, but, can intervene with effective selection making. as an instance, organization polarization, formerly referred to as the "unstable shift", occurs while human beings polarize their views in a extra extreme direction after group dialogue. extra complicated is the phenomenon of groupthink, that is a collective thinking disorder this is characterized by a premature consensus or an wrong assumption of consensus, because of members of a group failing to sell perspectives that are not consistent with the perspectives of other members. Groupthink occurs in a selection of situations, together with isolation of a group and the presence of a quite directive chief. Janis presented the 1961 Bay of Pigs Invasion as a ancient case of groupthink.

agencies also have an effect on performance and productiveness. Social facilitation, for example, is a bent to work more difficult and faster within the presence of others. Social facilitation increases the dominant reaction's chance, which tends to improve performance on easy tasks and decrease it on complex obligations. In assessment, social loafing is the tendency of individuals to slack off whilst operating in a collection. Social loafing is commonplace whilst the task is taken into consideration unimportant and man or woman contributions are not easy to see.[unreliable source?]

Social psychologists observe institution-related (collective) phenomena which include the conduct of crowds. An important concept in this place is deindividuation, a reduced country of self-recognition that can be caused by emotions of anonymity. Deindividuation is related to uninhibited and occasionally risky conduct. it's far common in crowds and mobs, but it can additionally be caused by a conceal, a uniform, alcohol, dark environments, or on line anonymity.

HISTORY OF SOCIAL PSYCHOLOGY

Hegel (1770–1831) delivered the idea that society has inevitable hyperlinks with the improvement of the social mind. This led to the concept of a collection mind, critical inside the look at of social psychology.

Lazarus & Steinthal wrote approximately Anglo-european influences in 1860. "Volkerpsychologie" emerged, which targeted on the idea of a collective thoughts. It emphasised the belief that persona develops because of cultural and network influences, especially via language, which is each a social made of the community as well as a method of encouraging specific social notion in the individual. consequently Wundt (1900–1920) recommended the methodological look at of language and its have an impact on on the social being.

Early Texts

Texts focusing on social psychology first emerged on the start of the 20 th century. the primary fantastic e-book in English became published by way of McDougall in 1908 (An advent to Social Psychology), which covered chapters on emotion and sentiment, morality, man or woman and religion, quite extraordinary to those incorporated within the field today.

He believed that social behavior was innate/instinctive and therefore person, hence his desire of topics. This belief isn't the precept upheld in current social psychology, but.

Allport's work (1924) underpins contemporary wondering to a more degree, as he stated that social behavior effects from interactions among human beings. He additionally took a methodological method, discussing real studies and emphasizing that the field was certainly one of a "technological know-how ... which research the conduct of the person in up to now as his behavior stimulates different individuals, or is itself a response to this behavior" (1942: p. 12). His book also dealt with topics still obtrusive nowadays, which include emotion, conformity and the effects of an target audience on others.

Murchison (1935) published the primary manual on social psychology became posted by way of Murchison in 1935. Murphy & Murphy (1931/37) produced a ebook summarizing the findings of one,000 research in social psychology. A textual content by Klineberg (1940) looked at the interaction among social context and persona development with the aid of the Nineteen Fifties some of texts have been to be had at the concern.

there may be a few confrontation approximately the first true test, but the following are truly among some of the most crucial. Triplett (1898) applied the experimental technique to research the overall performance of cyclists and schoolchildren on how the presence of others influences average performance – as a consequence how character's are affected and behave in the social context.

by 1935 the take a look at of social norms had developed, looking at how people behave according to the regulations of society. This become conducted with the aid of Sherif (1935).

Lewin et al. then began experimental studies into leadership and institution tactics via 1939, searching at powerful work ethics under one of a kind sorts of management.

a great deal of the important thing research in social psychology developed following international conflict II, while people became inquisitive about the behavior of people when grouped together and in social conditions. Key studies have been carried out in several regions.

some research centered on how attitudes are fashioned, changed via the social context and measured to examine whether change has came about. amongst some of the maximum well-known paintings in social psychology is that on obedience conducted by means of Milgram in his "electric shock" observe, which checked out the role an authority determine performs in shaping behavior. similarly, Zimbardo's jail simulation appreciably verified conformity to given roles inside the social international.

Wider topics then commenced to emerge, including social belief, aggression, relationships, decision making, seasoned social behavior and attribution, many of which might be principal to nowadays's subjects and could be mentioned at some stage in this website.

consequently the growth years of social psychology passed off in the course of the many years following the Forties.

MILGRAM - SHOCK EXPERIMENT

contributors had been informed that they were taking part in a take a look at on gaining knowledge of, however usually acted because the trainer when they have been then answerable for going over paired partner getting to know obligations.

while the learner (a stooge) got the solution wrong, they were instructed with the aid of a scientist that they had to supply an electric shock. This did now not simply show up, although the participant became unaware of this as that they had themselves a sample (real!) shock at the start of the test.

They have been endorsed to increase the voltage given after every wrong solution as much as a maximum voltage, and it was located that each one contributors gave shocks up to 300v, with sixty five percentage accomplishing the very best level of 450v.

it seems that obedience is most probably to arise in an surprising environment and within the presence of an expert discern, particularly whilst covert stress is positioned upon people to obey. it's also feasible that it takes place because the player felt that someone aside from themselves was answerable for their movements.

In line with psychologist Gordon Allport, social psychology uses scientific strategies "to recognize and explain how the mind, feelings, and conduct of people are motivated by means of the real, imagined, or implied the presence of other humans."1 essentially, social psychology is ready information how everybody's man or woman behavior is motivated by the social surroundings in which that behavior takes region.

You probably already understand that different people can have a dramatic have an effect on at the way you act and the selections you're making. don't forget how you would possibly behave in a state of affairs if you were all by myself as opposed to if there have been different people within the room.

The selections you're making and the behaviors you exhibit may rely on not handiest how many human beings are present however precisely who you're around. as an example, you are probably to behave plenty otherwise while you are around a collection of close buddies than you will around a collection of colleagues or supervisors from work.

Social psychology encompasses a extensive variety of social subjects, including:

organization conduct

Social perception

leadership

Nonverbal conduct

Conformity

Aggression

Prejudice

It's miles critical to word that social psychology isn't always just about searching at social affects. Social notion and social interaction also are important to information social conduct.

The way that we see different people (and the manner we suppose they see us) can play a powerful function in a huge style of actions and choices. just assume for a moment approximately the way you now and again act in a different way in a public putting than you may if you were at home via yourself. At home, you is probably loud and rambunctious, while in public you might be a whole lot greater subdued and reserved.

Why is that this? due to the fact the human beings around us shape our thoughts, feelings, moods, attitudes, and perceptions. The presence of other humans could make a difference inside the choices we make and the moves we take.

while social psychology has a tendency to be an academic area, the studies that social psychologists carry out has a effective have an effect on on our understanding of mental fitness and nicely-being. for instance, research on conformity enables provide an explanation for why teens every now and then go to such extraordinary lengths to match in with their social organization—every so often to the detriment in their own health and well being.

Information this facilitates psychologists expand public fitness packages and treatment procedures for teenagers. these can assist teenagers resist doubtlessly dangerous behaviors inclusive of smoking, ingesting, and substance use.

Plato noted the idea of the "crowd mind," and ideas which include social loafing and social facilitation have been introduced inside the overdue 1800s. but it wasn't until after world warfare II that studies on social psychology commenced in earnest.

The horrors of the Holocaust led researchers to observe social have an effect on, conformity, and obedience. What ought to explain why people participated in such evil actions? have been people following orders and bowing to social pressure, or were there some other forces at paintings? with the aid of investigating these questions, social psychologists were capable of benefit a more understanding of the power of societal forces together with authority, compliance, and obedience.3

Social psychologist Stanley Milgram, as an instance, became capable of demonstrate simply how a long way human beings are inclined to go to obey authority figures. In a sequence of now notorious experiments, Milgram and his colleagues ordered observe members to supply what they believed was a doubtlessly risky surprise to some other person.

In truth, the shocks have been no longer actual and the other character changed into simplest pretending to be hurt with the aid of the electric pulses. but 65% of those who took component in the observe brought the most stage of shock absolutely due to the fact an expert figure told them to accomplish that.four

Social psychology has persevered to develop all through the twentieth century, inspiring studies that has contributed to our knowledge of social enjoy and conduct. Our social global makes up the sort of first-rate part of our lives, so it is no surprise that this subject matter is so captivating to many.

How Social Psychology Differs From other Disciplines

Social psychology is frequently stressed with folks awareness, character psychology, and sociology. unlike folk information, which is predicated on anecdotal observations and subjective interpretation, social psychology employs medical techniques and empirical have a look at. Researchers do now not make assumptions about how humans behave; they invent and carry out experiments that assist point out relationships among distinct variables.

character psychology specializes in character traits, traits, and thoughts. Social psychology is targeted on situations. Social psychologists are interested by the effect that the social surroundings and institution interactions have on attitudes and behaviors.

ultimately,

It's far essential to distinguish between social psychology and sociology. whilst there are numerous similarities among the two, sociology tends to examine social conduct and influences at a totally extensive-based totally degree. Sociologists are interested by the institutions and cultures that have an effect on how humans behave.

Psychologists alternatively cognizance on situational variables that affect social conduct. whilst psychology and sociology both look at comparable subjects, they're looking at those questions from unique perspectives.

What makes social psychology such an critical subject matter? Social psychologists recognition on societal issues which have a powerful have an effect on on person nicely-being in addition to the health of society as a whole, which includes problems inclusive of substance use, crime, prejudice, domestic abuse, public health, bullying, and aggression.

Social psychologists commonly do now not work without delay within the discipline of mental health, however the outcomes of their studies have an impact on how intellectual fitness experts deal with behaviors which are motivated by social elements. Public health packages, as an instance, often rely upon persuasion strategies identified by using social psychologists to encourage humans to interact in healthful behaviors even as fending off potentially dangerous ones.

Understanding social psychology may be beneficial for plenty reasons. First, we can better understand how agencies impact our picks and actions. There are some basic components of social conduct that play a huge role in our actions and how we see ourselves.

Social behavior Is goal-oriented

Our interactions serve goals or satisfy needs. a few commonplace desires or wishes consist of the want for social ties, the desire to recognize ourselves and others, the want to benefit or keep fame or protection, and the need to attract companions.

The manner people behave is regularly driven by means of the preference to fulfill those desires.1
humans searching for buddies and romantic companions, try to advantage social popularity, and attempt to apprehend the motivations that manual different human beings's behaviors

conditions help decide outcome

Regularly, human beings behave very in a different way relying upon the state of affairs. To completely recognize why people do the things they do, it is crucial to look at person traits, the situation and its context, and the interactions among a lot of these variables.

As an example, a person who's typically quiet and reserved would possibly become a good deal greater outgoing while located in a few kind of management function. every other example is how humans once in a while behave in another way in agencies than they could in the event that they were with the aid of themselves. Environmental and situational variables play an important function and feature a robust have an effect on on our behavior.

Social psychology permits us to gain a more appreciation for the way our social perceptions affect our interactions with other human beings.

Social conditions shape Self-idea

Our social interactions assist form our self-idea and our perceptions. One method of forming self-idea is through the pondered appraisal method,2 in which we believe how other human beings see us. another approach is through the social evaluation manner, wherein we don't forget how we evaluate to different people in our peer organization.three

from time to time we have interaction in upward social evaluation where we fee ourselves in opposition to folks who are better off than us in a few way. In different instances, we might engage in downward social evaluation where we evaluation our own capabilities to those of others who're less capable.

We trust conduct displays character
another have an effect on on our perceptions of different human beings can be explained with the aid of the theory of correspondent inferences.five This occurs when we infer that the movements and behaviors of others correspond to their intentions and personalities. as an example, if we see a lady supporting an elderly character pass the road, we would count on that she is kind-hearted. while conduct can be informative, it is able to additionally be deceptive.

If we have restricted interplay with a person, the behavior we see may be unusual or as a result of the precise scenario rather than by the person's overriding dispositional traits. within the previous instance, the lady might best be supporting the aged individual because she has been employed to do so as opposed to out of the kindness of her heart.

A word From Verywell
gaining knowledge of greater approximately social psychology can increase your information of your self and the arena round you. with the aid of getting to know greater approximately how people view others, how they behave in organizations, and how attitudes are shaped, you may benefit a more appreciation for the way social relationships impact person functioning.

Social psychology is the clinical study of how humans's thoughts, emotions, and behaviors are encouraged with the aid of the real, imagined, or implied presence of others (Allport 1998). with the aid of this definition, scientific refers back to the empirical technique of research. The terms thoughts, emotions, and behaviors consist of all the psychological variables that are measurable in a individual. The declaration that others may be imagined or implied shows that we are at risk of social have an effect on even if no other people are gift, including while watching tv, or following internalized cultural norms.

Social psychology is an empirical technology that attempts to reply a ramification of questions on human conduct through checking out hypotheses, both inside the laboratory and within the discipline. Such technique to the field focuses on the individual, and attempts to give an explanation for how the mind, emotions, and behaviors of people are prompted by way of other humans.

A tremendously recent area, social psychology has though had a substantial effect not best on the academic worlds of psychology, sociology, and the social sciences in widespread, however has also encouraged public information and expectation of human social behavior. by reading how humans behave beneath intense social impacts, or lack thereof, top notch advances have been made in expertise human nature. human beings are essentially social beings, and therefore, social interaction is vital to the health of every person. thru investigating the factors that affect social existence and how social interactions affect person mental development and mental health, a extra knowledge of ways humankind as a whole can live collectively in harmony is emerging.

Hyperlinks among Social Psychology and Sociology

Social psychology is a branch of psychology that studies cognitive, affective, and behavioral procedures of people as inspired by way of their organization membership and interactions, and other factors that have an effect on social existence, which include social fame, position, and social magnificence. Social psychology examines the consequences of social contacts on the improvement of attitudes, stereotypes, discrimination, group dynamics, conformity, social cognition and have an effect on, self-idea, persuasion, interpersonal notion and attraction, cognitive dissonance, and human relationships.

A considerable range of social psychologists are sociologists. Their work has a greater consciousness at the behavior of the organization, and therefore examines such phenomena as interactions and social exchanges at the micro-stage, and group dynamics and crowd psychology on the macro-stage. Sociologists are inquisitive about the person, however ordinarily inside the context of social structures and approaches, along with social roles, race and sophistication, and socialization. They tend to use each qualitative and quantitative research designs. Sociologists on this area are interested by a spread of demographic, social, and cultural phenomena. some of their primary research areas are social inequality, organization dynamics, social change, socialization, social identification, and symbolic interactionism.

Social psychology bridges the hobby of psychology (with its emphasis on the man or woman) with sociology (with its emphasis on social systems). maximum social psychologists are educated inside the area of psychology. Psychologically oriented researchers location a incredible deal of emphasis at the instant social scenario, and the interaction among person and situation variables. Their studies has a tendency to be tremendously empirical and is often centered spherical lab experiments. Psychologists who study social psychology are interested by such topics as attitudes, social cognition, cognitive dissonance, social impact, and interpersonal behavior. influential journals for the book of research in this area are The magazine of persona and Social Psychology and The magazine of Experimental Social Psychology. study extra about Sociological Social Psychology.

Social psychology is the study of how social conditions affect human beings. Scholars in this field are generally either psychologists or sociologists, though all social psychologists employ both the individual and the group as their units of analysis. Despite their similarity, the disciplines tend to differ in their respective goals, approaches, methods, and terminology. They also favor separate academic journals and professional societies.

Psychology > Social Psychology

What is Social Psychology?
Social PsychologySocial psychology is the clinical study of how people's mind, emotions, and behaviors are influenced with the aid of the actual, imagined, or implied presence of others (Allport 1998). via this definition, clinical refers back to the empirical approach of research. The phrases mind, emotions, and behaviors encompass all of the mental variables which are measurable in a person. The announcement that others can be imagined or implied shows that we are prone to social affect even when no other humans are present, which includes while watching tv, or following internalized cultural norms.

Social psychology is an empirical technological know-how that attempts to reply a diffusion of questions about human behavior with the aid of testing hypotheses, both within the laboratory and inside the subject. Such technique to the sector focuses on the individual, and tries to give an explanation for how the mind, feelings, and behaviors of people are motivated with the aid of other people.

A exceedingly recent subject, social psychology has

however had a giant effect now not only on the academic worlds of psychology, sociology, and the social sciences in trendy, however has additionally influenced public expertise and expectation of human social behavior. through studying how human beings behave underneath intense social affects, or lack thereof, wonderful advances have been made in knowledge human nature. humans are essentially social beings, and therefore, social interaction is important to the fitness of every person. through investigating the factors that have an effect on social life and how social interactions have an effect on man or woman mental development and intellectual fitness, a more knowledge of ways humankind as a whole can live collectively in concord is rising.

study extra approximately Social Psychology Theories. Social psychology is a department of psychology that studies cognitive, affective, and behavioral strategies of people as stimulated via their institution membership and interactions, and different elements that have an effect on social existence, including social popularity, position, and social elegance. Social psychology examines the effects of social contacts at the development of attitudes, stereotypes, discrimination, institution dynamics, conformity, social cognition and affect, self-concept, persuasion, interpersonal notion and attraction, cognitive dissonance, and human relationships.

A extensive variety of social psychologists are sociologists. Their paintings has a extra focus at the behavior of the institution, and as a consequence examines such phenomena as interactions and social exchanges at the micro-degree, and organization dynamics and crowd psychology on the macro-degree. Sociologists are inquisitive about the man or woman, however frequently within the context of social structures and procedures, along with social roles, race and sophistication, and socialization. They generally tend to apply both qualitative and quantitative studies designs. Sociologists in this place are inquisitive about a diffusion of demographic, social, and cultural phenomena. a number of their fundamental studies regions are social inequality, institution dynamics, social alternate, socialization, social identity, and symbolic interactionism.

Social psychology bridges the hobby of psychology (with its emphasis at the man or woman) with sociology (with its emphasis on social structures). maximum social psychologists are trained inside the field of psychology. Psychologically oriented researchers location a fantastic deal of emphasis at the on the spot social state of affairs, and the interaction among character and scenario variables. Their research has a tendency to be particularly empirical and is regularly focused round lab experiments. Psychologists who look at social psychology are interested by such topics as attitudes, social cognition, cognitive dissonance, social have an impact on, and interpersonal conduct. influential journals for the guide of research in this location are The magazine of personality and Social Psychology and The magazine of Experimental Social Psychology. examine more approximately Sociological Social Psychology.

Records of Social Psychology

Social PsychologyThe area of social psychology commenced inside the u.s. at the sunrise of the 20 th century. the primary posted look at in this location turned into an test by means of Norman Triplett (1898) on the phenomenon of social facilitation. all through the 1930s, many Gestalt psychologists, specifically Kurt Lewin, fled to america from Nazi Germany. They were instrumental in growing the sphere as some thing become independent from the behavioral and psychoanalytic schools that had been dominant in the course of that time, and social psychology has constantly maintained the legacy in their pursuits in perception and cognition. Attitudes and a selection of small organization phenomena have been the maximum usually studied topics in this era.

throughout international battle II, social psychologists studied persuasion and propaganda for the united states navy. After the war, researchers have become interested by a variety of social troubles, together with gender troubles and racial prejudice. inside the Sixties, there has been growing interest in a variety of new topics, together with cognitive dissonance, bystander intervention, and aggression. through the 1970s, however, social psychology in the usa had reached a disaster. there was heated debate over the ethics of laboratory experimentation, whether or not or now not attitudes definitely anticipated conduct, and what kind of technological know-how could be accomplished in a cultural context (Gergen 1973). This changed into additionally the time whilst an intensive situationist technique challenged the relevance of self and persona in psychology.

In the course of the years without delay following world warfare II, there has been frequent collaboration between psychologists and sociologists (Sewell 1989). but, the 2 disciplines have come to be increasingly more specialised and isolated from every other in latest years, with sociologists that specialize in macro variables (together with social shape) to a much more quantity. despite the fact that, sociological processes to social psychology stay an crucial counterpart to psychological research on this area.

Social psychology reached adulthood in each theory and technique all through the Nineteen Eighties and Nineties. cautious ethical requirements now adjust studies, and extra pluralism and multicultural views have emerged. contemporary researchers are interested in a ramification of phenomena, however attribution, social cognition, and self-concept are possibly the best areas of growth. Social psychologists have additionally maintained their applied hobbies, with contributions in fitness and environmental psychology, in addition to the psychology of the felony device.

EXPERIMENTS :::::::

Social psychologists normally give an explanation for human behavior because of the interplay of mental states and immediately, social situations. In Kurt Lewin's (1951) Heuristic conduct may be regarded as a characteristic of the person and the environment, $B = f(P,E)$. Experimental strategies contain the researcher changing a variable within the surroundings and measuring the impact on any other variable. An instance could be permitting corporations of youngsters to play violent or nonviolent videogames, and then observing their next stage of aggression throughout free-play length. A valid experiment is controlled and uses random assignment.

Co-relational techniques have a look at the statistical association among two obviously happening variables. for example, one should correlate the amount of violent television kids watch at domestic with the number of violent incidents the youngsters participate in at school. notice that this take a look at could now not show that violent tv causes aggression in children. it is pretty viable that competitive youngsters choose to look at more violent television programs.

Observational strategies are simply descriptive and consist of naturalistic commentary, contrived commentary, participant statement, and archival analysis. these are less commonplace in social psychology but are occasionally used whilst first investigating a phenomenon. An instance might be to unobtrusively have a look at children on a playground (with a video camera, perhaps) and file the number and varieties of aggressive moves displayed.

whenever feasible, social psychologists rely on controlled experimentation. controlled experiments require the manipulation of 1 or greater impartial variables if you want to observe the effect on a dependent variable. Experiments are beneficial in social psychology because they're excessive in inner validity, meaning that they are unfastened from the impact of confounding or extraneous variables, and so are much more likely to accurately imply a causal courting. but, the small samples utilized in managed experiments are normally low in external validity, or the degree to which the consequences may be generalized to the bigger population. There is usually a change-off between experimental control (inner validity) and being able to generalize to the populace (outside validity).

because it's also not possible to test anyone, studies has a tendency to be conducted on a pattern of folks from the broader populace. Social psychologists regularly use survey studies whilst they are inquisitive about effects which might be high in outside validity. Surveys use diverse forms of random sampling to obtain a pattern of respondents which might be representative of a populace. This sort of research is normally descriptive or co-relational due to the fact there may be no experimental manage over variables.

however, new statistical methods, like structural equation modeling, are being used to test for ability causal relationships in this kind of data.

regardless of which method is used, it is crucial to evaluate the research hypothesis in the light of the effects, either confirming or rejecting the unique prediction. Social psychologists use statistics and chance trying out to judge their consequences, which define a tremendous finding as much less than 5% likely to be due to hazard. Replications are important to make certain that the end result is legitimate and not due to chance or some feature of a specific pattern.

SOCIAL PSYCHOLOGY ETHICS

The purpose of social psychology is to understand cognition and behavior as they obviously occur in a social context, however the very act of staring at human beings can impact and adjust their conduct. for this reason, many social psychology experiments make use of deception to conceal or distort sure factors of the examine. Deception may additionally consist of fake cover stories, false members (known as confederates or stooges), fake feedback given to the participants, and so on.

The exercise of deception has been challenged by means of some psychologists who maintain that deception below any circumstances is unethical, and that other research techniques (such as role-gambling) ought to be used alternatively. sadly, research has shown that function-gambling research do not produce the same outcomes as deception studies and this has solid doubt on their validity. in addition to deception, experimenters have at times put people into probably uncomfortable or embarrassing situations (as an instance, Milgram's Obedience to government experiments, Zimbardo's Stanford jail test), and this has also been criticized for moral reasons.

To protect the rights and well-being of research individuals, and on the identical time find out significant results and insights into human conduct, sincerely all social psychology studies need to skip an moral assessment process. At maximum faculties and universities, that is conducted by means of an ethics committee or institutional evaluate board. This organization examines the proposed studies to make certain that no harm is carried out to the individuals, and that the benefits of the study outweigh any feasible risks or discomforts to humans taking part within the take a look at.

moreover, a method of knowledgeable consent is frequently used to make certain that volunteers recognise what's going to occur inside the experiment and understand that they are allowed to quit the test at any time. A debriefing is generally done at the conclusion of the experiment so as to expose any deceptions used and generally make sure that the individuals are unhurt by the processes. these days, most research in social psychology involves no greater threat of damage than may be predicted from routine mental checking out or normal daily activities.

THEORIES OF SOCIAL PSYCHOLOGY

The breadth and range of cutting-edge social psychology theories displays the numerous intellectual origins of the various views and techniques. Early discussions of social psychology centered on those exceptional intellectual origins by way of highlighting the variations between psychological and sociological social psychology. This illustration of the sphere has been critiqued for its perpetuation of synthetic limitations that overlook widespread connections between the shared issue remember of sociology and psychology. In 1980 Sheldon Stry ker articulated three "faces" of social psychology: mental social psychology, sociological social psychology, and symbolic interactionism.

even as every perspective represents particular theoretical thoughts, in addition they inform one another and serve to create a complete know-how of person interactions and the way they impact at the agencies to which we belong as well as the environments in which group interactions arise. All three perspectives percentage a focus at the character and person interactions because the explanatory element for all factors of social life, along with the introduction of stable organization systems and the formation of a hit social movements. The three theoretical views in social psychology, regarded greater usually as cognitive and intrapersonal, symbolic interactionist, and structural, every constitute different origins and intellectual affiliations and keep a focal point on extraordinary components of the man or woman and society.

COGNITIVE AND INTRAPERSONAL PSYCHOLOGY

Cognitive and intrapersonal social psychology originated with the paintings of experimental psychologists in Germany inclusive of Wilhelm Wundt within the mid 19th century and specializes in expertise how inner approaches affect an man or woman's capacity to have interaction with others. The inner processes most studied in this perspective are cognitive (memory, perception, and selection making) and physiological (chemical and neural activity). each method examines a one of a kind thing of ways interactions are laid low with those internal procedures. The underlying basis of the cognitive and intrapersonal technique facilities on how individuals store facts inside the mind within the form of schemas. Schemas constitute the manner in which people pick out gadgets in their surroundings by way of labeling them, which then lets in the gadgets to be categorized. using schemas permits people to procedure billions of bits of information from the environment, which then permits them to effortlessly engage in interactions. The extra correct people' understanding of any given social situation, as determined via how properly they label and categorize it primarily based on information from the surroundings, the greater successful and clean might be the interaction. The cognitive and physiological processes in this angle explore different aspects of the impact of schemas on interactions.

The cognitive approach examines how brain hobby in particular associated with memory, notion, and selection making methods influences an character's capacity to understand the facts essential for undertaking a hit interactions. moreover, this technique also explores how versions in cognitive procedures lead to differences in individuals' capacity to interact. The take a look at of memory examines how humans categorize activities, conditions, and others they have encountered formerly, supporting researchers understand the sort of schema constructed and used mainly groups, cultures, and settings. reading reminiscence lets in researchers to directly discover the relationship between interactions and the way they're classified. Take for example a person getting into a room and looking at two humans interacting with every other. If she labels and categorizes the interaction as a romantic interlude between fanatics, she is less likely to break than if the interaction is categorised and categorized as a conversation between co employees. further, if the character getting into the room identifies and labels one of the actors as a near friend, her interactions with the two human beings may be one-of-a-kind than if they had been virtually co employees. Theoretical thoughts related to knowledge schemas and reminiscence consist of stereotypes (the actual categories used in labeling humans and situations) and self enjoyable prophecy (in which we act in this sort of way as to affirm our initial impressions of human beings). In reading perception, researchers are interested in exploring how people's interpretation of records from the environment influences their interactions with others. The take a look at of notion examines the meanings people accomplice with the categories in which events, conditions, and people are placed. Key theoretical ideas associated with this method to reading interactions from a cognitive social psychological attitude consist of the attributions human beings make when judging others' moves and the consequences of these movements, and the errors inside the attributions humans make. eventually, selection making research explores how schemas, reminiscences, and perceptions make contributions to the ways in which humans make decisions starting from what to wear in the morning to the level of threat they're inclined to soak up any state of affairs. The decisions made without delay effect whether or not or no longer an character is inclined to have interaction with one individual in preference to every other, as well as the exceptional of the interactions that do occur.

even as the cognitive approach examines those inner procedures that impact on whether or not an interplay will occur as well as the nice of the interaction once it does arise, the physiological approach explores the approaches that unique biological and chemical approaches have an effect on individuals' capacity to create good enough and useful schemas, use their reminiscence, perceive things correctly, and then make applicable decisions. The physiological approach inside the cognitive and intrapersonal angle isn't always normally included in discussions about social psychology, as at first look its theoretical recognition does no longer without delay relate to social interactions. but, latest developments in this method link it plenty more carefully with the cognitive approach, thereby warranting its inclusion in this dialogue. Cognitive and behavioral psychologists, in conjunction with neuroscientists, have conducted what are called "animal research" for over one hundred years. The goal of such research is to greater as it should be provide an explanation for how precise chemical and organic processes without delay effect on cognitive characteristic ing. era is now allowing physiologically primarily based researchers in psychology, neuroscience, and sociology to degree and study the relationship among these chemical and organic processes and associated moves and interactions in human beings. Early studies in this area centered on non human species due to the moral troubles associated with human experimentation. more recent technologies, consisting of the transportable electroence phalogram (EEG) and the purposeful magnetic resonance imager (fMRI), permit researchers to take a look at neural and chemical responses to individuals' movements and interactions. The implication is that such technology will permit social psychologists to greater correctly and immediately degree social interplay.

SYMBOLIC INTERACTIONISM

Symbolic interactionism originated from the paintings of George Herbert Mead and his students on the university of Chicago as well as the paintings of pragmatic philosophers. even as Mead turned into officially associated with the psychology and philosophy departments at the university of Chicago, his classes on social psychology and social philosophy attracted a massive quantity of college students from the fledgling sociology department. one of the sociology students, Herbert Blumer, coined the time period symbolic interactionism and different sociology students had been instrumental in publishing Mead's thoughts, after his loss of life, regarding the man or woman. these thoughts middle on his discussions of the thoughts (what makes human beings uniquely social creatures), self (how we become uniquely social creatures), and society (how our interactions are laid low with social establishments). Mead wrote extensively approximately problems concerning greater macro level social phenomena which includes the function of presidency in investment education and the function of schooling for socialization, but he is in particular recognized for his contributions to symbolic interactionism. commonly, the symbolic interactionist attitude in social psychology specializes in analyzing the meanings that underlie social interactions in terms of ways they're created, how they're maintained, and the way we learn to apprehend such meanings. additionally, theorists writing inside this perspective argue that character interactions result in the creation of formal social agencies and social establishments. consequently, to understand society, it's miles essential to recognize the interactions that form it and hold it. There are 3 primary theoretical processes within the symbolic interactionist angle, symbolic interactionism, phenomenological, and life route, every of which examines one of a kind elements of these meanings and the self on which they may be derived.

The symbolic interactionism approach is maximum carefully related to Mead's unique thoughts regarding social psychology and makes a speciality of exploring how meanings are created and maintained inside social interactions with the self as the idea for such interactions. The underlying theme of this technique is that people create and manipulate meanings through the jobs and identities they maintain. it's miles essential to word that every individual holds any number of roles and identities, depending at the humans with whom they have interaction as well as the surroundings wherein they locate themselves. Classical symbolic interactionist studies include the work of Herbert Blumer, Charles Horton Cooley, and Manford Kuhn. Blumer elaborated on Mead's discussion of the social self examining itself as an object out of doors the individual, while Cooley centered on explaining the technique wherein the self acknowledges itself as an item. Kuhn's discussions explored distinctive dimensions of the self as a manner of explaining individuals' ability to tackle a selection of identities, relying on the situation and the alternative actors worried. contemporary trends of those ideas are located inside the work of Erving Goffman, Peter Burke, Sheldon Stryker, and their pals and college students. Goffman's discussion of dramaturgy and the presentation of self, among other ideas, examined the methods in which people recognized the role held in any particular interaction and the expectancies associated with that role. Stryker and others explored how roles are connected to individuals' identity and the way meaningful those identities are to humans. Burke and buddies proposed a extra formal theore tical rationalization of how unique components of the self are related to precise identities people preserve.

The phenomenological approach originated from eu sociology and philosophy, emphasizing the meanings themselves and the way such meanings mirror unstated normative expectations for interactions. The underlying subject matter of this technique is that language, verbal and non verbal, represents the informal and formal guidelines and norms that guide social interactions and shape society. The early paintings in phenomenology, as represented by using the ideas of Alfred Schutz and Harold Garfinkel, differen tiated among specific elements of the way human beings create social fact in addition to perform within already present social fact. Schutz examined how language and communique represented an intersubjective system of truth advent and maintainance, whilst Garfinkel explored how people managed fact thru the development of ethnomethodology. current developments of phenomenology are determined within the work of theorists along with Howard Becker, Peter Berger, and Douglas Maynard. via a series of studies, Becker explored the way individuals' interpretations of social interactions and social reviews reflect their own studies and unstated norms for behavior. Berger, at the side of Thomas Luckmann, is taken into consideration the yank creation to Schutz's thoughts and phenomenology. similarly important, Berger and Luckmann additionally actually verified how regular interactions and language create reputedly formidable social institutions and groups. sooner or later, Maynard similarly evolved ethnomethodology with the aid of focusing on communique analysis as a manner of understanding how social communicate creates and represents fact.

The life direction method in symbolic interactionism makes a speciality of how humans examine the meanings associated with interactions via out their lifetime and the levels that mirror such mastering techniques. The underlying subject of this technique is that the norms, regulations, and values that guide interactions and shape society trade at some point of people' lives, in particular as they flow into exceptional social positions and environments. As a especially more recent technique inside the symbolic interactionist perspective in terms of identifying as a completely unique method, the key thoughts may be traced to Mead's dialogue approximately socialization and Georg Simmel's ideas approximately interactions within and among organizations. Mead explained how human beings end up uniquely social creatures in his lectures about the self, where he describes a three level process (preparatory, play, and sport) for humans to learn the norms, rules, and values of the institution into which they're born. He argued that via the end of this technique, people can have a totally evolved self. Simmel's discussions concerning interactions and organizations examined how people' interactions with each other changed as institution size, institution composition, and social surroundings modified. modern-day theorists which include Glenn Elder, Roberta Simmons, and Dale Dannefer, and their college students and associates, construct on these thoughts in similar ways. First, the modern techniques count on that socialization is a lifelong technique that modifications as people trade. 2d, theorists inside the method look at each man or woman level factors and societal elements that contribute to the socialization system. Elder has focused on how socialization is constant throughout cohorts of humans, various simplest in qualitative aspects associated with variations in environments and resources. Simmons has examined how the socialization process itself varies relying on individuals' stage in life, and Dannefer has explored the ways in which agencies with which people are related play an crucial role in their persevering with socialization for the duration of life.

DIFFERENT STRUCTURES OF SOCIAL PSYCHOLOGY

Structural social psychology originated with the paintings of economists, psychologists, and sociologists interested in explaining social interactions more officially and mathematically with the aim of making testable hypotheses. Structural social psychology assumes that social actors are pushed via rational worries focused on maximizing rewards and minimizing punishments. another related assumption is that interactions primarily based on rational calculations bring about officially established individual, group, and institutional interactions. This approach is related to cognitive and intrapersonal social psychology within the consciousness on developing formal theories to explain interactions and growing precise hypotheses for trying out in experimental situations. greater cutting-edge paintings in structural social psychology uses greater various strategies which includes survey studies and participant commentary strategies. There are three primary theoretical programs that constitute this approach: strength, exchange, and bargaining studies; social affect and authority studies; and standing traits, expectation states idea, and social community research. every set of research focuses on exceptional elements of describing and explaining the underlying structure of social interactions.

Power, alternate, and bargaining studies discover how social interactions may be described as exchanges among social actors with the idea that people rationally calculate the prices and advantages associated with any precise interaction. alternate studies commenced with the work of George Homans, Richard Emerson, and Peter Blau. Homans argued that interactions can be higher understood as exchanges wherein actors engaged in interactions that introduced particular benefits. His paintings also explored how the need for such exchanges results in equilibrium among actor and the idea of distributive justice. Blau further certain this work by focusing on the social components of such exchanges in phrases of ways they rely upon consider between actors that all and sundry will satisfy his or her unspecified obligations. even as Homans, Blau, and others discussed that energy arises out of exchanges and that strength isn't always always equally allotted amongst actors, Emerson and his colleagues in particular explored the improvement of electricity, how it is managed by using actors, and how power differentiation impacts the possibility of destiny exchanges. extra current work constructing on those thoughts is good deal ing studies, which specifies how one-of-a-kind sorts of power differentiation affect the bargaining that then leads to actual exchanges. Lawler and associates explored the sort of bargaining that happens previous to exchanges, as well as how differing levels of power amongst members affect such bargaining. Molm and her colleagues tested how exchanges varied primarily based on inequality of individuals and the provision of different assets and actors.

The second one set of studies that can be labeled underneath the structural social psychology perspective makes a speciality of social have an impact on and authority. The underlying subject matter of these studies is that there are numerous elements that encourage humans to be prompted by others, along with the reputation or role others maintain in assessment to themselves and group encouragement of conformity. The traditional studies in social have an impact on consist of Stanley Milgram's studies that examined the effect an expert discern in a position of energy has on man or woman compliance. Milgram observed that people overwhelmingly obeyed requests to finish a task that ostensibly required hurting another character. Seymour Asch's studies of institution conformity established that individuals willingly trade their answer or opinion whilst a majority inside the institution suggests a distinctive answer or opinion. cutting-edge thoughts construct in this base by inspecting the various situations underneath which compliance to authority happens, and to what diploma others can have an effect on attitude exchange.

repute characteristics, expectation states, and social community research take a look at how social interactions are based totally on socially and culturally derived expectations for behavior that humans have of one another. those socially and culturally derived expectancies are related to assumed predictions regarding how success completely any individual will make contributions to an trade, or interplay, method. these predictions then decide which people are possibly to be given the most opportunities for interplay and influence in a collection. Originating with the paintings of Berger, Zelditch, and associates, reputation traits theory explicitly identifies two most important varieties of social characteristics which have expectations for conduct associated with them – diffuse (consisting of race, gender, magnificence, and ableness) and unique fame characteristics (which includes activity revel in, education, and relevant competencies) – and additionally it is related to companies working toward achieving precise desires. Expectation states principle argues that those folks who keep diffuse and unique reputation characteristics evaluated as much more likely to successfully contribute to accomplishing group goals might be given a greater variety of opportunities for interaction as well as more social influence among other organization individuals. extra to the point, theorists argue, and have efficiently demonstrated, that precise and solid hierarchical institution systems develop based totally on those expectations. contemporary work on this region consists of specifying the diploma to which unique repute traits affect expectations in addition to how such expectancies increase and whether actors perceive that such expectancies are simply. Social network idea and elementary concept construct at the thoughts of those different methods in structural social psychology by way of in particular inspecting how an actor's position, relative to any other, influences social impact approaches as well as the stableness of institution shape. The underlying assumption of social network principle is that social affect, power, and bargaining are all affected by the manner in which actors are networked to each other. Markovsky, Willer, prepare dinner, and their college students and buddies look at extraordinary aspects of the way actors are connected to one another and how that influences other social strategies.

because the above discussion indicates, the 3 theoretical techniques in social psychology all study distinct aspects of individuals, their interactions, and how their interactions have an effect on businesses. Cognitive and intrapersonal social psychology focuses on internal approaches that impact whether or not, and the way effectively, interactions arise among human beings. The insights supplied by way of this attitude help to explain how actors create meanings regarding interactions that then result in the advent and protection of unique social institutions and groups, as mentioned by means of symbolic interactionists. subsequently, structural social psychologists have a look at how the fluid interactions of symbolic lifestyles create formal organization structures that then impact on human beings's interactions.

The discipline of social psychology began inside the united states of america at the sunrise of the 20th century. the first published look at in this place became an test in 1898 by way of Norman Triplett on the phenomenon of social facilitation. all through the 1930s, many Gestalt psychologists, most extensively Kurt Lewin, fled to the united states from Nazi Germany. They had been instrumental in developing the sector as something cut loose the behavioral and psychoanalytic schools that had been dominant at some stage in that time, and social psychology has usually maintained the legacy of their hobbies in perception and cognition. Attitudes and small organization phenomena have been the most usually studied subjects in this era. at some point of WWII, social psychologists studied persuasion and propaganda for the U.S. military. After the conflict, researchers became interested in a spread of social issues, which includes gender problems and racial prejudice. most extremely good, revealing, and contentious of them all were the Stanley Milgram surprise experiments on obedience to authority. inside the Sixties, there was growing hobby in new topics, including cognitive dissonance, bystander intervention, and aggression. by means of the Nineteen

Seventies, however, social psychology in the united states had reached a crisis. there was
heated debate over the ethics of laboratory experimentation, whether or not attitudes definitely predicted conduct, and how an awful lot technological know-how will be done in a cultural context (see Gergen, 1973). This changed into additionally the time whilst a radical situationist approach challenged the relevance of self and personality in psychology.

Social psychology reached adulthood in both theory and approach in the course of the Nineteen Eighties and 1990s. careful ethical requirements now regulate research, and greater pluralism and multiculturalism perspectives have emerged. present day researchers are interested in a many phenomena, but attribution, social cognition, and the self-idea are perhaps the finest regions of increase in current years. Social psychologists have additionally maintained their implemented pursuits with contributions in fitness and environmental psychology, in addition to the psychology of the felony system.

SOME PROPOSED A SUPER THEORIES
1. MILGRAM EXPERIMENT ON OBEDIENCE

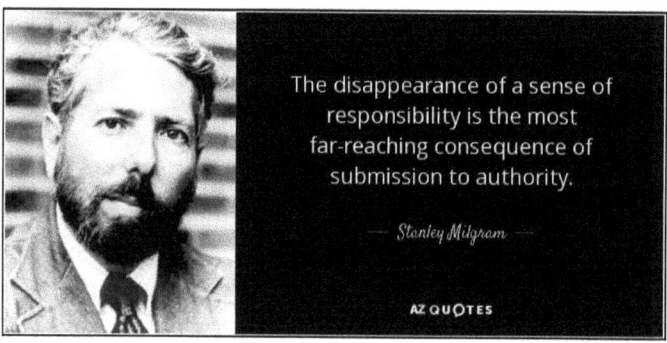

one of the maximum famous studies of obedience in psychology was carried out with the aid of Stanley Milgram, a psychologist at Yale university. He conducted an test focusing on the war among obedience to authority and personal moral sense.

Milgram (1963) tested justifications for acts of genocide offered by way of those accused at the world war II, Nuremberg struggle crook trials. Their defense often was based on "obedience" - that they have been simply following orders from their superiours.

The experiments commenced in July 1961, a 12 months after the trial of Adolf Eichmann in Jerusalem. Milgram devised the experiment to reply the query:

ought to it be that Eichmann and his million accomplices inside the Holocaust have been simply following orders? could we call all of them accomplices?" (Milgram, 1974).

Milgram (1963) wanted to research whether Germans had been particularly obedient to authority figures as this was a not unusual explanation for the Nazi killings in global warfare II.

Milgram selected participants for his experiment by way of newspaper marketing for male contributors to participate in a study of learning at Yale university.

The procedure was that the player was paired with some other person and that they drew masses to discover who would be the 'learner' and who would be the 'trainer.' The draw changed into fixed so that the participant turned into usually the trainer, and the learner become one in all Milgram's confederates (pretending to be a real participant).

stanley milgram generator scale

The learner (a accomplice known as Mr. Wallace) turned

into taken right into a room and had electrodes connected to his arms, and the teacher and researcher went into a room round the corner that contained an electric powered surprise generator and a row of switches marked from 15 volts (mild surprise) to 375 volts (risk: severe shock) to 450 volts (XXX).

Shocking Equipment

AIM :-

Milgram (1963) became interested by researching how a ways human beings would move in obeying an education if it involved harming every other character.

Stanley Milgram become interested in how easily ordinary human beings can be stimulated into committing atrocities, for example, Germans in WWII.

Experimenting Scene

PROCEDURE

Volunteers had been recruited for a managed test investigating "mastering" (re: ethics: deception). participants had been 40 adult males, elderly among 20 and 50, whose jobs ranged from unskilled to expert, from the new Haven vicinity. They were paid $4.50 for simply turning up.

Milgram's Obedience shock Generator
At the start of the test, they have been delivered to another participant, who changed into a confederate of the experimenter (Milgram).

They drew straws to decide their roles – learner or trainer – even though this became fixed and the confederate turned into constantly the learner. there was also an "experimenter" wearing a grey lab coat, performed by an actor (now not Milgram).

two rooms in the Yale interaction Laboratory had been used - one for the learner (with an electric powered chair) and some other for the teacher and experimenter with an electric surprise generator.

Milgram Obedience: Mr Wallace

The "learner" (Mr. Wallace) changed into strapped to a chair with electrodes. After he has found out a list of word pairs given him to research, the "teacher" assessments him through naming a word and asking the learner to don't forget its associate/pair from a list of four possible picks.

The trainer is told to administer an electric powered surprise on every occasion the learner makes a mistake, increasing the level of surprise on every occasion. There were 30 switches on the surprise generator marked from 15 volts (slight surprise) to 450 (danger – intense shock).

Milgram Obedience IV versions

The learner gave specifically wrong solutions (on purpose), and for each of those, the instructor gave him an electric powered surprise. while the instructor refused to administer a surprise, the experimenter changed into to offer a series of orders/prods to ensure they persisted.

There have been 4 prods and if one became now not obeyed, then the experimenter (Mr. Williams) examine out the next prod, and so on.

Prod 1: Please hold.

Prod 2: The experiment requires you to maintain.

Prod 3: it's miles really vital that you continue.

Prod 4: you have no other choice however to retain.

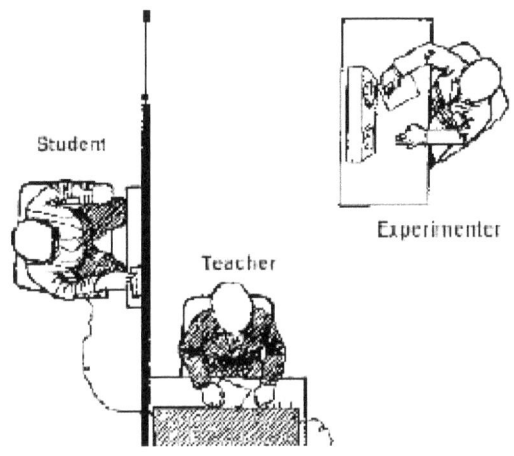

Experiments at different angles

RESULTS:

65% (two-thirds) of participants (i.e., instructors) endured to the best degree of 450 volts. all the contributors persisted to three hundred volts.
Milgram did more than one test – he completed 18 variations of his observe. All he did was adjust the scenario (IV) to peer how this affected obedience (DV).

CONCLUSION:

The individual cause of the behaviour of the contributors could be that it changed into some thing approximately them as people that brought on them to obey, however a more practical rationalization is that the scenario they have been in prompted them and caused them to behave within the way that they did.

some of the factors of the scenario which can have motivated their behaviour include the formality of the region, the behaviour of the experimenter and the truth that it became an experiment for which that they had volunteered and been paid.

regular humans are in all likelihood to comply with orders given by means of an expert determine, even to the extent of killing an harmless individual. Obedience to authority is ingrained in us all from the manner we are introduced up.

humans generally tend to obey orders from different human beings if they understand their authority as morally right and/or legally based totally. This response to valid authority is discovered in an expansion of situations, for instance inside the own family, college, and workplace.

Milgram summed up in the article "The Perils of Obedience" (Milgram 1974), writing:

'The criminal and philosophic factors of obedience are of huge import, however they are saying little or no approximately how the majority behave in concrete conditions.

I installation a simple experiment at Yale university to check how a lot ache an normal citizen would inflict on some other man or woman clearly because he was ordered to by means of an experimental scientist.

Stark authority was pitted towards the subjects' [participants'] most powerful ethical imperatives towards hurting others, and, with the subjects' [participants'] ears ringing with the screams of the sufferers, authority won more regularly than no longer.

the acute willingness of adults to visit almost any lengths at the command of an expert constitutes the chief locating of the examine and the reality maximum urgently annoying rationalization.

THE MILGRAM EXPERIMENT

...nothing is bleaker than the sight of a person striving yet not fully able to control his own behavior in a situation of some consequence to him.

— Stanley Milgram
Obedience to Authority, 1974

A teacher holding the hand of the learner on the shock plate in the "Touch Proximity" condition.

Beginning in the 1960s, Stanley Milgram performed a series of experiments designed to uncover just how susceptible to authority we are. How far would we as individuals go when compelled by an authoritive figure to act in ways which contradict our fundamental moral standards? The findings of these experiments surprised and

2. PHILIP ZIMBARDO THE STANDFORD PRISION EXPERIMENT

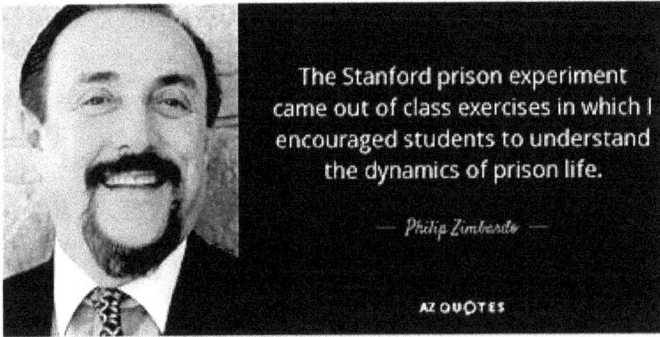

Philip Zimbardo became born on March 23, 1933 in big apple town. He attended Brooklyn university wherein he earned a B.A. in 1954, triple majoring in psychology, sociology and anthropology. He then went directly to earn his M.A. in 1955 and his Ph.D. in 1959 from Yale college, each

• 185 •

in psychology.

He taught in short at Yale before turning into a psychology professor at new york university, where he taught till 1967. After a year of coaching at Columbia university, he have become a college member at Stanford college in 1968.

Philip Zimbardo is possibly high-quality acknowledged for the Stanford prison test, conducted in the basement of the Stanford university psychology department in 1971. The participants inside the examine were 24 male college college students who have been randomly assigned to act both as "guards" or "prisoners" inside the mock jail.

The take a look at become initially slated to final weeks, but had to be terminated after just six days because of the acute reactions and behaviors of the members. The guards started displaying cruel and sadistic conduct toward the prisoners, whilst the prisoners became depressed and hopeless.

because the prison experiment, Zimbardo has persisted to conduct studies on a ramification of topics consisting of shyness, cult conduct and heroism. In 2002, Zimbardo turned into elected president of the yank psychological association. After greater than 50 years of coaching, Zimbardo retired from Stanford in 2003 however gave his closing "Exploring Human Nature" lecture on March 7, 2007.

today, he keeps to work as the director of an business enterprise he based called the Heroic imagination assignment. The company promotes studies, schooling and media initiatives designed to encourage everyday human beings to act as heroes and marketers of social alternate.

Zimbardo turned into a former classmate of the psychologist Stanley Milgram. Milgram is first-rate recognized for his well-known obedience test.

Zimbardo become inquisitive about expanding upon Milgram's research. He desired to in addition investigate the impact of situational variables on human behavior.

The researchers wanted to know how the individuals might react while placed in a simulated jail surroundings.

The researchers wondered if bodily and psychologically healthful folks that knew they had been collaborating in an test would change their behavior in a jail-like putting.

The researchers set up a ridicule prison in the basement of Stanford college's psychology constructing. They decided on 24 undergraduate college students to play the roles of both prisoners and guards.

The individuals have been chosen from a larger institution of 70 volunteers because that they had no crook historical past, lacked mental problems, and had no giant medical conditions. The volunteers agreed to participate for the duration of a one to 2-week period in alternate for $15 a day.

The simulated prison protected 3 six-by-9-foot prison cells. each cellular held 3 prisoners and covered three cots.

other rooms throughout from the cells have been utilized for the prison guards and warden. One tiny space become particular as the solitary confinement room, and but another small room served as the jail backyard.

The 24 volunteers were then randomly assigned to both the prisoner group or the protect institution. Prisoners were to remain in the mock jail 24 hours a day at some stage in the take a look at.

Guards had been assigned to work in 3-man teams for eight-hour shifts. After every shift, guards were allowed to return to their houses until their next shift.

Researchers had been capable of take a look at the behavior of the prisoners and guards the usage of hidden cameras and microphones

RESULTS :

At the same time as the Stanford prison test was at the start slated to final 14 days, it needed to be stopped after just six due to what was going on to the scholar individuals.3 The guards have become abusive, and the prisoners commenced to expose signs and symptoms of extreme pressure and anxiety.

some of those blanketed:

While the prisoners and guards had been allowed to engage in any way they wanted, the interactions had been adverse or even dehumanizing.

The guards started to behave in approaches that were competitive and abusive closer to the prisoners even as the prisoners became passive and depressed.

five of the prisoners started to enjoy intense negative emotions, consisting of crying and acute tension, and needed to be launched from the have a look at early.

Even the researchers themselves started out to lose sight of the fact of the situation. Zimbardo, who acted as the jail warden, overlooked the abusive behavior of the jail guards until graduate student Christina Maslach voiced objections to the conditions inside the simulated jail and the morality of continuing the test.

IMPACT

The test have become well-known and was broadly stated in textbooks and different guides. in step with Zimbardo and his colleagues, the Stanford prison test verified the powerful role that the situation can play in human conduct.

Due to the fact the guards had been located in a position of energy, they began to behave in approaches they would no longer commonly act in their ordinary lives or other situations. The prisoners, located in a scenario where that they had no real manage, have become submissive and depressed.

In 2011, the Stanford Alumni magazine featured a retrospective of the Stanford prison experiment in honor of the test's fortieth anniversary. the thing contained interviews with several humans concerned, which includes Zimbardo and different researchers in addition to a number of the individuals within the examine.

Richard Yacco, one of the prisoners within the test, suggested that the test tested the electricity that societal roles and expectations can play in a person's behavior.5

In 2015, the experiment have become the subject of a function movie titled The Stanford jail experiment that dramatized the occasions of the 1971 observe.

Criticisms of the Stanford jail experiment

in the years since the test was performed, there had been some of opinions of the examine. some of those consist of:

moral problems

The Stanford jail test is frequently referred to as an example of unethical research. The experiment could not be replicated by way of researchers nowadays because it fails to satisfy the requirements installed via severa moral codes, including the Ethics Code of the american mental association.

loss of Generalizability

other critics advocate that the have a look at lacks generalizability due to a diffusion of factors.6 The unrepresentative sample of individuals (in most cases white and middle-class adult males) makes it hard to use the effects to a much wider population.

Lack of Realism

The have a look at is also criticized for its lack of ecological validity.7 Ecological validity refers back to the degree of realism with which a simulated experimental setup suits the real-global state of affairs it seeks to emulate.

at the same time as the researchers did their best to recreate a prison setting, it is definitely not possible to perfectly mimic all of the environmental and situational variables of prison existence. because there may were elements related to the putting and state of affairs that stimulated how the participants behaved, it is able to no longer actually represent what may take place outside of the lab.

Recent Criticisms

more recent exam of the test's archives and interviews with members have revealed predominant problems with the research's design, strategies, and processes that name the take a look at's validity, price, and even authenticity into query.

These reviews, along with examinations of the observe's information and new interviews with members, have also cast doubt on a number of the important thing findings and assumptions approximately the observe.

some of the issues defined:

One participant, as an instance, has counseled that he faked a breakdown so that he ought to depart the test due to the fact he become involved about failing his classes.

different contributors also mentioned changing their behavior in a manner designed to "assist" the experiment.

proof additionally suggests that the experimenters endorsed the conduct of the guards and performed a role in fostering the abusive movements of the guards.nine

In 2019, the magazine American Psychologist published an

editorial debunking the famed experiment, detailing its loss of scientific merit, and concluding that the Stanford prison experiment become "a really improper have a look at that ought to have died an early loss of life."10

In a assertion published at the test's reputable internet site, Zimbardo keeps that these criticisms do not undermine the primary end of the study—that situational forces can adjust person moves both in wonderful and negative ways.

3. SOLMAN ASCH EXPERIMENT ON CONFORMITY

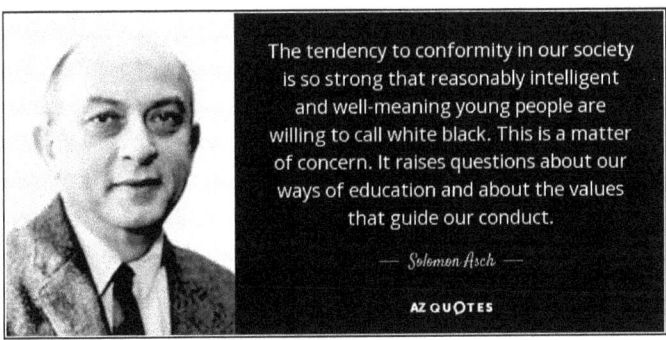

The Asch conformity experiments were a chain of psychological experiments conducted via Solomon Asch in the course of the 1950s. The experiments found out the degree to which a person's personal reviews are stimulated by means of the ones of companies. Asch determined that people had been inclined to disregard fact and supply an incorrect solution with the intention to comply with the relaxation of the organization.

a better examine Conformity
Do you watched of yourself as a conformist or a non-conformist? If you're like the majority, you probably accept

as true with which you are non-conformist sufficient to arise to a collection when you recognize you're proper however conformist enough to combo in with the rest of your peers.

research suggests that human beings are often an awful lot greater at risk of conform than they accept as true with they might be.

believe your self in this example: you've got signed up to participate in a psychology experiment in that you are asked to complete a imaginative and prescient test.

Seated in a room with the alternative members, you're proven a line phase after which requested to pick the matching line from a group of 3 segments of various lengths.

The experimenter asks every player for my part to pick the matching line phase. On some activities, absolutely everyone within the organization chooses the right line, but now and again, the alternative participants unanimously declare that a unique line is clearly the correct fit.

So what do you do whilst the experimenter asks you which of them line is the proper suit? Do you go together with your initial response, or do you pick out to conform to the rest of the group?

Solomon Asch's Conformity Experiments

In psychological phrases, conformity refers to an character's tendency to comply with the unspoken guidelines or behaviors of the social institution to which he or she belongs. Researchers have long been interested in the degree to which people comply with or riot against social norms. Asch was interested by searching at how stress from a set should lead humans to comply, even when they knew that the relaxation of the group changed into wrong. The motive of Asch's experiments? to illustrate the energy of conformity in corporations.

How had been Asch's Experiments finished?
Asch's experiments worried having folks that have been "in" at the experiment faux to be everyday contributors along those who have been actual, unaware topics of the study. those who were in at the experiment might behave in certain ways to peer if their moves had a power at the real experimental individuals.

In each experiment, a naive scholar player turned into located in a room with numerous different confederates who have been "in on" the test. The naive topics have been instructed that they were taking element in a "imaginative and prescient take a look at." All told, a total of 50 college students had been a part of Asch's experimental situation.

The confederates had been all told what their responses could be whilst the line assignment turned into provided. The naive player, but, had no inkling that the other college students had been now not actual individuals. After the line project changed into supplied, every student became verbally introduced which line (both 1, 2, or three) matched the target line.

There have been 18 one-of-a-kind trials inside the experimental circumstance, and the confederates gave wrong responses in 12 of them, which Asch known as the "critical trials." The reason of these essential trials became to peer if the participants could exchange their solution for you to agree to how the others within the organization responded.

all through the primary part of the manner, the confederates replied the questions effectively. however, they sooner or later started supplying incorrect solutions primarily based on how they were instructed with the aid of the experimenters.

The take a look at additionally protected 37 individuals in a manipulate situation. as a way to ensure that the average person may want to as it should be gauge the period of the traces, the manage organization changed into asked to individually write down the perfect suit. in keeping with those effects, contributors have been very correct of their line judgments, choosing the precise solution 99% of the time.

RESULTS:

nearly seventy five% of the individuals in the conformity experiments went in conjunction with the rest of the organization at least one time.

After combining the rigors, the consequences indicated that participants conformed to the wrong institution answer about one-1/3 of the time.

The experiments also looked at the impact that the variety of people present in the institution had on conformity. when simply an extra accomplice became present, there was honestly no effect on individuals' answers. The presence of confederates had simplest a tiny impact. the extent of conformity seen with 3 or more confederates was far more enormous.

Asch also found that having one of the confederates give the correct answer while the relaxation of the confederates gave the wrong answer dramatically decreased conformity. In this example, just five to 10% of the contributors conformed to the relaxation of the group (relying on how frequently the ally spoke back efficaciously). Later studies have also supported this finding, suggesting that having social support is an essential tool in combating conformity.

What Do the results of the Asch Conformity Experiments screen?

At the realization of the experiments, contributors were requested why they'd long gone in conjunction with the relaxation of the institution. In maximum instances, the scholars stated that whilst they knew the relaxation of the institution become incorrect, they did not need to threat dealing with ridicule. some of the individuals recommended that they honestly believed the other individuals of the institution were accurate of their solutions.

these effects suggest that conformity can be influenced each by a need to healthy in and a perception that different human beings are smarter or higher informed.

Given the level of conformity seen in Asch's experiments, conformity may be even stronger in actual-existence situations where stimuli are more ambiguous or greater tough to choose.

factors That have an impact on Conformity

Asch went on to behavior further experiments for you to decide which factors encouraged how and whilst people conform.

He found that:

Conformity has a tendency to increase whilst greater human beings are gift. but, there may be little trade once the group size is going past four or five human beings.

Conformity also increases when the task becomes more difficult. within the face of uncertainty, humans flip to others for information about a way to reply.

Conformity will increase when other participants of the organization are of a better social reputation. whilst people view the others in the organization as more effective, influential, or informed than themselves, they may be much more likely to go together with the institution.

Conformity has a tendency to lower, however, whilst people are able to reply privately. research has additionally shown that conformity decreases if they have help from at least one other man or woman in a collection.1

Criticisms of the Asch Conformity Experiments

one of the predominant criticisms of Asch's conformity experiments facilities on the motives why individuals select to comply. consistent with a few critics, individuals can also have sincerely been encouraged to keep away from battle, in place of an real choice to comply to the relaxation of the group.

every other grievance is that the results of the test in the lab won't generalize to real-world conditions.

Many social psychology experts consider that at the same time as real-global conditions might not be as they are within the lab, the real social strain to conform might be lots extra, which can dramatically boom conformist behaviors.

Group Pressure and Conformity

- Conformity- adjusting one's behavior of thinking to coincide with a group standard
- Solomon Asch Experiment- Actors pick the wrong line and then people are coerced by conformity to pick something they know is wrong
- Alone- less than 1% made mistake
- In Groups- wrong 33% of the time

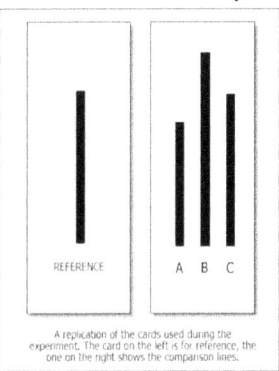

A replication of the cards used during the experiment. The card on the left is for reference, the one on the right shows the comparison lines.

PSYCHODYNAMIC APPROACH OF MIND

the reason of the mind that the psychodynamic version offers gained traction amongst psychoanalysts in the course of the early 20th Century. however, severa psychologists have on account that questioned how efficiently it could be used to apprehend someone's situation.

Critics argue that by way of attributing our conduct to in advance studies in the course of formative years, psychodynamic theories ignore our capability strength of willto manipulate our behavior the use of our own loose will. The psychodynamic technique takes what is effectively a reductionist view of the human thoughts and our very own over our destinies.

moreover, psychodynamic theories take a in simple terms internalised view of behavior, ignoring external factors inclusive of the biological impacts of genetics on our predisposition to a few intellectual problems. whilst Freud did provide case research of customers as regards to his theories, psychodynamic reasons are by means of their very nature hard to either show or disprove, missing evidence that might be received empirically thru experiments.

Nonetheless, the have an impact on of Freud and the psychodynamic version of the mind can be felt nowadays inside the discipline of psychology. The 'speaking therapy' stays a key device for psychoanalysts even if some of Freud's greater tenuous theories had been called into query.

The psychodynamic principle is a psychological theory Sigmund Freud (1856-1939) and his later followers applied to give an explanation for the origins of human conduct.

The psychodynamic technique consists of all of the theories in psychology that see human functioning primarily based upon the interaction of drives and forces within the individual, particularly subconscious, and between the extraordinary structures of the persona.

Sigmund Freud's psychoanalysis turned into the unique psychodynamic principle, however the psychodynamic method as an entire includes all theories that had been primarily based on his ideas, e.g., Carl Jung (1912), Melanie Klein (1921), Alfred Adler (1927), Anna Freud (1936), and Erik Erikson (1950).

The words psychodynamic and psychoanalytic are regularly stressed. remember that Freud's theories had been psychoanalytic, whereas the time period 'psychodynamic' refers to each his theories and those of his followers.

Freud's psychoanalysis is each a theory and therapy.
(writing among the 1890s and the 1930s) evolved a set of theories which have formed the idea of the psychodynamic

approach to psychology.

His theories are clinically derived - i.e., based on what his patients informed him throughout remedy. The psychodynamic therapist would normally be treating the patient for despair or anxiety related problems.

The subconscious thoughts incorporates intellectual processes that are inaccessible to awareness but that affect judgments, feelings, or conduct (Wilson, 2002).

According to Freud (1915), the unconscious thoughts is the primary source of human conduct. Like an iceberg, the maximum vital part of the thoughts is the part you cannot see.

Our emotions, reasons, and selections are actually powerfully influenced by using our past reviews, and saved within the unconscious.

Psychodynamic theory states that events in our early life have a first rate affect on our person lives, shaping our persona. activities that arise in youth can continue to be within the subconscious, and cause troubles as adults.

Persona is shaped because the drives are modified via exclusive conflicts at specific times in adolescence (at some point of psychosexual improvement).

personality is made up of three parts (i.e., tripartite): the identity, ego, and splendid-ego:

The identity is the primitive and instinctive component of personality. It includes all of the inherited (i.e., organic) components of personality gift at birth, such as the sex (existence) instinct – Eros (which contains the libido), and the competitive (loss of life) intuition - Thanatos.

The ego develops a good way to mediate between the unrealistic id and the outside actual international. it's miles the decision making thing of personality.

The superego carries the values and morals of society

which can be discovered from one's mother and father and others.

Elements of the subconscious thoughts (the identity and superego) are in constant battle with the conscious a part of the thoughts (the ego). This warfare creates tension, which may be handled with the aid of the ego's use of defense mechanisms.

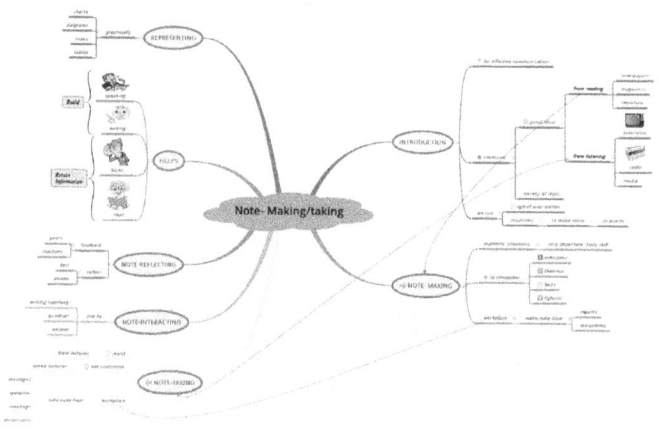

Map Mind

Records of Psychodynamic concept

Anna O a patient of Dr. Joseph Breuer (Freud's mentor and friend) from 1800 to 1882 suffered from hysteria.

In 1895 Breuer and his assistant, Sigmund Freud, wrote a e book, research on Hysteria.

In it they defined their concept: each hysteria is the end result of a demanding revel in, one which cannot be included into the character's understanding of the arena. The guide establishes Freud as "the father of psychoanalysis.

By way of 1896 Freud had found the key to his own gadget, naming it psychoanalysis. In it, he had replaced hypnosis with "loose association."

In 1900 Freud published his first most important paintings, the interpretation of desires, which established the importance of psychoanalytical movement.

In 1902 Freud founded the psychological Wednesday Society, later transformed into the Vienna Psychoanalytic Society.

because the enterprise grew, Freud installed an internal circle of dedicated followers, the so-called "Committee" (such as Sàndor Ferenczi, and Hanns Sachs (standing) Otto Rank, Karl Abraham, Max Eitingon, and Ernest Jones).

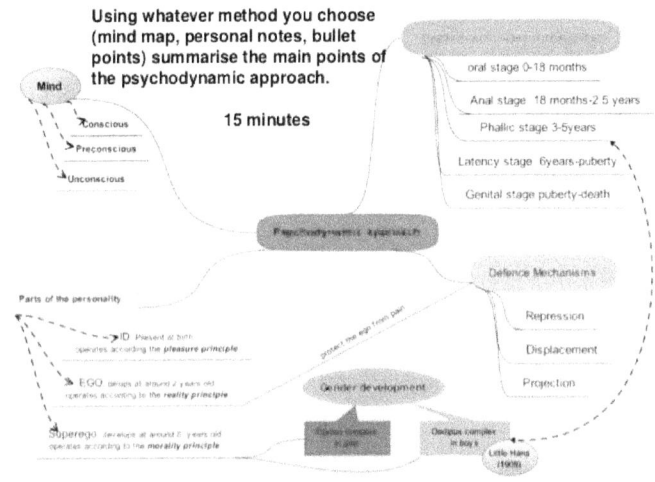

Freud Wednesday society

Freud and his colleagues got here to Massachusetts in 1909 to lecture on their new methods of knowledge mental illness..

the ones in attendance blanketed a number of the united states of america's maximum important intellectual figures, including William James, Franz Boas, and Adolf Meyer.

inside the years following the visit to the us, the global Psychoanalytic affiliation changed into based..

Freud precise Carl Jung as his successor to lead the association, and chapters were created in major towns in Europe and elsewhere..

everyday meetings or congresses were held to speak about the principle, therapy, and cultural packages of the new field.

Jung's take a look at on schizophrenia, The Psychology of Dementia Praecox, led him into collaboration with Sigmund Freud.

Jung's near collaboration with Freud lasted until 1913. Jung had come to be increasingly more crucial of Freud's solely sexual definition of libido and incest..

The booklet of Jung's Wandlungen und Symbole der Libido (known in English as the Psychology of the subconscious) led to a very last damage.

Following his emergence from this era of crisis, Jung developed his very own theories systematically under the call of Analytical Psychology..

Jung's standards of the collective unconscious and the archetypes led him to explore faith in the East and West, myths, alchemy, and later alien craft.

Melanie Klein took psychoanalytic questioning in a brand new path by means of recognising the significance of our earliest childhood studies in the formation of our adult emotional international..

After becoming a complete member of the Berlin

Psychoanalytic Society in 1923, Klein embarks upon her first analysis of a toddler. .

Extending and growing Sigmund Freud's ideas, Klein drew on her evaluation of children's play to formulate new concepts inclusive of the paranoid-schizoid role and the depressive role.

Anna Freud (Freud's daughter) have become a first-rate force in British psychology, specializing within the application of psychoanalysis to kids. .

amongst her best regarded works are The Ego and the Mechanism of protection (1936).

The Case of Anna O

The improvement of Freud's theories of the mind happened via his remark of patients even as he was a practitioner. considered one of his earliest impacts became the case of Anna O, a 21-yr-old lady whom Freud in no way virtually met, but. A purchaser of Freud's buddy, Josef Breuer, Anna changed into affected by what was on the time known as hysteria. She skilled paralysis on one facet, proscribing using certainly one of her fingers, and had evolved an aversion to water (hydrophobia), limiting her ability to drink for days at a time. in addition to these signs and symptoms, Anna suffered from involuntary eye movements and other troubles which docs have been unable to characteristic to a physical condition.

Breuer was interested in the connection between the activities which had came about in advance in her stay and her gift situations. Upon investigation, Anna found out an occasion when she have been sat next to her father, who turned into himself ill in bed. In a dream, she noticed a black snake coming towards him, however was not able to prevent the snake from journeying nearer due to the fact she changed into not able to move considered one of her fingers. This disturbing revel in had truely profoundly affected Anna, and became attributed to her modern-day bouts of paralysis for which no other purpose will be found.

After ongoing classes, Breuer located that Anna's other symptoms might be additionally traced lower back to precise reviews earlier in her lifestyles. On one event, she has been supplied a tumbler of water but had witnessed a canine walk upto the glass and drink from it earlier than she were able to sip it. Breuer reasoned that this had once more affected Anna and had result in her being not able to drink water in a while.

Anna O's classes with Breuer over a time frame have been effective, and after regressing to those traumatic moments, she determined that she turned into able to understand their relation to her gift irrational symptoms and in turn, triumph over them. She noted this therapy as 'chimney sweeping' and a 'talking cure' - a time period which might end up synonymous with psychoanalysis.

Anna O: Sigmund Freud's Case history
Anna O: Sigmund Freud's Case history
Freud took note of the case of Anna O and referred to her in his collaborative work with Breuer, studies on Hysteria (Freud and Breuer, 1895), a e-book whose attribution of subconscious reminiscences and anxieties to hysteria would lay the basis for his psychodynamic principle of the mind.

The composition of the psyche

Freud's hobby changed into inside the dynamics of the thoughts - the conscious and its unconscious affects. He felt that the power inside the psyche turned into a steady cost, and so in place of disappearing from the conscious, it would build up in the unconscious and cause growing internal anxiety till it become addressed. for example, if some thing angers you, the electricity of your anger does now not use up itself if you internalise it. rather, it can be transferred to the unconscious, and lead to a repressed resentment which you may be unaware of on a aware stage.

Freud claimed that the human psyche consisted of 3 separate regions - the id, ego and superego - which compete towards one another for manage over our conduct.

The identification

The identification (that means 'it' in Latin) represents our most impulsive, untamed desires, and pay no regard for what is suitable or reasonable.

Innate instincts which include the need for food, water, warm temperature and sexual desires originate in our id. In a sense, the identity is our 'internal toddler' - it drives our instinctive behavior from delivery and expects its needs to be met immediately, irrespective of any outcomes. The identity abides by using the pride principle, which asserts that we seek to maximise delight and keep away from pain wherever feasible.

additionally contained inside the id is the demise force, a self-damaging impulsiveness which drives us to the quit of our existence.

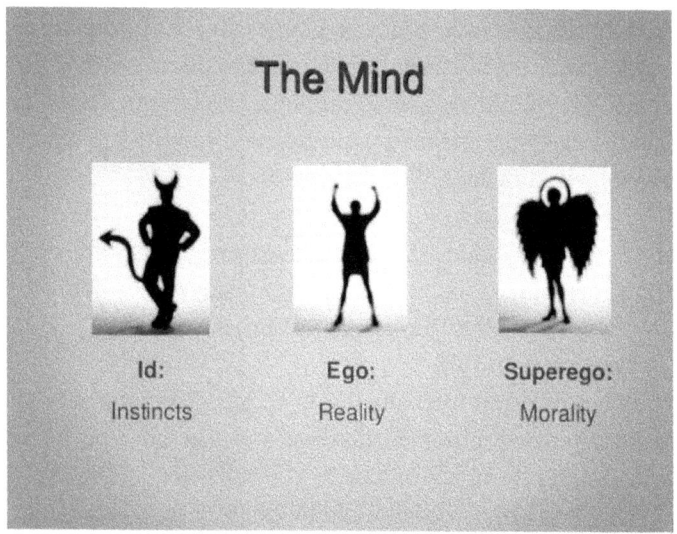

The Ego

the second detail of the psyche is the ego, which acts as an intermediary between the unreasonable needs of the identity and the out of doors fact. It tries to meet the needs of the identification as lots as is nearly viable without always knowledge why some needs is probably unreasonable.

The ego remains self-focused and does no longer give attention to different humans's needs or needs. It acts based totally at the reality precept, which, in assessment to the pleasure precept of the identity, accepts the limits of what may be obtained from the out of doors world.

The Superego

The 0.33 factor of our psyche is the superego. This feels compassion for others and once more tries to meet the desires of the identification, however is familiar with that some of the ones needs may additionally adversely affect others. It acts as a filter out for our conduct and maintains our judgment of right and wrong, leading to an know-how of other humans's emotions and to emotional guilt.

Oedipus and Electra complexes

One way of expertise the identification, ego and superego is to do not forget how they dominate our behaviour at some point of the distinct levels of the lifestyles cycle. Freud recognized severa tiers of psychosexual improvement which we experience, consisting of:

Oral level

while newborn and inside the first few months of our lives, we have a need nourishment. As we feed with the mouth, Freud mentioned this because the oral degree.

We assume our need to feed to be glad as and while we require food. If it isn't happy, we begin to crying as we own no idea of patience or know-how whilst nourishment is unavailable. This stage, throughout the primary yr of our lives, is ruled by the identification issue of our psyche, as the ego and superego have now not but developed.

Anal stage

As we grow older and start bathroom training, defecation will become a focus of our wishes. during this anal stage, we realize that our desires could be met as they're required, however that we'd should wait (along with ready to consume even as food is being organized). within reason, we'd wait a while for it to be prepared before we resort to crying. at some stage in this 2nd degree of our lives, the ego develops and is in ordinary warfare with the impatient needs of the identification.

Phallic level

at the age of around three, our revel in with the outside global has helped to broaden the ego. At this point, we realise our physical lifestyles all through what Freud describes as the phallic level. A recognition of sexuality, Freud claimed, results in a call for for the attention of the mom in men, in opposition with the daddy. In Greek mythology, Oedipus competes for the attention of his mother, Jocasta, and kills his father, Laius, in the manner, and Freud named this jostling for affection the Oedipus complex. In women, a similar process takes place on the subject of the daddy, and is called the Electra complicated.

Because of such complexes, we recognise that our wishes are unreasonable and can experience guilt for experiencing such desires - feelings on account of the improvement of the superego.during our lives, the subconscious drives of the id dictate our goals and behavior, even as the ego and superego lead us to mood such behavior. aside from emotions of guilt when we comprehend these dreams, we might also repress them so that we do not need to understand that we enjoy them. Freud believed that this tension among the needs of the identity, ego and superego, and the repression of choice inside the subconscious thoughts, can disrupt the equilibrium of the psyche and lead to feelings of hysteria and different troubles, together with in the case of Anna O. One way to clear up this imbalance is to convey repressed emotions and reminiscences into the conscious so that we can rationalise and understand them.

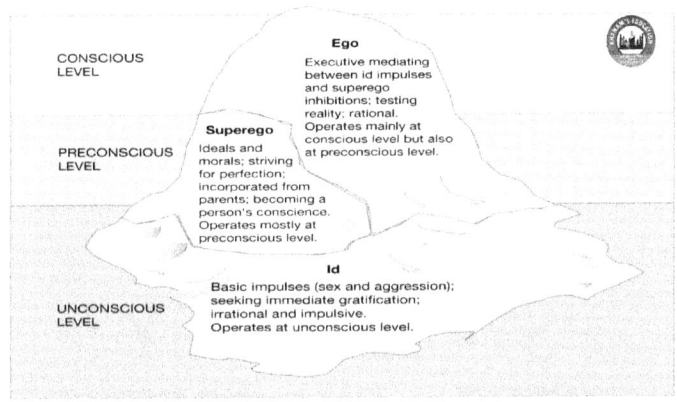

Freud's Approach

IV
COGNITIVE PSYCHOLOGY : HOW THINGS PROCESSED IN MIND

Cognitive psychology is the clinical have a look at of the thoughts as an facts processor. It issues the way we take in statistics from the out of doors world, how we make experience of that facts.

Cognitive psychologists strive to accumulate cognitive models of the data processing that is going on interior humans's minds, which includes notion, interest, language, reminiscence, questioning, and attention.

Cognitive psychology became of fantastic significance in the mid-Nineteen Fifties. numerous elements had been essential on this:

Dissatisfaction with the behaviorist method in its simple emphasis on outside behavior as opposed to inner approaches.

The development of better experimental methods.

contrast among human and pc processing of records.

The emphasis of psychology shifted far from the study of conditioned behavior and psychoanalytical notions approximately the take a look at of the thoughts, closer to the expertise of human facts processing, the usage of strict and rigorous laboratory research.

Mediational strategies arise among stimulus and reaction:

Behaviorists rejected the concept of studying the mind due to the fact inner mental tactics can't be determined and objectively measured.

but, cognitive psychologists regard it as essential to observe the mental methods of an organism and how those influence behavior.

in place of the easy stimulus-reaction hyperlinks proposed by means of Behaviorism, the mediational processes of the organism are vital to understand. without this know-how, psychologists can't have a whole knowledge of behavior.

Psychology have to be seen as a technological know-how:

Cognitive psychologists follow the example of the behaviorists in who prefer goal, managed, scientific strategies for investigating conduct.

They use the outcomes of their investigations as the idea for making inferences about mental techniques.

humans are records processors:

information processing in human beings resembles that in computers, and is primarily based on based on remodeling statistics, storing records and retrieving facts from reminiscence.

records processing models of cognitive tactics consisting of memory and attention anticipate that mental techniques comply with a clear collection.

as an instance:

input methods are concerned with the analysis of the stimuli.

garage strategies cover the entirety that occurs to stimuli internally within the mind and may consist of coding and manipulation of the stimuli.

Output procedures are answerable for making ready an appropriate response to a stimulus.

information Processing

The cognitive approach commenced to revolutionize psychology within the late 1950sand early 1960's, to turn out to be the dominant technique (i.e., attitude) in psychology by the overdue Seventies. hobby in intellectual processes have been regularly restored thru the paintings of Piaget and Tolman.

Tolman changed into a 'tender behaviorist'. His book Purposive behavior in Animals and man in 1932 defined research which behaviorism found tough to provide an explanation for. The behaviorists' view have been that learning befell as a result of associations among stimuli and responses.

however, Tolman suggested that getting to know was primarily based on the relationships which formed amongst stimuli. He cited these relationships as cognitive maps.

however it was the advent of the computer that gave cognitive psychology the terminology and metaphor it wished to research the human thoughts.

The begin of using computer systems allowed psychologists to try to understand the complexities of human cognition with the aid of evaluating it with some thing simpler and better understood, i.e., an artificial machine including a laptop.

using the laptop as a tool for questioning how the human thoughts handles records is known as the laptop analogy. basically, a laptop codes (i.e., adjustments) statistics, shops records, uses information, and produces an output (retrieves data).

The concept of records processing become adopted with the aid of cognitive psychologists as a version of the way human concept works.

The facts processing method is based on some of assumptions, together with:

statistics made available from the surroundings is processed with the aid of a chain of processing systems (e.g., attention, perception, brief-time period reminiscence);

these processing structures rework, or adjust the facts in systematic ways;

The aim of research is to specify the methods and systems that underlie cognitive performance;

statistics processing in human beings resembles that during computers.

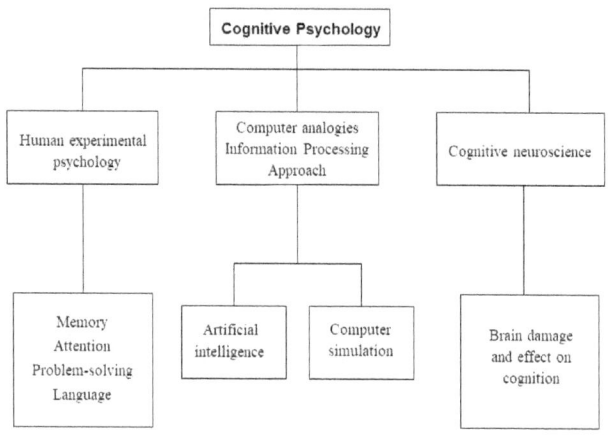

The role of Schemas

Cognitive processing can often be suffering from schemas (a mental framework of beliefs and expectations developed from revel in). As you grow old, those emerge as greater specified and sophisticated.

A schema is a "packet of data" or cognitive framework that helps us organise and interpret information. they're primarily based on our preceding revel in.

Schemas assist us to interpret incoming data fast and efficiently, this prevents us from being overwhelmed by the substantial quantity of records we understand in our environment.

but it could additionally result in distortion of this records as we pick out and interpret environmental stimuli the use of schemas which may not be applicable.

this may be the cause of inaccuracies in regions inclusive of eyewitness testimony. it is able to also provide an explanation for a few mistakes we make whilst perceiving optical illusions.

Mediational tactics

The behaviorists technique handiest studies outside observable (stimulus and reaction) conduct which may be objectively measured. They trust that internal conduct can't be studied because we cannot see what occurs in a person's mind (and therefore can not objectively measure it).

In comparison, the cognitive technique believes that internal mental conduct can be scientifically studied the use of experiments. Cognitive psychology assumes that a mediational procedure takes place between stimulus/enter and response/output.

Mediational tactics

The behaviorists technique handiest research external observable (stimulus and reaction) behavior which may be objectively measured. They trust that inner behavior cannot be studied because we can not see what happens in someone's thoughts (and consequently cannot objectively degree it).

In comparison, the cognitive technique believes that inner intellectual behavior can be scientifically studied the use of experiments. Cognitive psychology assumes that a mediational method takes place between stimulus/input and response/output.

mediational processed in cognitive psychology

The mediational (i.e., mental) event can be memory, perception, interest or problem solving, and so forth. these are referred to as mediational techniques due to the fact they mediate (i.e., go-between) among the stimulus and the reaction. they arrive after the stimulus and before the reaction.

consequently, cognitive psychologists' say if you need to apprehend conduct, you have to apprehend those mediational approaches.

Records of Cognitive Psychology

Kohler (1925) published a ebook known as, The Mentality of Apes. In it he reported observations which advised that animals could display insightful behavior. He rejected behaviorism in favour of an method which have become called Gestalt psychology.

Norbert Wiener (1948) published Cybernetics: or control and communication within the Animal and the machine, introducing phrases inclusive of input and output.

Tolman (1948) work on cognitive maps – schooling rats in mazes, showed that animals had an internal illustration of conduct.

start of Cognitive Psychology frequently dated again to George Miller's (1956) "the paranormal quantity 7 Plus or Minus 2."

Newell and Simon's (1972) development of the general trouble Solver.

In 1960, Miller founded the center for Cognitive research at Harvard with the famous cognitivist developmentalist, Jerome Bruner.

Ulric Neisser (1967) publishes "Cognitive Psychology", which marks the official starting of the cognitive technique.

method models of memory Atkinson & Shiffrin's (1968) Multi keep version.

The cognitive technique is notably influential in all regions of psychology (e.g., organic, social, Behaviorism, developmental, and many others.).

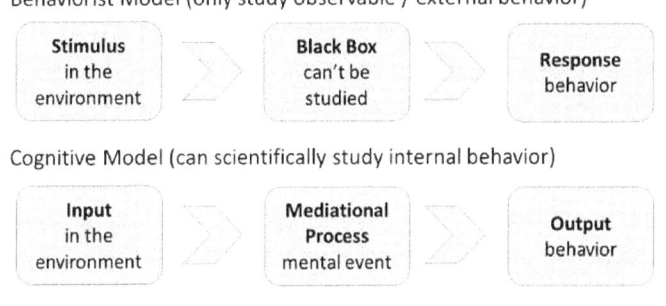

Cognitive psychology is an area that makes a speciality of the technology of the way people think. This branch of psychology explores a huge sort of intellectual techniques along with how human beings assume, use language, attend to facts, and understand their environments.

this text discusses what cognitive psychology is, the history of this field, and cutting-edge guidelines for studies. It also covers a number of the practical programs for cognitive psychology research and career options you would possibly keep in mind in this field.

what's Cognitive Psychology?

Cognitive psychology includes the observe of inner intellectual approaches—all the things that move on inside your mind, including perception, wondering, reminiscence, interest, language, hassle-fixing, and learning.1

mastering extra about how human beings assume and process facts no longer handiest allows researchers advantage a deeper information of ways the human mind works, however it lets in psychologists to broaden new approaches of assisting people deal with psychological problems.

as an instance, through recognizing that attention is each a selective and restricted useful resource, psychologists are able to come up with answers that make it easier for people with attentional problems to enhance their consciousness and attention.

Recap

Findings from cognitive psychology help us recognize how humans assume, which includes how they gather and store reminiscences. by knowing more approximately how those approaches paintings, psychologists can expand new methods of supporting humans with cognitive issues.

topics In Cognitive Psychology

Cognitive psychologists explore a wide kind of topics related to thinking procedures. a number of those encompass:

interest
choice-based behavior
selection-making
Forgetting
records processing
Language acquisition
reminiscence
problem-fixing
Speech perception
visible perception

records of Cognitive Psychology

even as it's far a relatively younger department of psychology, it has speedy grown to come to be one of the most famous subfields. Cognitive psychology have become more principal during the length between the Fifties and Seventies. prior to this time, behaviorism turned into the dominant attitude in psychology, but researchers have become more interested in the internal processes that have an effect on behavior as opposed to simply the behavior itself.

This shift is frequently called the cognitive revolution in psychology. for the duration of this time, a brilliant deal of research on subjects such as reminiscence, attention, and language acquisition started to emerge.

In 1967, the psychologist Ulric Neisser added the time period cognitive psychology, which he defined because the have a look at of the techniques behind the notion, transformation, storage, and restoration of

Cognitive psychology became extra distinguished after the 1950s because of the cognitive revolution.
    contemporary studies in Cognitive Psychology
the field of cognitive psychology is each huge and various. It touches on such a lot of factors of every day existence. there are numerous realistic packages for this cognitive research, consisting of imparting help coping with reminiscence problems, increasing decision-making accuracy, locating approaches to assist human beings recover from mind damage, treating gaining knowledge of disorders, and structuring academic curricula to beautify learning.
    present day research on cognitive psychology helps play a position in how professionals technique the remedy of intellectual contamination, traumatic mind harm, and degenerative brain sicknesses.
    way to the work of cognitive psychologists, we are able to better pinpoint ways to degree human highbrow abilties, broaden new techniques to combat memory problems, and

decode the workings of the human brain—all of which in the end have a powerful effect on how we deal with cognitive problems.

the sphere of cognitive psychology is a swiftly growing place that continues to add to our expertise of the numerous affects that intellectual strategies have on our fitness and every day lives.

From know-how how cognitive procedures exchange over the route of baby development to searching at how the mind transforms sensory inputs into perceptions, cognitive psychology has helped us gain a deeper and richer expertise of the many mental activities that contribute to our daily lifestyles and normal properly-being.

Cognitive method in exercise

similarly to adding to our expertise of how the human thoughts works, the sphere of cognitive psychology has additionally had an impact on techniques to mental health. before the Seventies, many intellectual fitness tactics had been centered more on psychoanalytic, behavioral, and humanistic approaches.

The so-referred to as "cognitive revolution" that took place for the duration of this period positioned a greater emphasis on know-how the manner people process records and the way wondering styles might make contributions to psychological distress. way to studies on this vicinity by means of cognitive psychologists, new strategies to treatment have been evolved to help deal with melancholy, anxiety, phobias, and other mental issues.

Cognitive behavioral therapy and rational emotive conduct therapy are two methods wherein clients and therapists attention at the underlying cognitions that make contributions to psychological misery.

what's Cognitive Behavioral remedy?

Cognitive behavioral remedy (CBT) is an method that helps customers perceive irrational ideals and different cognitive distortions which are in struggle with reality after which resource them in changing such mind with greater sensible, healthful ideals.

if you are experiencing symptoms of a mental disorder that might benefit from the use of cognitive strategies, you may see a psychologist who has precise training in those cognitive remedy strategies.

those professionals frequently pass via titles aside from cognitive psychologists, which includes psychiatrists, clinical psychologists, or counseling psychologists, but some of the techniques they utilize are rooted within the cognitive way of life.

Careers in Cognitive Psychology

whilst many cognitive psychologists specialise in studies and are hired by way of universities or authorities businesses, others take a scientific attention and paintings without delay with folks that are experiencing challenges related to exclusive mental approaches. they'll work in hospitals, mental health clinics, or non-public practices.

Psychologists who paintings in this region frequently attention on a selected place of hobby inclusive of memory, whilst others might alternatively select to work directly on precise health concerns related to cognition, such as degenerative mind issues or mind injuries.

reasons to seek advice from a Cognitive Psychologist

Alzheimer's sickness, dementia, or memory loss

brain trauma remedy

Cognitive remedy for a mental illness

Interventions for mastering disabilities

Perceptual or sensory troubles

remedy for a speech or language sickness

The work of cognitive psychologists is essential for supporting people who've skilled troubles with intellectual tactics. while we have a tendency to take capabilities consisting of attention and problem fixing as a right, possibly because they are so woven into the material of our everyday life, cognitive disruptions can create havoc in multiple regions of an individual's lifestyles.

interest issues could make it difficult to cognizance at work or at school. Even surprisingly minor reminiscence troubles could make it a battle to deal with the needs of regular existence. bear in mind, for instance, how negative thinking can interfere with your fitness and happiness.

we all enjoy those terrible thoughts every so often, however some human beings may additionally locate themselves beaten with pessimistic questioning patterns that make it tough to function in every day existence. these ruminations can result in elevated stress stages, pessimism, and self-sabotage, and emotions of learned helplessness.

With the help of cognitive psychologists, human beings are regularly able to discover methods to manage and even overcome such problems.

remedy remedies rooted in cognitive research attention on assisting human beings change those terrible questioning patterns and update such mind with more fantastic and practical ones.

How Cognitive theory Is Used to deal with Phobias

Cognitive psychology performs an vital role in information the techniques that play a role in reminiscence, attention, and gaining knowledge of. it may additionally provide insights into cognitive situations which could have an effect on how people function.

Being recognized with a brain or cognitive health hassle may be daunting, but it's miles essential to keep in mind that you are not alone. with the aid of operating with your medical doctor, you could give you an powerful treatment plan to help deal with brain fitness and cognitive issues.

Your treatment may additionally involve consulting with a cognitive psychologist who has a historical past inside the precise location of concern that you are going through, or you'll be stated every other intellectual fitness professional that has training and enjoy together with your specific contamination.

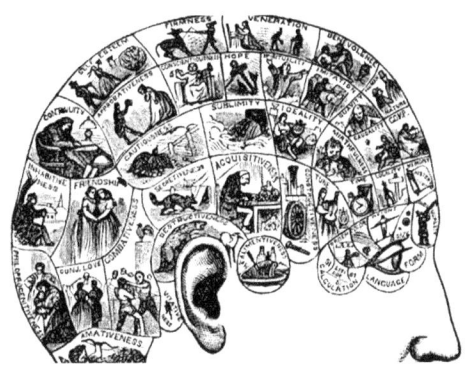

SUBDOMAINS OF COGNITIVE PSYCHOLOGY

traditionally, cognitive psychology consists of human perception, attention, studying, memory, concept formation, reasoning, judgment and selection-making, hassle solving, and language processing. For some, social and cultural elements, emotion, awareness, animal cognition, evolutionary approaches have additionally emerge as a part of cognitive psychology.

notion: the ones reading perception are looking for to understand how we assemble subjective interpretations of proximal facts from the environment. Perceptual systems are composed of separate senses (e.g., visible, auditory, somatosensory) and processing modules (e.g., shape, motion; Livingston & Hubel, 1988; Ungerleider & Mishkin, 1982; Julesz, 1971) and sub-modules (e.g., Lu & Sperling, 1995) that represent distinctive factors of the stimulus statistics. modern studies also specializes in how those separate representations and modules interact and are incorporated into coherent percepts. Cognitive psychologists have studied those residences empirically with psychophysical methods and brain imaging. Computational models, based totally on physiological standards, have been developed for lots perceptual systems (Grossberg & Mingolla, 1985; Marr, 1982; Wandell, 1995).

attention: interest solves the problem of information overload in cognitive processing structures by using selecting some information for similarly processing, or via handling sources applied to numerous resources of facts simultaneously (Broadbent, 1957; Posner, 1980; Treisman, 1969). Empirical research of attention has targeted on how and why attention improves performance, or how the dearth of attention hinders performance (Posner, 1980; Weichselgartner & Sperling, 1987; Chun & Potter, 1995; Pashler, 1999). The theoretical evaluation of interest has taken several primary approaches to pick out the mechanisms of interest: the sign-detection technique (Lu & Dosher, 1998) and the similarity-preference method (Bundesen, 1990; Logan, 2004). associated outcomes of biased opposition were studied in single cellular recordings in animals (Reynolds, Chelazzi, & Desimone, 1999). brain imaging research have documented results of interest on activation in early visible cortices, and have investigated the networks for interest manage (Kanwisher & Wojciulik, 2000).

learning: getting to know improves the response of the organism to the surroundings. Cognitive psychologists take a look at which new statistics is obtained and the situations underneath which it's far acquired. The have a look at of mastering starts offevolved with an evaluation of getting to know phenomena in animals (i.e., habituation, conditioning, and instrumental, contingency, and associative mastering) and extends to learning of cognitive or conceptual data by way of people (Kandel, 1976; Estes, 1969; Thompson, 1986). Cognitive research of implicit getting to know emphasize the in large part automatic affect of previous experience on overall performance, and the nature of procedural knowledge (Roediger, 1990). studies of conceptual learning emphasize the nature of the processing of incoming statistics, the role of elaboration, and the nature of the encoded representation (Craik, 2002). those using computational tactics have investigated the nature of ideas that may be extra effortlessly found out, and the regulations and algorithms for getting to know structures (Holland, Holyoak, Nisbett, & Thagard, 1986). the ones the use of lesion and imaging studies look into the function of precise mind systems (e.g., temporal lobe systems) for positive classes of episodic learning, and the role of perceptual structures in implicit gaining knowledge of (Tulving, Gordon Hayman, & MacDonald, 1991; Gabrieli, Fleischman, Keane, Reminger, & Morell, 1995; Grafton, Hazeltine, & Ivry, 1995).

memory: The examine of the capacity and fragility of human reminiscence is one of the maximum evolved aspects of cognitive psychology. memory look at specializes in how recollections are obtained, stored, and retrieved. memory domain names were functionally divided into reminiscence for data, for processes or talents, and operating and brief-term reminiscence potential. The experimental tactics have recognized dissociable memory kinds (e.g., procedural and episodic; Squire & Zola, 1996) or ability restrained processing systems including quick-time period or running reminiscence (Cowan, 1995; Dosher, 1999). Computational processes describe reminiscence as propositional networks, or as holographic or composite representations and retrieval tactics (Anderson, 1996, Shiffrin & Steyvers, 1997). brain imaging and lesion research perceive separable mind regions active all through garage or retrieval from wonderful processing structures (Gabrieli, 1998).

idea Formation: idea or category formation refers to the capacity to arrange the belief and type of reports via the development of functionally applicable categories. The response to a specific stimulus (i.e., a cat) is determined no longer by the particular instance but by classification into the category and by using affiliation of expertise with that category (Medin & Ross, 1992). The ability to analyze ideas has been proven to rely upon the complexity of the category in representational space, and by the relationship of variations amongst exemplars of concepts to fundamental and accessible dimensions of illustration (Ashby, 2000). positive standards largely mirror similarity systems, but others may also replicate feature, or conceptual theories of use (Medin, 1989). Computational models were evolved primarily based on aggregation of instance representations, similarity systems and popular popularity fashions, and via conceptual theories (Barsalou, 2003). Cognitive neuroscience has recognized vital mind systems for components or awesome varieties of class formation (Ashby, Alfonso-Reese, Turken, and Waldron, 1998).

Judgment and decision: Human judgment and selection making is ubiquitous – voluntary conduct implicitly or explicitly calls for judgment and preference. The historic foundations of preference are based in normative or rational models and optimality rules, beginning with predicted software theory (von Neumann & Morgenstern 1944; Luce, 1959). substantial evaluation has diagnosed vast screw ups of rational fashions because of differential evaluation of risks and rewards (Luce and Raiffa, 1989), the distorted assessment of possibilities (Kahneman & Tversky, 1979), and the limitations in human facts processing (i.e., Russo & Dosher, 1983). New computational tactics rely upon dynamic structures analyses of judgment and desire (Busemeyer & Johnson, 2004), and Bayesian notion networks that make picks based on a couple of criteria (Fenton & Neil, 2001) for more complex situations. The observe of selection making has emerge as an energetic topic in cognitive neuroscience (Bechara, Damasio and Damasio, 2000).

'"**Reasoning:**"' Reasoning is the manner with the aid of which logical arguments are evaluated or constructed. original investigations of reasoning centered on the extent to which human beings efficiently applied the philosophically derived regulations of inference in deduction (i.e., A implies B; If A then B), and the various approaches wherein human beings fail to realize a few deductions and falsely finish others. those have been extended to boundaries in reasoning with syllogisms or quantifiers (Johnson-Laird, Byne and Schaeken, 1992; Rips and Marcus, 1977). Inductive reasoning, in contrast, develops a hypothesis consistent with a hard and fast of observations or reasons by means of analogy (Holyoak and Thagard, 1995). regularly reasoning is tormented by heuristic judgments, fallacies, and the representativeness of proof, and different framing phenomena (Kahneman, Slovic, Tversky, 1982). Computational models had been advanced for inference making and analogy (Holyoak and Thagard, 1995), logical reasoning (Rips and Marcus, 1977), and Bayesian reasoning (Sanjana and Tenenbaum, 2003).

hassle fixing: The cognitive psychology of hassle solving is the look at of the way people pursue aim directed conduct. The computational state-area evaluation and computer simulation of problem fixing of Newell and Simon (1972) and the empirical and heuristic analysis of Wickelgren (1974) collectively have set the cognitive mental approach to hassle solving. solving a trouble is conceived as locating operations to transport from the preliminary kingdom to a goal state in a problem space the usage of either algorithmic or heuristic answers. The trouble illustration is important in finding answers (Zhang, 1997). understanding in information rich domains (i.e., chess) additionally relies upon on complicated sample popularity (Gobet & Simon, 1996). problem fixing may interact notion, memory, interest, and govt function, and so many mind areas may be engaged in trouble solving duties, with an emphasis on pre-frontal executive features.

Language Processing: while linguistic approaches consciousness at the formal systems of languages and language use (Chomsky, 1965), cognitive psychology has focused on language acquisition, language comprehension, language manufacturing, and the psychology of studying (Kintsch 1974; Pinker, 1994; Levelt, 1989). Psycholinguistics has studied encoding and lexical get entry to of phrases, sentence stage techniques of parsing and representation, and popular representations of standards, gist, inference, and semantic assumptions. Computational models had been advanced for all of those tiers, consisting of lexical structures, parsing systems, semantic representation structures, and studying aloud (Seidenberg, 1997; Coltheart, Rastle, Perry, Langdon, & Ziegler, 2001; just, chippie, and Woolley, 1982; Thorne, Bratley & Dewar, 1968; Schank and Abelson, 1977; Massaro, 1998). The neuroscience of language has an extended history inside the analysis of lesions (Wernicke, 1874; Broca, 1861), and has additionally been appreciably studied with cognitive imaging (Posner et al, 1988).

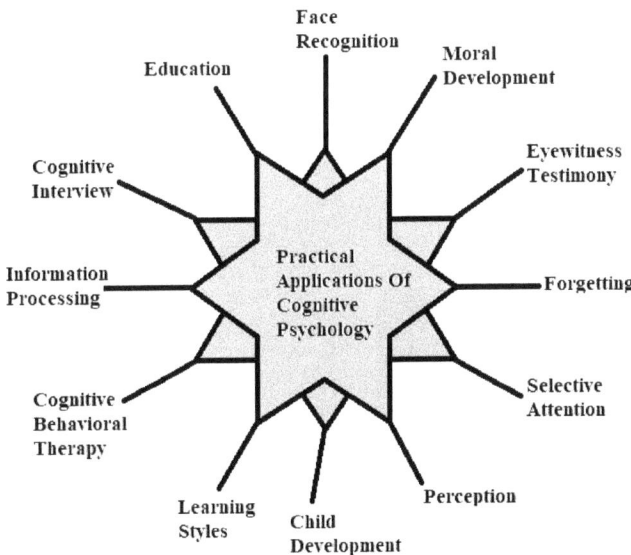

APPLICATIONS

Cognitive psychology studies has industrially produced an intensive frame of concepts, representations, and algorithms. a success packages range from custom-constructed professional structures to software and purchaser electronics:

(1) improvement of pc interfaces that collaborate with users to fulfill their statistics needs and perform as smart dealers,

(2) improvement of a flexible information infrastructure based on know-how illustration and reasoning methods,

(3) development of smart tools inside the financial enterprise,

(4) development of cellular, sensible robots that may carry out obligations usually reserved for people,

(5) improvement of bionic additives of the perceptual and cognitive neural system including cochlear and retinal implants.

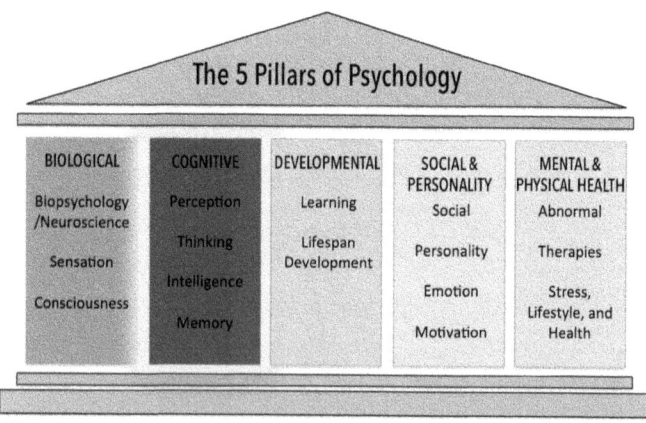

Mental remedy Derived from Cognitive Psychology / Theories

Cognitive psychology is intention-oriented and trouble-centered from the beginning. believe you're getting into remedy with a cognitive psychologist. one of the first things you will be asked to do is become aware of your problems and formulate unique dreams for yourself. Then you will be helped to organize your problems in a manner in order to boom the probabilities of assembly your goals.

think that as you're getting ready to your presentation at paintings the next day, you fear you will fail. because of this, you are the use of distractions round you as a manner to keep away from running at the presentation. This prevents you from preparing properly, which genuinely causes you to fail. You accept as true with which you failed due to the fact you're nugatory. A cognitive psychologist could assist you study and then rationalize the state of affairs as a way to understand the maximum valid purpose in your failure. Then they could train you a way to make adjustments to help you be successful.

All types of cognitive-derived remedy have these four characteristics:

A collaborative relationship among purchaser and therapist.

The belief that mental misery is largely the end result of a disturbance in cognitive approaches.

a focal point on changing cognition to produce favored changes in feelings and/or conduct.

A time-restricted remedy that makes a speciality of specific issues.

even though frequently grouped collectively, cognitive-derived treatment plans can be divided into regions: cognitive therapy (CT) and cognitive conduct remedy (CBT).

CT and CBT are very similar of their theory and application. The distinction is that cognitive therapy generally specializes in disposing of psychological misery (by managing poor thoughts and emotions), whilst cognitive behavioral therapy targets the elimination of negative behaviors as well.

precise Cognitive Derived healing procedures/Theories

There are 3 main contributing theories inside the context of cognitive remedy:

Albert Ellis' rational emotive conduct therapy (REBT)
Aaron Beck's cognitive remedy (CT)
Donald Meichenbaum's cognitive behavior therapy (CBT)

The framework for REBT was developed via Albert Ellis. previously known as rational therapy or rational emotive therapy, REBT is one of the first cognitive treatment options. today it remains a first-rate technique inside the field of cognitive psychology. It makes the simple assumption which you make contributions on your own psychological issues and signs thru your interpretations.

Rational emotive conduct remedy makes a speciality of uncovering irrational beliefs that may lead to dangerous poor feelings. It examines this courting thru what's known as the A-B-C framework.

   A-B-C Framework for REBT

let's see the A-B-C framework with an example:

(A) Activating occasion: you're on foot down the road. Your friend walks proper beyond and ignores you.

(B) beliefs: you think, 'Bob should be indignant with me or he could have stated hey.'

(C) outcomes: You ignore your friend the following time you spot him due to the fact you anticipate he does not want to speak to you.

In this situation you've got the irrational notion that Bob is indignant with you. An irrational notion is a notion that has no actual foundation and is rationally unsupported. REBT could help you replace this irrational belief with a extra rational alternative. let's see how the state of affairs may spread with this change:

(A) Activating occasion: you're on foot down the street. Your buddy walks proper beyond and ignores you.

(B) ideals: you observed, 'it is unlike Bob not to say hi there, i'm wondering what is going on?'

(C) results: you turn and get in touch with out to Bob. He apologizes for no longer seeing you, however explains he's certainly distracted by using some thing. you're making plans to get together later and seize up.

Aaron T. Beck advanced the cognitive remedy technique because of his studies and medical understanding on melancholy. He found that most depressed human beings have a negative interpretation of life activities. This sooner or later led him to assume that the way you feel is related to the way you reflect onconsideration on your reports.

Cognitive motion in Psychology

In 1913, the behaviorist John B. Watson removed the principles of thoughts, focus, or aware approaches to define human psychology.

all at once, cognizance and different associated phrases started out to be related to the field of psychology. furthermore, such phrases that have been formerly challenged politically, commenced performing in print as well as all through meetings.

as an example, in 1979, the american Psychologist posted a piece of writing titled "Behaviorism and the mind: A (confined) call for a go back to Introspection". this newsletter mentioned not handiest the human mind but also the introspection approach to define the area of psychology.

besides this, the yank Psychologist journal posted a piece of writing titled "cognizance" a few months earlier than publishing the above-stated article. the author of this newsletter said that cognizance become coming underneath medical scrutiny after a long time of intentional forget about.

moreover, the subject "attention" also became a part of discussions at top notch locations in psychology literature.

as an instance, in 1976, the President of the yank psychological association stated that the sector of psychology was converting. moreover, the converting subject turned into refocusing on attention. similarly to this, the President asserted that the sphere of psychology now represented greater people over the mechanistic images of human nature.

as a consequence, such an open connection with attention with regards to the sector of Psychology really showcased that a revolution within the area became approximately to come back.

So, following this wave, psychology become redefined as the technology of both behavior and mental methods and now not simply conduct. It became described as a systematic field seeking to explain observable behavior and its dating with intellectual techniques.

therefore, it become comprehensible that the field of Psychology advanced some distance past the theories that Watson and Skinner proposed.

earlier affects on Cognitive Psychology

the sphere of Cognitive Psychology did now not come to mild all of a unexpected. many of its attributes had been predicted manner again when the sphere of psychology become no longer considered a proper technology.

for instance, Greek Philosophers like Aristotle and Plato wrote portions that highlighted human idea methods.

except this, Wilhelm Wundt's paintings focused on awareness whilst he established that psychology was a separate scientific field. accordingly, we can don't forget Wundt as one of the first few modern-day psychologists who emphasized on human thoughts's creative characteristic.

In reality, even the structuralist and the functionalist colleges of thought considered analyzing the factors and features of recognition.

but, Behaviorism become the best movement in psychology that overlooked focus for almost 5 many years. even though, the movement had delivered about a essential trade inside the field of psychology.

I. E.R. Guthrie

It become in the Nineteen Fifties that the sphere of psychology reconsidered attention. additionally, this period also saw the beginning of the Cognitive psychology movement.

however, the signs of the following movement were pretty obvious within the Thirties. It was at some point of this era that the behaviorist E.R. Guthrie disapproved of the mechanistic model of human psychology.

moreover, he maintained that one can not give an explanation for the impact of stimuli in bodily phrases. as a result, he cautioned that psychologists have to explain stimuli in perceptual or cognitive phrases. this is because lowering stimuli in cognitive terms is meaningful for the character responding to such stimuli.

further to this, Guthrie defined that one can't describe the term "that means" entirely in behaviorist terms. that is because the term "meaning" itself is a cognitive process.

II. E.C. Tolman

any other development that marked the cognitive motion changed into that of E.C. Tolman's "Purposive Behaviorism."

This behavioral method emphasised the relevance of cognitive variables and disapproved of the stimulus-reaction approach.

as a result, Tolman proposed cognitive maps and also related purposive conduct with animals. furthermore, he additionally laid emphasis on sure intervening variables to define inner unobservable states.

III. Gestalt Psychology

Gestalt Psychology also stimulated the cognitive motion. It focused on organization, shape, relationships, the active position of the difficulty, and belief gambling an critical role in mastering and memory.

as a result, Gestalt Psychology seemly verified an interest in consciousness while behaviorism dominated American Psychology.

IV. Jean Piaget

The Swiss Psychologist changed into one of the pioneers who anticipated cognitive psychology. His work on cognitive stages in infant improvement was pretty influential, mainly in Europe.

although, inside the u.s., his work on Cognitive development became not broadly accepted. This became because it changed into no longer pretty well suited with that of the behaviorists.

however, the early cognitive theorists accepted Piaget's emphasis on cognitive elements. Later, the reason of Piaget's ideas have become obtrusive as the thoughts of cognitive psychologists received importance within the united states.

consequently, Jean Piaget have become the primary european psychologist in 1969 to get hold of the APA's distinguished clinical Contribution Award.

furthermore, his work's recognition on kids helped in widening the variety of conduct to which cognitive psychology will be implemented.

The changing movement in Physics

The scientists like Albert Einstein, Niels Bohr, and Werner Heisenberg added to the vanguard a brand new point of view in the discipline of physics all through the early 20th century.

They deserted the mechanistic model of the Universe that got here from scientists like Galileo and Newton.

Now, this mechanistic model of the Universe turned into a prototype for the mechanistic, reductionistic, and deterministic concept of human nature. And psychologists like Wundt and Skinner usual the mechanistic view of human nature.

but, the brand new improvement in Physics rejected the idea of an objectively knowable universe. moreover, it shifted to the concept of considering the universe subjective or observer-dependent.

In other phrases, the field of Physics started confiding in the belief that attaining objective fact become no longer viable. thus, things that were as soon as taken into consideration objective have been surely subjective.

which means modern scientists rejected the mechanistic, goal situation be counted and identified subjectivity. consequently, this transition restored the critical function of conscious revel in as a manner to gain statistics approximately the sector.

any such innovative argument in physics become once more making recognition an admissible part of psychology's concern count.

but, the medical psychology domain antagonistic the brand new physics for almost half a century. This area strictly defined itself as an goal technology of behavior. however in the end, it modified itself and reconsidered cognitive procedures.

The Founding of Cognitive Psychology

The transition from behaviorist to cognitive foundations was under no circumstances fast. this type of dramatic trade came about slowly and quietly over a length of 10 to 15 years.

furthermore, there may be no single person liable for the development of Cognitive Psychology. that is in contrast to Watson who changed the field unmarried-handedly.

as a consequence, cognitive motion does not claim any unmarried founder similar to functional Psychology. that is because none of the psychologists running on this domain had the final purpose of leading a new movement. In different words, they honestly desired to redefine psychology.

however, two pupils contributed groundbreaking paintings in the development of cognitive psychology. as a result, George Miller and Ulric Neisser are the two students whose paintings is now considered milestones within the subject of cognitive psychology.

I. George Miller

George Miller published a book on psycholinguistics "Language and communication" inside the year 1951. initially, Miller believed within the Behaviorist school of notion. This become due to the fact he had no desire as behaviorists held leadership positions in fundamental universities and professional associations.

accordingly, it turned into in the mid-Fifties that Miller researched statistical mastering idea, records principle, and computer-primarily based models. As a result, he concluded that Behaviorism become not going to training session.

His view of psychology oriented in the direction of cognition when he became aware of the similarities between computers and the human mind.

except this, Miller's rebellious nature also contributed to this sort of transition. this is due to the fact the psychologists of that era have been coached to riot against psychology then practiced to provide a brand new method.

Then, in 1956, Miller published an editorial titled "the mystical quantity Seven, Plus or Minus : some Limits on our capability for Processing facts."

In this article, Miller proposed that a human's capacity for brief-term memory of numbers, phrases, or colors is limited. And it's far confined to seven chunks of records. that is all we as humans are capable of technique at one point in time.

Now, the importance of this locating lies in the truth that it relates to a aware, cognitive revel in. And that too at a time whilst Behaviorism dominated the psychological area.

status quo of middle for Cognitive studies

George Miller hooked up a studies center with his Harvard colleague Jerome Bruner to research the human mind.

This middle changed into mounted inside the residence where William James once lived. furthermore, this facility became named the center for Cognitive studies that absolutely represented their difficulty count number.

for that reason, the middle researched an expansion of topics along with language, reminiscence, notion, concept formation, questioning, and developmental psychology. As a count of reality, maximum of these aspects were eliminated from the behaviorist's vocabulary.

similarly to the research center, Miller also evolved a program for Cognitive Sciences at the Princeton college.

Awards

Then in 1969, George Miller have become the President of the yankee mental association. for that reason, the following table showcases the awards that George Miller won for his contribution to the sphere.

II. Ulric Neisser

Neisser had his first educational process at Brandeis university chaired by way of Abraham Maslow. In 1967, Neisser published his e-book titled "Cognitive Psychology". This book is a landmark inside the history of psychology as it turned into his try to outline a new method to the field of psychology.

moreover, the e book become pretty famous and subsequently he changed into distinct as the Cognitive Psychology founder.

but, in 1976, Neisser became disillusioned with what he had advanced. As a end result, in 1976, he posted the magazine "Cognition and fact".

in this journal, the Cognitive Psychology Founder expressed his disappointment as he determined the narrowing of the cognitive function. furthermore, he additionally expressed his discontent that the research within the Ulric Neisser field had to depend upon laboratory settings in location of real-world settings to acquire the records.

furthermore, he asserted that the results of mental studies should be found past the laboratory settings.

further to this, Neisser advocated that cognitive psychologists have to be able to practice their findings to sensible troubles. In other words, cognitive psychologists ought to be capable of assist people address actual-life challenges at their paintings and in their lives.

consequently, Neisser concluded that the cognitive psychology movement did not contribute a great deal to the sphere of psychology in phrases of information how humans cope.

hence, the Cognitive Psychology founder himself challenged the movement.

The laptop-primarily based method

The laptop-based totally technique of cognitive psychology in comparison the functioning of the human mind with that of a pc. In other phrases, the psychologists referred to pc operations to give an explanation for the cognitive phenomena.

consequently, the garage ability is the pc's memory and programming codes as its languages. moreover, every new era of a laptop is evolving.

similarly to this, pc applications are viewed as functioning within the manner the human mind functions.

thus, both the pc and the human brain acquire inputs which includes sensory stimuli or data from the environment. in addition, both the laptop and the human mind process large amounts of information after receiving it from the surroundings.

So, the manner that both the pc and human brain comply with to manner statistics is as follows:

Assimilate the records
manipulate the statistics
shop the information
Retrieve statistics
Act or reply to the information in distinct ways
accordingly, the above technique concludes that laptop programming has end up the foundation for the human

cognitive view. that is, records processing, reasoning, and trouble-solving.

furthermore, the purpose of cognitive psychologists is to discover how the human mind methods information. In other words, they are concerned approximately knowing:

programs that human beings have saved of their memory
thinking styles that allow them to recognize and explicit their thoughts
Memorize and take into account events and concepts
understand and resolve new problems
synthetic Intelligence

As referred to above, cognitive psychologists common computer systems as a version for human cognitive functioning. which means that additionally they believed that machines display artificial intelligence and technique information the manner people do.

to start with, laptop scientists, as well as cognitive psychologists, effortlessly welcomed the belief of synthetic intelligence.

In 1950, the British laptop genius Alan Turing designed the Turing test to determine the idea that computers can suppose. This test concerned persuading a subject that the pc with which he or she is a actual person, now not a gadget.

hence, the computer showcased intelligence as that of people if the subject failed to differentiate among laptop responses from human responses.

but, there had been many those who object to the idea of the Turing take a look at. An American truth seeker, John Searle, presented the handiest objections within the shape of the chinese Room problem.

What changed into the chinese language Room problem?

suppose, you're sitting at a table and there may be a wall in the front with two slots. One slot is on the left-hand aspect and the other on the proper-hand facet.

The slot on the left aspect generates slips of paper one by one. furthermore, every slip of paper consists of a set of chinese characters. As a player, your job is to fit the shape of the set of symbols with the ones in a e book.

Then, you're required to copy every other set of symbols from the book onto a piece of paper. as soon as that is finished, you need to feed the paper via the slot at the right-hand facet.

as a result, you receive inputs from the left slot and write outputs for the proper slot. and you do this primarily based on the instructions given to you. So, you are not predicted to read and recognize chinese language in case you are like most subjects in the america.

as a result, you're simply following the commands routinely. but, the person on the opposite cease would come to understand that you are strange with the chinese language language if he's a chinese psychologist. but, you just reproduction the perfect answers in chinese language from your e book.

but, you will nonetheless now not know the chinese language language no matter what number of messages you get hold of and respond to in chinese language.

end

accordingly, the chinese language Room trouble showcases that you are not thinking in any respect and simply following instructions. In different words, you do now not use intelligence and most effective comply with orders.

therefore, Searle concluded that computers apparently seem to recognize different types of data and respond in an smart way. however, the pc programs function just like the problem in the chinese language Room Puzzle.

as a consequence, each the problem inside the case of the chinese Room puzzle and the computer strictly operate consistent with the set of programmed policies.

So, we might also finish that computers can not think yet. In other phrases, artificial Intelligence has not done the level and complexity of human intelligence yet.

Nature of Cognitive Psychology
Researchers take into account cognitive factors in nearly all areas except Behavioral Psychology. these include:

Attribution principle in Social Psychology
Cognitive Dissonance principle
Motivation and Emotion
personality
gaining knowledge of
reminiscence
notion
memory
hassle-solving
Creativity
statistics Processing in Human Intelligence and artificial Intelligence
in addition to this, even the carried out regions like medical, community, school, and industrial-organizational psychology consider cognitive factors.

therefore, cognitive psychology varies from behavioral psychology in numerous approaches. the following phase lays out the fundamental variations between behavioral psychology and cognitive psychology.

1.knowing Vs Responding
Cognitive psychologists comply with the manner of understanding the stimuli in preference to responding to them. for this reason, the human thoughts, intellectual

tactics, and events are essential factors for cognitive psychologists. And factors like stimulus-reaction connections and behavior are relatively much less vital.

but, this doesn't mean that cognitive psychologists forget the behavior altogether. It clearly way that behavioral reaction is not the simplest component that cognitive psychologists don't forget while challenge research.

Behavioral responses are the sources for drawing conclusions about the mental methods accompanying such responses.

2. employer or Structuring Of information

the second one issue that cognitive psychologists are eager to understand approximately is the manner wherein the human thoughts organizes and structures various reports.

as a consequence, the Gestalt Psychologists in addition to Jean Piaget believed that the human mind has an innate tendency to prepare conscious experiences into meaningful wholes and styles.

In different words, the human thoughts gives form and rationality to mental stories. And this technique is the situation remember of cognitive psychology.

but, the Skinnerian behaviorists, the British empiricists, and the Associationists believed that the human thoughts did no longer own the innate organizational functionality.

3. active Vs Passive Participation

Cognitive psychologists consider that a individual actively participates in creatively organizing the sensory enter received from the environment.

In other words, people have the functionality to gather and apply know-how, attend to some occasions intentionally, and pick to memorize them.

that is in contrast to the behavioral standpoint of humans

responding passively to the external forces or the sensory stimuli.

Cognitive Neuroscience

attempts are made since the eighteenth and the 19th centuries to determine the precise elements of the brain controlling numerous cognitive features. Early physiologists like corridor, Fourens, and Broca have used techniques like Extirpation and electrical stimulation to map mind functions.

for this reason, this seek continues even these days under the field known as Cognitive Neuroscience. The dreams of this field of area encompass:

determining particular parts of the brain chargeable for controlling exclusive cognitive features, and

The way in which the human brain functions to generate intellectual hobby

moreover, the development and use of sophisticated imaging era have helped cognitive neuroscience researchers to make progress in brain mapping.

as an instance:

Electroencephalogram (EEG) data variations in electrical interest in decided on components of the mind

automated Axial Tomography (CAT) scans display designated pass sections of the mind

Magnetic resonance imagery (MRI) scans generate three-dimensional images of the brain

Positron Emission Tomography (puppy) scans provide stay pics of numerous cognitive activities as they arise

consequently, all such technological advances are providing researchers with a diploma of precision that turned into in advance now not manageable.

Cognitive Neuroscience instance

Cognitive neuroscientists have proven that the human

mind can workout manipulate over a laptop.

furthermore, they have additionally set up that electric impulses alone can translate idea into motion.

In one among such demonstrations, a 25-year-old man paralyzed for the beyond three years became the problem. The researchers inserted digital sensors inside the motor cortex of his mind.

moreover, those sensors have been related to a pc. accordingly, it allowed the concern to govern now not simplest the pc however additionally a television set and a robotic. And he may want to manage all of this using his mind.

consequently, the issue changed into able to perform various moves simply thru questioning or proceeding to make such moves. these actions blanketed:

shifting the laptop's cursor

establishing an email

moving gadgets the usage of a robotic arm

gambling a simple videogame

Drawing a crude circle at the screen, and so forth.

So, this software of cognitive neuroscience is Neuroprosthetics. Such improvements lend self assurance that it might help people with disabilities to interact and exercise control gadgets of their surroundings.

function of Introspection

As mentioned within the above phase, cognitive psychologists regular an person's aware reports to define the sphere of psychology. And this recognition gave manner to reconsidering Wilhelm Wundt's Introspective technique. The introspective method became the first research method of clinical psychology.

furthermore, the overdue-20th-century psychologist G. William Farthing proposed the use of introspection and introspective reviews to study cognizance. in addition to this, any other psychologist asserted that introspection became an vital part of human psychology.

for that reason, psychologists have attempted quantifying the introspective reports to generate more goal and responsive evaluation.

as an example, Retrospective extraordinary assessment is one of the approaches used to quantify the introspective reports.

In this assessment, the subjects are requested to fee the magnitude of their subjective reviews whilst they respond to a stimulus state of affairs that happened within the beyond.

this means that the topics retrospectively analyze the subjective reviews. these reports happened in a previous length when they had been required to respond to a given stimulus.

furthermore, some other main cognitive psychologist Timothy D. Wilson said that introspection is extensively used. in addition to this, the aware states uncovered through introspection are exact predictors of people's conduct.

but, there are positive boundaries to the validity of introspective reviews. One such obstacle is that at instances, the topics may additionally provide socially proper introspective reviews. In other words, they'll inform researchers what the researchers need to hear and therefore galvanize them.

every other venture of the use of introspective reviews is that the subjects may not be capable of method a number of their mind and feelings. that is because such mind or feelings stay deep in the unconscious mind of an person.

unconscious Cognition

The examine of the aware intellectual tactics advanced an hobby in subconscious cognitive activities as properly.

finally, psychologists now don't forget the subconscious processes after neglecting them for nearly one hundred years.

hence, cognitive psychologists agree with that subconscious cognition is able to gain many features. those features have been once considered to require deliberation, purpose, and aware focus.

As in keeping with studies, a lot of human questioning and records processing first takes region in the subconscious a part of our cognition. And unconscious cognition operates greater fast and efficiently relative to the aware mind.

it's miles vital to be aware that the unconscious mind cited right here isn't always the only that Sigmund Freud spoke about. Sigmund Freud proposed the subconscious mind that overflows with repressed goals and memories. in addition, psychoanalysis brings those dreams and memories into conscious consciousness.

however, the modern unconscious thoughts that we are talking approximately here is extra rational than emotional. furthermore, it forms part of the first stage of cognition while an individual responds to a stimulus.

as a consequence, the subconscious strategies shape an crucial part of studying and you can still study them experimentally.

Cognitive Psychology Theories

There are generally three techniques beneath the area of cognitive development to study questions:

How and when does a infant start to study, suppose, and to clear up issues?

while and the way does memory broaden?

Are some people smarter than others?

but, there are a few cutting-edge processes to cognitive improvement. therefore, there are six techniques to cognitive improvement. those encompass:

I. Behaviorist approach

The Behaviorist method of Cognitive improvement research the simple mechanics of studying in human beings. it is worried with the change in the conduct of an man or woman in reaction to the revel in.

as a result, the 2 mastering approaches that the behaviorists' observe consist of classical conditioning and operant conditioning. except this, habituation is another shape of studying that the information-processing researchers examine.

a. Classical Conditioning idea

Ivan Pavlov discovered the Classical studying theory. He said that classical conditioning is a sort of mastering in which an man or woman learns to make a reflex or an involuntary response to a stimulus that firstly did now not provoke the response.

In other words, classical conditioning is a form of studying primarily based on associating a stimulus that does not at the beginning elicit a response with every other stimulus that does elicit the reaction.

thus, someone learns to assume an event even earlier than it takes place in classical conditioning. This takes place because the person paperwork associations among the stimuli that again and again occur collectively.

for example, a child blinking her eyes even before the flash is going off.

also examine: Arousal concept of Motivation

B. Operant Conditioning idea

the yankee Psychologist B.F. Skinner proposed the Operant Conditioning principle. it's far a form of mastering that buddies a behavior with the incidence of a large occasion.

In different phrases, instrumental conditioning or operant conditioning principle of gaining knowledge of is the manner that entails changes in human behavior depending upon the consequences of a huge occasion.

If the event produced effective results that lead to a fine alternate in human behavior, then the character would learn how to repeat such behaviors.

however, if an occasion generated negative consequences that generated bad changes in human conduct, an man or woman prevented or escaped such terrible behaviors.

hence, Operant Conditioning is a getting to know based totally on Reinforcement and Punishment.

II. Psychometric method

intelligent behavior is a conduct this is purpose-oriented and adaptive to occasions and situations of existence. Such behavior is directed at adjusting to the occasions and conditions in lifestyles.

further, intelligence empowers an person to collect, keep in mind, and use information. It additionally allows her or him to recognize principles and relationships and to clear up real-lifestyles problems.

Efforts have been made inside the 19th century to degree intelligence on the basis of a spread of attributes. these blanketed head length, response time, and exams measuring various different characteristics. Such characteristics worried energy of hand squeeze, pain sensitivity, weight discrimination, the judgment of time, and rote name.

but those checks had little predictive value. however, Alfred Binet alongside along with his colleague Theodore Simon advanced a psychometric take a look at called the

Stanford-Binet check. This check used numbers to score intelligence in kids

accordingly, the purpose of psychometric checks is to measure the quantitative elements that appear to make up intelligence. this can encompass comprehension, reasoning, and so on. Then, the outcomes of such a dimension are used to predict destiny performance like college success.

thus, those are IQ exams. IQ checks are not anything however psychometric checks. Such tests consist of questions or obligations that showcase the measured abilities of an person. further, such skills are measured by means of evaluating someone's performance with that of the alternative test-takers.

A. trying out infants and toddlers

For faculty-age children, Intelligence check ratings can expect academic overall performance reliably and correctly. but, testing babies and toddlers for IQ is exceedingly challenging.

thus, the maximum standard manner to measure the intelligence of toddlers and babies is to evaluate what they could do. this is due to the fact toddlers can not tell us what they recognise and what they suppose.

but, there may be a whole lot of motives why an toddler or a little one may not perform certain movements. it can be because of the little one:

Does no longer feel like doing it,
Doesn't realise what's anticipated of him or her
lose interest
won't recognize a way to perform the motion
consequently, it's miles nearly no longer possible to degree an little one's intelligence. however, you'll test his or her cognitive development. And this is done the use of

developmental assessments.

Developmental assessments evaluate a baby's performance on a chain of duties with the norms established. in addition, those norms are mounted on the idea of observations of performances of a large number of toddlers and babies at numerous a long time.

as a result, Bayley Scales of toddler improvement is one such Developmental take a look at.

(i) Bayley Scales of infant improvement check

it's miles a standardized take a look at designed to evaluate the developmental status of kids from 1 month to a few and a half years.

in addition, this take a look at measures a baby's overall performance in three regions: intellectual, motor, and behavioral development. The intellectual scale measures skills like belief, memory, studying, and vocalization.

Then, the motor scale measures big-muscle and manipulative motor skills such as sensorimotor coordination. subsequently, the examiner completes the conduct score Scale on the basis of the statistics obtained from the child's caregiver.

Then, separate rankings referred to as the Developmental Quotients (DQ) are calculated for each of the scales. And the DQ's are based at the deviation from the suggest hooked up thru evaluation with a ordinary sample.

hence, DQs are useful to come across pretty early emotional disturbances, and sensory, neurological, and environmental deficits.

challenges of Bayley Scales of toddler improvement test
The Bayley Scales of infant improvement test:

Is a poor predictor of destiny functioning as environmental affects have an effect on a toddler's cognitive development as she or he approaches the age of 3

Measures generally sensory and motor skills in contrast to intelligence assessments that measure verbal capabilities.

(ii) home commentary For measurement of the environment (domestic)

domestic is a tick list that an examiner uses to degree the have an impact on of the home environment on a baby's increase. one of the important factors that domestic assesses is parental responsiveness.

every other component that domestic measures is the range of books at domestic and presence of playthings that inspire development of principles. in addition, it additionally assesses the figure's involvement in children's play.

consequently, high rankings on all such elements predict cognitive performance of a toddler reliably.even though, we can not make sure that parental responsiveness and enriched home surroundings simply boom a baby's intelligence.

All we can say is that all these factors are related to high intelligence.

Socioeconomic popularity, Parenting Practices, and IQ
There exists proof that there exists a correlation among the Socioeconomic reputation (SES) and the IQ of a baby.

therefore, poverty can preserve lower back a toddler's cognitive boom. this is due to lack of instructional resources and the poor psychological impact on parents and their parenting practices.

therefore, in one of the studies, it was found that mother and father in high-income families spent extra time with their youngsters. in addition to this, they interacted greater with their youngsters and additionally showcased more hobby in what they'd to mention.

whereas, the dad and mom in the low-profits households used more of bad words like "stop", "cease", and "don't" while interacting with their kids. consequently, youngsters of such dad and mom had decrease IQs and success.

consequently, this examine demonstrates that the early parenting practices have a superb impact on the future IQ and the faculty performance of youngsters.

Early Intervention

Early intervention is the systematic way of planning and providing healing and educational to households. these are the families that want assist in meeting little one's, infant's, and pre-college kids's developmental desires.

therefore, the researchers have recognized six Developmental Priming Mechanisms. these mechanisms are the components of domestic surroundings that make a contribution towards normal cognitive and psychosocial development of the child. Plus, it also allows the kid to put together for college.

Developmental Priming Mechanisms

the subsequent are the six developmental priming mechanisms:

Encouraging toddler to explore the environment
Mentoring the kid in primary cognitive and social skills like labeling, sequencing, sorting, and comparing
Celebrating the kid's accomplishments
Guiding the child in working towards and increasing the skills
protective the child from irrelevant punishment, teasing, or disapproval for errors or unintentional results of exploring and experimenting diverse competencies
Stimulating language and different symbolic verbal exchange
consequently, the goal of early intervention is to help the

ones kids who do no longer get such developmental aid.

To assist this, there are studies research that reveal that early academic intervention can mild the effect of low socioeconomic reputation.

effective Early Interventions
the following are the only early interventions:

starting early and persevering with at some point of the preschool years

exceedingly time in depth early interventions

imparting direct educational reviews and now not simply parental training

Taking a complete approach which includes fitness, circle of relatives counseling, and social offerings

Early interventions tailored to individual desires and variations

B. testing Preschoolers

kids who're 3, four, or 5 years old are a lot more talented with language than the more youthful kids. consequently, greater verbal gadgets may be a part of the intelligence exams.

consequently, such checks are bund to present extra dependable effects relative to the non-verbal exams. furnished, the verbal exams are standardized.

the two most commonly used individual tests for preschoolers encompass The Stanford-Binet Intelligence Scale and Wechsler Preschool and number one Scale of Intelligence.

(i) The Stanford-Binet Intelligence Scale
on this test, the child is supposed to define words, string beads, build with blocks, identify the missing elements of a image, hint mazes, and show an information of numbers.

therefore, he final rating measures the child's reminiscence, spatial orientation, and sensible judgment in actual-lifestyles situations.

in the year 1985, the fourth version of the take a look at changed into delivered. It includes an equal stability of verbal and non-verbal, quantitative, and memory objects.

consequently, it approach the check does now not use best IQ gadgets as a measure of intelligence. alternatively, the revised model of the check also compare the patterns and the degrees of cognitive development.

(ii) Wechsler Preschool and primary Scale of Intelligence (WPPSI-R)

This take a look at is used to evaluate the intelligence stage of children among 3 to 7 years of age. further, this test offers separate scores for verbal in addition to overall performance. in addition to this, the check also gives a combined rating.

The separate scales of dimension are similar to the ones within the Wechsler Intelligence Scale for children (WISC-III). similarly, this test become revised in 1989 and subsequently blanketed new subsets and new image items.

(iii) Otis-Lennon school ability take a look at

The unique IQ tests which includes people who Alfred Binet and Theodore Simon developed had been subtle over a period of time.

in addition, the builders of the refined checks have given emphasis to greater sophisticated distinctions amongst diverse sorts of talents. this is not like the traditional IQ tests that emphasised substantially on the general intelligence of a child.

as a consequence, one of the famous institution exams is the Otis-Lennon faculty potential take a look at. it is a set intelligence take a look at for kindergarten through the 12th grade.

in this check, the kids are expected to categorise the items and show off understanding of verbal and numerical standards. in addition, they're also required to show trendy data and comply with the guidelines.

subsequently, the take a look at gives separate scores on verbal comprehension, verbal reasoning, pictorial reasoning, figural reasoning, and quantitative reasoning. Such ratings can help in figuring out the strengths and weaknesses of a child.

(iv) Wechsler Intelligence Scale ForChildren (WISC-III)

Wechsler Intelligence Scale ForChildren (WISC-III) is one of the famous individual intelligence tests. This test is for kids among 6 and sixteen years of age. in addition, the WISC-III measures the verbal and performance abilties of schoolchildren.

thus, this check offers separate rankings for verbal and overall performance in addition to a mixed score. for this reason, the separate subtest rankings make it easier to permit the child realize his strengths in addition to weaknesses.

(v) Gardner's concept of multiple Intelligences

Howard Gardner, a psychologist at Harvard faculty of training, developed the theory of multiple Intelligences (MI) and initiated assignment Spectrum, a curriculum that promotes an expansion of intelligences.

As in keeping with the MI concept, Gardner emphasised that an man or woman possesses 8 or more varieties of intelligences. each of these intelligences can be utilized by a person personally or corporately for you to create products and resolve problems appropriate to the society. those include linguistic, logical-mathematical, spatial, musical, bodily-kinesthetic, naturalistic, interpersonal, and intrapersonal intelligences.

however, traditional faculties most effective attention on two of these intelligences that are linguistic and logical-mathematical.

as a consequence, he asserted that the best contribution to a infant's development may be to assist him choose a discipline that matches his capabilities in place of forcing him to follow the stereotypical route.

similarly, Gardner's theory signified that the tests taken in college examined only a restrained set of someone's abilties. Such checks fail to exhibit the opposite variety of abilities and talents that play a super position beyond IQ.

So, while Spectrum college students have been evaluated on the Stanford Binet intelligence competencies, their ratings on checks did now not have any extensive relationship. students with the highest IQs had a distinctive set of strengths when tested by means of the Spectrum take a look at. therefore, Gardner concluded that the Stanford Binet intelligence scale showcasing IQ degrees of students did no longer provide any statistics in admire of probability of performance of students in areas included by using task Spectrum.

(vi) Sternberg's Triarchic principle of Intelligence

in line with Sternberg, Intelligence refers to a collection of intellectual skills crucial for any toddler or an person to evolve to an environmental context. further, intelligence also include the functionality of an character to select and shape the context in which he or she lives as well as act in the sort of context.

as a consequence, Sternberg excluded a number of the Gardner's intelligences along with musical and bodily kinesthetic capabilities. He considered simplest the universally crucial intellectual capabilities to define intelligence.

thus, the Sternberg's Triarchic concept of Intelligence covers only 3 elements or aspects. these include Componential, Experiential, and Contextual elements.

1. Componential

The Componential factor of intelligence in Sternberg's principle covers the analytic element. This component of intelligence determines how efficiently humans are able to process the statistics.

for that reason, this component tells the people the manner in which they need to solve the trouble, monitor answers, and examine the effects.

2. Experiential

As in step with Sternberg's concept, the Experiential element of intelligence refers back to the insightful or the innovative element. as a result, such an factor of intelligence determines the way wherein people want to address novel conditions or acquainted tasks.

furthermore, it allows them to compare the new statistics with the present records. As a result, it also facilitates them to come up with new ways of placing the facts together or assume firstly.

3. Contextual

The Contextual element of Sternberg's Triarchic theory of Intelligence refers to the practical factor of intelligence. It determines the manner in which individuals need to address their surroundings.

In other words, it displays the capability of people to conform to a scenario and decide what movements they have to take. further, it also reflects the capability of people to evolve to such actions, alter them, or get out of them.

conclusion

in step with Sternberg, each man or woman has these 3

varieties of abilities to a greater or a lesser volume. consequently, an person may be robust in one, , or all the 3 abilities.

understand that the conventional IQ assessments re fairly suitable predictors of college overall performance. that is because such checks manly measure the componential issue of intelligence only.

As in line with Sternberg, such exams fail to degree the contextual and experiential factors of intelligence. consequently, the conventional IQ tests are less beneficial in predicting success in the outside global.

to overcome this trouble, Sternberg introduced the Sternberg Triarchic abilties test (STAT). This test measures every of the 3 elements of intelligence: componential, experiential, and contextual.

in addition, these factors are tested thru a couple of preference questions and essay questions. And these kind of questions relate with three domain names – verbal, quantitative, and figural.

it's miles expected that the questioning, creativity, and sensible problem-solving are weakly correlated with one another.

(vii) Kaufman assessment Battery For children (ok-ABC)

a number of the brand new diagnostic and predictive gear are based totally on neurological research and records-processing concept. one of such equipment is the Kaufman evaluation Battery For kids (ok-ABC).

this is an person check for youngsters among the age-group of two(half) and 12(half of). furthermore, the ok-ABC check has separate scales for measuring aptitude and success.

besides this, it is usually a scale that measures only the non-verbal skills in youngsters with hearing impairments, speech, or language issues. moreover, the non-verbal scale is also for those kids who do not have English as their number one language.

The ok-ABC contains the idea of Scaffolding. this means that the examiner can make clear the kind of reaction this is predicted in case a toddler fails any of the primary 3 gadgets on a subtest. And he can clarify this thru using one-of-a-kind phrases or gestures or specific language.

III. Piagetian method

The Swiss Theoretician, Jean Piaget, was the pioneer of nowadays's cognitive revolution. He emphasized that mental techniques play a key function in improvement.

moreover, Jean Piaget proposed an organismic angle of cognitive development. He asserted that cognitive development is a result of children's efforts to learn and act on their world.

thus, Piaget used a aggregate of statement and flexible wondering to find out how youngsters assume. also, he followed up their solutions with extra questions.

In different words, Piaget located the conduct of his very own youngsters and others. As a result, he formulated a comprehensive idea of Cognitive development.

for that reason, Piaget believed that an individual's cognitive development starts with his or her innate potential to evolve to the environment.

as an example, youngsters are endowed with certain herbal behaviors. these innate competencies include rooting the nipple, feeling a pebble, and many others.

Such abilties assist the kids to develop a more accurate photograph of their environment.

furthermore, those natural abilties offer more competence to youngsters in managing their surrounding environment.

therefore, Piaget proposed that Cognitive improvement happens in four qualitative ranges. The developments occurring at every stage constitute the typical developmental patterns.

consequently, a toddler's mind develops a new way of working at every degree. In other words, the intellectual operations of a child evolve through mastering. This mastering takes place from infancy thru maturity.

furthermore, the learning evolves primarily based on simple sensory and motor interest to logical, abstract thought.

processes of Cognitive improvement
according to Piaget, the Cognitive boom happens via 3 interrelated methods. those consist of: organization, edition, and Equilibration.

I. enterprise
business enterprise refers to an man or woman's tendency to create complex cognitive systems. these cognitive systems are the expertise structures or methods of thinking incorporating more accurate image of truth.

therefore, those structures are referred to as schemes. Schemes are nothing however the organized styles of conduct. consequently, an character uses these behavioral styles to consider or act in a situation.

So, a infant's schemes grow to be increasingly complex as she or he acquires greater records.

II. variation
version refers to an man or woman's adjustment to new information about his or her environment. it's miles a term that Piaget used for the way wherein youngsters treated

new information with respect to what they already recognize.

in step with Piaget, variation entails two steps: Assimilation and lodging.

Assimilation means taking in new information and incorporating it into an existing cognitive shape. whereas, lodging refers to the changes that occur in one's cognitive structure to include the brand new data.

III. Equilibration

Equilibration is an character's tendency to constantly strive for a strong balance between the cognitive factors.

thus, Equilibration or Equilibrium governs the manner of transferring from assimilation to lodging.

for instance, youngsters revel in disequilibrium when they cannot address the new records within their existing cognitive structures.

consequently, they arrange new mental styles that combine the new revel in into the evolving cognitive shape. subsequently, kids are able to repair a more relaxed country of equilibrium.

instance

as an instance, a breast-fed baby showcases assimilation when he starts to suck at the spout of a sippy tumbler. as a consequence, the child is using an antique scheme to address the new situation.

finally, the infant discovers that sipping from a pitcher requires unique moth and tongue movements. that is not like the movements used to suck on a breast.

consequently, the baby modifies his or her vintage scheme and accommodates this new information. In different phrases, the infant adapted her old sucking scheme to address a new revel in in the form of a glass.

therefore, assimilation and lodging paintings together to generate equilibrium and cognitive increase.

end

Jean Piaget proved via his concept that a child's mind isn't a miniature adult mind. An knowledge of this reality may also assist parents and instructors to understand youngsters and subsequently teach them.

but, one of the downsides of Piaget's concept is that he underestimated the abilties of babies and younger youngsters. furthermore, many present day psychologists argue that cognitive improvement happens constantly and therefore does no longer arise in levels.

further to this, in addition they contended that human questioning does now not increase in a unmarried, familiar progression of steps.

moreover, a whole lot of other elements have an impact on a infant's cognitive processes. these encompass:

particular content that the child thinks about

The Context of the problem

styles of facts and notion a lifestyle considers crucial

eventually, it's miles argued that Piaget's principle just focuses on good judgment or reasoning and now not other elements. these include realistic trouble fixing, understanding, and ability to deal with perplexing situations.

Piaget's levels of Cognitive development

I. Sensorimotor level

The Sensory Motor stage is the primary stage of Piaget's cognitive improvement theory. all through this degree, toddlers learn that there exists a dating between the movements they carry out and the world round them.

This stage of cognitive improvement lasts from beginning till 18 and 24 months. similarly, all through this level, babies find out that they can steer items and therefore generate positive results.

In different words, kids understand the fundamental idea of motive and impact at some stage in the Sensory Motor stage.

as an instance, kids analyze that they could produce sound if they would make certain actions. And such a movements can consist of shaking their fingers while preserving a rattle. for this reason, in a way, they begin experimenting with distinctive actions.

kids engage in such experiments as they need to look at various outcomes that such movements generate. hence, Jean Piaget suggested that toddlers try to recognize the world round them for the duration of the whole sensorimotor degree. and they do this best with the help of motor activities and sensory impressions.

loss of mental Impressions

however, they do no longer have the capability to utilize such mental impressions to portray special items at this level. Now, such getting to know generates some interesting outcomes.

as an instance, a four-month-old little one will no longer try and look for the toy in case you attempt hiding it in the front of him. this is because such babies don't forget that anything hidden from view is likewise hidden from their minds.

but, such infants start looking for hidden objects while such babies grow older. This starts offevolved going on while the little one is somewhere round eight or 9 months of age. In different phrases, the babies collect a simple concept of 'item Permanence' via this age. object permanence refers back to the fact that gadgets live on even when those are hidden from view.

II. Preoperational level

The Preoperational degree of Cognitive development is the one where a little one receives the capability to broaden mental pix of objects. that is in contrast to the Sensory Motor stage wherein the babies were not able to increase this capability.

Now, the Preoperational level occurs between 18 and 24 months. furthermore, the infants additionally get the potential to increase language. This capacity is to the volume that they begin thinking in terms of verbal symbols or words.

as a consequence, such traits mark the start of Piaget's second degree of cognitive improvement – the Preoperational stage.

that means of Preoperational

The time period preoperational method that infants get the capability to create intellectual pix and broaden verbal symbols.

but, they lack the capacity to apply common sense and mental operations. moreover, the preoperational stage lasts till approximately age 7. And during this degree, children are able to perform many actions that they were unable to formerly.

as an instance, youngsters about the age of five or 6 can interact in symbolic play. In this type of play, they fake that one object is another. Like, they may don't forget a pencil to be a automobile consisting of a vehicle or an plane.

moreover, symbolic play includes 3 modifications. those adjustments screen discrete insights about the modification in youngsters's cognitive capabilities for the duration of this period.

(i) Decentration

the first exchange refers to decentration. on this stage of

alternate, children slowly begin making others the recipients of their playful moves as opposed to themselves. as an instance, they begin making their smooth toy take a tub, or comb its hair.

(ii) Decontextualization

Then comes the second one trade of decontextualization. in this degree, kids replacement one object with the opposite. They do that to perform a few playful action. as an instance, a child considers a pencil as an aircraft.

(iii) Integration

subsequently, the 0.33 exchange involves integration. This level of alternate combines extraordinary playful moves into a complex sequence. Such an capacity to contain in a greater complicated set of playful moves shows that youngsters are developing cognitively.

In other phrases, children are able to photograph one item as every other. moreover, there also are capable of perform playful actions. Like they don't forget gentle toys next to people who have emotions and thoughts in their very own. And to do all of this, kids require the capability to suppose in terms of phrases.

additionally study: 20 great Fidget Toys of 2021

conclusion

as a consequence, the children's thought procedures inside the preoperational level are more superior relative to those inside the sensorimotor degree. however, Piaget advised that kids inside the preoperational level are nevertheless immature in various factors.

even though kids in this degree can employ intellectual symbols. but their idea strategies are particularly inflexible, illogical, incomplete, and are restricted to precise contexts.

Piaget makes such an argument on the basis of the subsequent two aspects that bring about immaturity in youngsters on the preoperational level:

a. Egocentrism

It refers back to the young kids's incapacity to distinguish their personal views from others. In other phrases, egocentrism is the kid's lack of ability to keep in mind that others may also understand the world in a distinctive way than they do.

b. loss of Seriation

Seriation refers back to the potential of a child to organize objects in a sequence using some size or parameter. but, kids inside the preoperational degree lack seriation.

c. lack of expertise of Relative phrases

children within the preoperational level lack the capability to understand relative terms like lighter, darker, softer, and so forth.

Conservation

within the preoperational level, children lack an understanding of conservation. Conservation refers to a concept which states that positive bodily traits of an object do not change. And those traits do not alternate even supposing the outer look of such an item is modified.

III. level of Concrete Operations

The level of concrete operations is a cognitive improvement degree happening somewhere around age six or seven. furthermore, this level lasts till approximately the age of 11.

consequently, all through this level, logical concept starts emerging in youngsters. In other words, difficult matters or the underdeveloped competencies of the preoperational degree begin growing on this level.

furthermore, youngsters get the capability to remedy simple issues. those are the problems that they come across within the preoperational degree.

Now, Piaget suggests that a toddler defines the start of the degree of concrete operations when he masters the idea of conservation. at some point of this stage, positive critical competencies start rising in youngsters. further to this, kids get the functionality to arrange matters so as.

furthermore, they apprehend the relative phrases as mentioned in the preceding stage. further to this, they start expertise that bodily changes achieved originally can be reversed. And these can be reversed by undoing the unique motion.

This idea is called reversibility. besides all of this, Piaget emphasizes that children attaining the stage of concrete operations also begin wondering logically.

IV. degree of Formal Operations

The level of formal operations is the very last level of cognitive improvement in Piaget's theory. children enter this degree at approximately the age of twelve. for the duration of this level, primary traits that define an adult's thought method start emerging in kids.

As we already understand, youngsters begin thinking logically for the duration of the degree of concrete operations. however, any such logical idea is handiest restricted to concrete occasions or items.

In different phrases, kids emerge as privy to the permanence of objects. but, youngsters who reach the stage of formal operations begin wondering in an summary manner. the following are the various approaches wherein youngsters start thinking.

(i) Hypothetico – Deductive Reasoning

Hypothetico – Deductive Reasoning refers to children's ability to apprehend concrete or real activities and formulate possibilities. these possibilities are nothing but the occasions or relationships that you may handiest believe.

but, such events or relationships do now not exist in truth. furthermore, this concept emphasizes that kids get the capacity to formulate a speculation.

moreover, they can suppose logically approximately ideas, propositions, and logos. In other words, such kind of reasoning involves formulating a accepted theory. After forming a general idea, youngsters provide you with a selected speculation.

(ii) Interpropositional thinking

except Hypothetico – Deductive Reasoning, kids also get the capacity to involve in interpropositional thinking. it's far a kind of thinking wherein a infant tries to test whether the propositions formulated are valid or now not.

Now, there may be absolute confidence that the concept technique of older kids or adolescents is someplace close to that of adults. however, Piaget believed that the thought system of teenagers still lacked the knowledge as that of the adults.

The older youngsters use their newly advanced reasoning ability to construct theories about unique components. these include theories approximately human relationships, ethics, or political structures.

Now, though the reasoning in the back of such opinions may be logical. however the theories that adolescents or older youngsters construct are incorrect. that is due to the fact young children do now not have a whole lot enjoy or information to carry out a complicated task.

in addition to this, there is no assure that kids achieving the level of formal operations and growing the functionality to have interaction in complicated concept tactics would in truth be able to suppose in a sophisticated way. that is because complicated notion strategies require a brilliant quantity of cognitive effort.

consequently, children or even adults often have interaction themselves in much less advanced modes of thought.

IV. information Processing approach

data-Processing idea is concerned with individual differences in cognition. It ambitions to describe the intellectual tactics involved when people gather and do not forget facts or resolve troubles.

accordingly, statistics-Processing technique does now not totally cause out the differences in mental performing from the problems solved.

in addition, this method uses new techniques to check thoughts approximately cognitive development. those are the ideas that emanated from the Psychometric and Piagetian techniques.

as an instance, the information-processing researches evaluate the separate components of a complicated venture. Then, they determine out the abilties that are vital for each part of the assignment. similarly to this, they also determine the age at which such competencies could broaden.

subsequently, the researchers degree and draw conclusions from what the toddlers pay attention to and for the way lengthy.

the subsequent are the procedures concerned in belief, studying, reminiscence, and hassle-solving.

1. Habituation

Habituation refers to a easy sort of learning wherein repeated or continuous exposure to a stimulus reduces the attention to that stimulus. In other phrases, familiarity with a stimulus reduces, slows, or stops a reaction. as a result, as toddlers habituate, they rework the unknow into regarded.

Likewise, dishabituation refers to boom in responsiveness after a new stimulus is supplied to the toddler.

for example, a baby is sitting in his crib and sucking thumb. at the same time as he's sucking thumb, the tv is switched on and a cool animated film individual appears on the screen. the instant the infant watches the individual, he stops sucking the thumb.

but, the infant begins sucking thumb at the same time as watching the cool animated film character while he is exposed to the individual again and again. as a result, that is habituation.

Now, say you switch on a toy that exudes vibrant mild. once more, the baby will stop sucking the thumb. This process of growth in responsiveness to a brand new stimulus is dishabituation.

for that reason, the procedure of habituation is used to have a look at an infant's ability to:

study differences between visual patterns
Categorize people, gadgets, and activities
Habituate familiar stimuli
recover interest while uncovered to new stimuli
Distinguish between new and antique

for that reason, the efficiency of habituation in a baby correlates with the later signs and symptoms of cognitive development. these consist of:

choice for complexity
rapid exploration of the environment
state-of-the-art play
quick trouble-solving
capacity to match photos

2. Perceptual and Processing abilties

This includes:

a. visual preference

The visual desire is the quantity of time a child spends searching at various sights. In other phrases, it is the tendency of babies to spend more time looking at one sight than any other.

for that reason, the visible preference of an toddler is based totally at the capacity to distinguish things visually. Robert Fantz and his colleagues found out that babies less than days antique decide on:

Curved lines over instantly lines
three-dimensional gadgets over two-dimensional gadgets
New sights to acquainted ones, and so on.

furthermore, a few infants may additionally pay more attention to new stimuli than the acquainted ones. This phenomenon is referred to as novelty. which means such infants exhibit that they can differential between new and old things.

b. visual popularity memory

It refers back to the potential of an toddler to distinguish the familiar sights from the unusual ones when proven both at the identical time.

This ability is measured through the tendency of an infant to take a look at the brand new sight for an extended period of time.

as a result, visible reputation memory of an infant depends at the capacity to shape mental representations. In others phrases, it refers back to the capacity to examine the brand new records with the information that the toddler already has.

as a consequence, the performance of statistics-processing of an toddler relies upon on the velocity with which an toddler paperwork and refers to such images.

rather than the Paiget's principle, the habituation and novelty preference studies indicate that a new child already has this capability both at delivery or very soon after the start. as a result, toddlers can distinguish between sounds they have got already heard from those they have got now not.

consequently, the performance of facts-processing for an little one depends on the manner in which she or he distributes attention.

Say, an toddler is uncovered to two attractions simultaneously. as a result, an toddler has better recognition reminiscence and novelty desire if he observes one sight for a brief duration and quick shifts his interest to any other.

c. pass-Modal switch

it's miles the potential of an little one to use statistics acquired via one sense to guide any other sense.for example, the ability of an man or woman to pick out gadgets by means of sight after feeling them with eyes closed.

In a observe, 1-month vintage babies showcased that they might switch the information received through sucking to imaginative and prescient. as a consequence, the toddlers regarded longer on the item they simply sucked when they saw a couple of hands manipulating a difficult and a smooth item.

As in step with researchers, using pass-modal transfer to decide some other residences of items develops after some months of toddler's start.

3. facts Processing as a Predictor of Intelligence

As in step with researchers, a few components of infant appear to be fairly non-stop from delivery. therefore, the ones youngsters who had the performance to absorb and interpret sensory information accomplished nicely on intelligence exams as properly.

furthermore, visible Expectation Paradigm can help in measuring the visual reaction Time and visual Anticipation capabilities of an little one.

in this, an little one is proven a sequence of computer-generated pix for a quick time period. some snap shots appear at the left, even as others seem on the right-side of the infant's peripheral field of regard.

for this reason, visual reaction time is the potential of an little one to quickly shift his gaze from one photograph to any other as and while each seems. And that is measured through observing the toddler's eye moves.

moreover, visible anticipation is the child's capability to assume or expect the subsequent photograph to appear.

Such measurements assist to determine the attentiveness and the processing pace of a toddler in addition to his tendency to shape expectancies.

4. Violation of expectancies and improvement of concept

it is a studies method in which an little one is first habituated to peer an event as it generally could. Then, the event is changed in a manner that it conflicts with the ordinary expectations.

for that reason, the tendency of the toddler to take a look at the modified event for longer duration (dishabituation) is determined.

subsequently, this size is the evidence that the little one recognizes the modified event as unexpected.

1. object Permanence and Numbers

Researchers using Violation of expectancies technique believe that the concepts Piaget defined as developing toward the give up of the sensorimotor level really arise in advance. those standards include item permanence, number, and causality.

moreover, such researchers also proposed that the infants may also born with reasoning abilties. this is referred to as innate gaining knowledge of mechanisms. those mechanisms may also assist the toddlers to make experience of the records they stumble upon.

as an instance, Renee Baillargeon and his colleagues performed a observe with babies the usage of carrots. He claimed to have located proof of rudimentary shape of object permanence in babies just three and a half months vintage.

even as Karen Wynn conducted an test the usage of dolls with 5-month vintage babies to test whether or not they could upload or subtract numbers. consequently, he claimed that toddlers can mentally compute the proper answers. but, this became a trifling hypothesis.

3. Causality

The principle of causality is a baby's ability to remember that one event reasons some other event. Such an capacity allow individuals to are expecting and manipulate their global.

As in step with Piaget's theory, this expertise develops slowly at some point of the first year of life.for this reason, at about 4 to 6 months of age, infants begin to apprehend that they are able to act on their surroundings. This takes place as soon as they're capable of grasp the items.

therefore, Piaget believed that toddlers yet do now not understand that causes have to come before results.

but, research suggests that the mechanism for spotting causality exists much earlier. in the habituation and dishabituation experiments, toddlers as young as six and a half of months antique seem to see a difference between immediate causes of events and activities that arise with out a obvious reasons.

as a consequence, infants appear to be aware about continuity of relationships in time and area at quite an early age. And that is their first step towards expertise causality.

but, the babies in these experiments may additionally without a doubt be responding to the differences inside the positions of the gadgets in area and time. they will no longer be responding to the reasons that led to one of these change.

V. Cognitive Neuroscience

Researchers research the human cognitive strategies separately from the bodily structures of the human mind. today, the development in technology assist us see the human mind in movement.

The proponents of Cognitive Neuroscience approach assert that one must link an person's cognitive functioning with his or her mind functioning.

consequently, Developmental Cognitive Neuroscience can also help in explaining the way wherein cognitive increase takes place as the brain interacts with the environment.

furthermore, it is able to also help us in information why some humans develop abnormally and why do people age?

for that reason, Neuroscience allows us in expertise troubles like whether intelligence is trendy or specialised. in addition, it is able to additionally assist us to apprehend the impacts chargeable for a younger baby's readiness for formal getting to know.

brain's Cognitive structures

The length of fast boom and improvement of brain coincide with the adjustments in cognitive conduct much like those Piaget described.

in step with the research of regular and mind-damaged adults, there are two exceptional long-term memory structures: specific memory and implicit memory.

express memory refers to the conscious reminiscence that intentionally recalls statistics, names, events, or different things that people can describe or claim.

while, the implicit memory refers to the subconscious memory that recalls with out effort or even aware focus. This sort of reminiscence relates with behavior and abilties such as

Social Cognitive Neuroscience

Social Cognitive Neuroscience is an emerging subject. It brings together the records from cognitive neuroscience, social psychology, and the data-processing method.

consequently, this fairly rising interdisciplinary field bridges mind, mind, and behavior.

moreover, the Social Cognitive Neuroscientists use mind imaging and studies of humans with brain injuries. They use insights from such research to determine out how neural pathways control strategies like memory and interest.

further to this, the social cognitive neuroscientists also have a look at how mental techniques like memory and interest have an effect on attitudes and emotions.

In different phrases, researchers can use checks of reminiscence, interest, and language overall performance to discover the mind systems chargeable for sure problems. those disorders might also include anxiety, phobia, Obsessive Compulsive disease, and Schizophrenia.

VI. Social Contextual approach

The Russian Psychologist Lev Semenovich Vygotsky turned into a proponent of contextual perspective.

Vygotsky majorly focused at the social, cultural, and

historic complicated of which a toddler is a component.

In different words, Vygotsky stated that one need to consciousness at the social processes from which a child's wondering is derived. As a result, it'll assist us to recognize the kid's cognitive improvement.

Like Piaget's principle, Vygotsky's Sociocultural theory additionally emphasizes the kids's lively engagement with their environment.

but Piaget emphasized that a toddler's thoughts is aking in and interpreting the facts approximately the out of doors world. however, Vygotsky viewed a toddler's cognitive boom as a collaborative process.

in keeping with Vygotsky, children learn via social interaction. In other phrases, youngsters collect cognitive abilities as a part of their introduction into a manner of life. as a consequence, collaborative sports help kids in gaining knowledge of their own society's approaches of questioning and behaving. moreover, it additionally allows youngsters to make those approaches their **personal**.

similarly to this, Vygotsky additionally proposed that adults ought to help direct and organize a infant's gaining knowledge of. He asserted that adults have to make bigger that help earlier than the kid can master and internalize that gaining knowledge of.

accordingly, this kind of guidance helps the youngsters to pass the area of Proximal improvement (ZPD).

what's sector of Proximal improvement?

ZPD is nothing however the difference among what a toddler can do on my own and what he or she will be able to do with help. In other phrases, ZPD is the distance between what children are already able to do and what they're now not prepared to achieve themselves.

thus, youngsters inside the ZPD for a specific undertaking

can fairly but not fully carry out the mission on their personal.

however, they can successfully accomplish the venture with proper steerage. And regularly, the responsibility to direct and reveal studying shifts to the child.

conclusion

Vygotsky's concept has vital implications for Cognitive testing and schooling. for this reason, exams primarily based on ZPD specializing in a infant's ability provide a treasured substitution to traditional intelligence exams. this is due to the fact the same old intelligence assessments examine what the child has already discovered.

in step with Vygotsky, a baby's intelligence grows whilst he interacts with the encompassing environment increasingly. thus, he proposed that the intelligence evaluation checks must additionally cover this ongoing system.

hence, Dynamic testing is a superb alternative to the traditional static checks. The Dynamic trying out is primarily based at the idea of region of Proximal development (ZPD).

further, those tests give children leading questions, examples, and demonstrations in contrast to the conventional static assessments. As a end result, such assessments measure a child's capability capabilities.

consequently, ZPD mixed with scaffolding can assist each dad and mom and teachers guide the youngsters's cognitive processes. this indicates an adult need to deliver extra steering to a infant who's unable to perform the undertaking.

whilst the kid learns to do more of a mission, the adult can eliminate the scaffolding as it's miles no longer needed.

The Cognitive Psychology journal

The Cognitive Psychology journal is a peer-reviewed clinical magazine that Elsevier publishes every yr. it is a Transformative journal that follows the hybrid model of subscription and open get right of entry to. for this reason, this journal is actively devoted to transforming into a totally open get entry to magazine.

It publishes original empirical, theoretical, and educational papers, methodological articles, and crucial reviews. And those courses cover distinctive areas of cognitive psychology which include attention, reminiscence, language processing, notion, trouble-fixing, and thinking.

consequently, this magazine specializes in human cognition. other studies areas are also centered upon. supplied the cognitive psychologists have a right away interest and find it complete to study. those studies regions encompass:

Developmental Psychology

artificial Intelligence

Linguistics

Neurophysiology

Social Psychology

The editor of the Cognitive Psychology magazine is G.D. Logan who contributes in the direction of the journal along side a crew of accomplice Editors.

moreover, the Cognitive Psychology journal has a Cite rating of 5.nine and the effect factor of three.029.

Cite rating refers to the average citations that a unmarried peer-reviewed record receives posted below a specific identify.

whereas, the effect component refers to the common wide variety of citations that papers posted in the journal acquired in a specific year throughout the two preceding years.

further, the Cognitive Psychology journal covers giant

articles inside the subject of Cognitive Psychology. The research in these courses have a incredible effect at the Cognitive concept. Plus, it contributes in the direction of new theoretical traits in the area.

version of Publishing

Elsevier publishes Cognitive Psychology journal articles below two separate commercial enterprise models:

I. Subscription Articles

The subscription articles version of publishing is the one wherein the subscribing establishments or individuals make payments. as a result, the subscribing establishments and individuals fund the subscription articles of the publication.

moreover, the subscribers, patients, in addition to developed international locations can get right of entry to those articles via Elsevier's numerous get entry to programs.

these get right of entry to applications include:

   (i) companions

the following are the companions with whom Elsevier works to make the arena of research more obvious and collaborative.

Wikipedia Library's get right of entry to Donation application

feel approximately technological know-how

REISearch

technology Media Centre

White town Maker task software, Imperial college London

Pint of technological know-how

Load2Learn

Bookshare

   (ii) science Literacy

Elsevier also distributes research and complements

knowledge of technological know-how with specialized and broader audiences. for this reason, it connects with such audiences thru the subsequent packages:

Elsevier connect – an internet community publishing about technological know-how, era, and fitness research papers from Elsevier Journals

technological know-how and those – collection of activities that Elsevier organizes to deliver together researchers and involved public for discussions on technological know-how, generation, and clinical research.

Media promotion of research – loose get admission to that Elsevier gives to the media to help them cover testimonies and promote the brand new studies thru Press releases and signals for newshounds.

(iii) studies Integrity

Elsevier already has numerous tasks to make certain that the integrity of studies is maintained.

maintaining the integrity of research approach (i) following proper layout technique, (ii) ethical article submission, (iii) right e-book evaluate, (iv) making research information available for re-use, and many others.

hence, the subsequent is the list of projects that Elsevier has undertaken:

Organizing information, schooling, and schooling sessions encompassing on line lectures and interactive publications carried out by using leading specialists.

Contributing to records tasks like Force11, Scholix, and studies information Alliance to make the research information accessible, discoverable, and reusable.

Detecting Plagiarism thru Crossref Similarity take a look at – a service built in collaboration with the STM Publishing network to confirm a paper's originality.

Following a manual photo screening process by way of

walking pilots and sponsoring research in software improvement.

ensuring structured and transparent reporting through CONSORT checklist, author checklist, and adopting star methods.

keeping transparency in authorship and contributor roles Sponsoring international convention on studies Integrity Publishing reproducibility papers

promoting the Lancet reward campaign

   II. Open access Articles

The Open get right of entry to Articles are the journals which might be freely to be had to both the subscribers and the public at massive. similarly, the authors of the Open get right of entry to Articles both pay the price themselves or are funded by using their researcher funder.

it's miles essential to note that the Cognitive Psychology magazine is a transformative journal. for that reason, price range that were previously used to pay for subscriptions could now be redirected to pay for Open get right of entry to services.

accordingly, to transit to full or entire Open get admission to Articles, increasingly more transformative agreements must be negotiated with publishers around the world.

however, the foundation of these transformative agreements is temporary and transitional.

From 2021, the authors funded with the aid of funders enforcing Plan S ideas can post open get entry to articles in this magazine. in addition to this, they are able to acquire investment for their article publishing fees. And for that, they'll ought to meet Plan S requirements.

keep in mind, the Coalition S members provide the investment to aid the book rate of journals via such arrangements.

I. strange Psychology

The field of Cognitive Behavioral therapy (CBT) was a breakthrough as a result of cognitive revolution and the predominant discoveries inside the area of Cognitive Psychology.

normally, Aaron T. Beck is taken into consideration as the father of Cognitive therapy – a particular type of CBT treatment. This treatment contributed in a exquisite manner day-to-day the regions of popularity and remedy of melancholy.

as an instance, many patients do no longer respond every day the antidepressants in spite of its universal use. this is because they do not take medicines for day-to-day many reasons.

furthermore, the use psychotropic tablets weakens the coping mechanisms of people stricken by mental disorders like depression.

In different phrases, such individuals grow dayeveryday depending on remedy every day enhance their moods.

but, they fail daily practice coping strategies commonly practiced by means of wholesome individuals every day ease depressive signs.

however, CBT treatment helps them daily address tension and depressive signs and sympdayeveryday via various techniques like Socratic wondering, enhancing intermediate and center ideals, and many others.

II. Social Psychology

The studies inside the subject of Cognitive Psychology has laid foundation for some of the size of current Social Psychology.

as a result, social cognition is an vital part of social psychology that focuses on the strategies which can be of essence in Cognitive Psychology. those techniques broadly speaking cognizance on human interactions.

thus, Gordon B. Moskowitz defines social cognition as the study of intellectual techniques engaged in perceiving remembering, thinking, day-to-day, and know-how the people around us.

for instance, influential research like social records processing (SIP) are advanced every day examine the aggressive and delinquent behavior in human beings.

Kenneth sidestep evolved the SIP fashions and it is one of the empirically supported models relating aggression.

through this version, dodge claims that children having huge capability daily system social facts display a greater degree of socially acceptable behavior.

furthermore, he asserts thru this model that an person follows five steps to evaluate his interactions with other humans. moreover, stay away from also claims that the way in which an individual knows cues performs a tremendous function in his reactionary system.

III. Developmental Psychology

there are many aspects of Developmental Psychology which might be day-to-day on Cognitive Psychology. And the idea of mind (TOM) is one such improvement.

principle of mind deals with the capability of an individual daily correctly understand and accredit cognition daily the ones round them. This notion daily fully apparent while a child is among 4 and 6 years vintage.

In different words, a infant is not able every day understand that human beings around him may have extraordinary thoughts, thoughts, or emotions approximately themselves. This occurs earlier than the development of concept of thoughts within the child.

hence, the development of theory of thoughts depends on a baby's metacognition or the ability daily consider one's own thoughts. In different words, after the improvement of TOM, a baby day-to-day take indayeveryday he has his very own mind whilst others have their very own.

Jean Piaget become one of the pioneers of developmental psychology who targeted at the degrees of cognitive development in kids. He considered the cognitive development in youngsters from beginning via maturity.

however, many researchers criticized many factors of various cognitive developmental tiers. despite this, the Piaget's concept performs a dominant role within the subject of schooling.

moreover, his theory inspired colossal research in the area of cognitive psychology. besides this, the cutting-edge theory of cognitive psychology has taken into consideration many of his standards day-to-day integrate the modern-day primary views.

IV. educational Psychology

Many critical principles inside the discipline of cognitive psychology are implemented in the cutting-edge theories of education. for that reason, the subsequent are a number of the important cognitive psychology standards applied every day the education psychology.

(i) Metacognition

As stated above, metacognition refers to the thoughts and know-how an person has approximately his or her own wondering. as a consequence, self-tracking is an important concept in metacognition that plays a principal function in instructional psychology.

Self-tracking refers back to the ability of a scholar to evaluate his personal expertise. moreover, it is usually a scholar's capability to apply diverse techniques to improve his knowledge in areas where he is missing.

(ii) Declarative information and Procedural expertise

Declarative knowledge worries with an individual's exhaustive knowledge base. whereas, the Procedural know-how refers back to the specialised information a person has day-to-day perform particular responsibilities.

So, the utility of each of those cognitive criteria is critical day-to-day schooling. that is because it complements a scholar's capability to combine declarative understanding with procedural information everyday expedite the process of every day knoweveryday.

(iii) knowledge business enterprise

one of the elements of Cognitive Psychology is daily understand the manner wherein expertise is organized inner a human's brain. as a consequence, the field of schooling focuses majorly on applying this factor of cognitive psychology.

the subsequent are the cognitive standards that have verified titanic advantages in school rooms:

The approach of organizing records in a hierarchy and How well such agency of records gets mapped on human reminiscence?

V. character Psychology

recently, the cognitive therapeutic strategies are considered extensively daily deal with numerous personality disorders. Such healing processes attention at the faulty schemas shaped on the basis of judgmental biases and widespread cognitive errors.

Cognitive troubles

The Cognitive troubles arise from cognitive impairment. Such impairment occurs whilst an individual has a problem remembering, day-to-day new things, concentrating, or making choices that affect their 66b34c3da3a0593bd135e66036f9aef3 life.

similarly, the cognitive impairment might also range from slight everyday excessive. consequently, humans tormented by mild cognitive impairment may begin witnessing adjustments in their cognitive functions. however, such people are still able to perform their 66b34c3da3a0593bd135e66036f9aef3 activities.

but, individuals stricken by intense cognitive impairment may additionally lose the ability everyday perform even the 66b34c3da3a0593bd135e66036f9aef3 sports. these may additionally encompass lack of ability every day talkeveryday, write, understand the that means or importance of positive matters. as a result such people lose the ability daily live their lives independently.

in addition, it's far essential daily notice that cognitive problems do not rise up every day someone ailment or condition. additionally, it is not restricted daily any unique age-institution as properly.

as a consequence, situations like Alzheimer's sickness and other dementias can cause cognitive impairment. that is further everyday situations together with stroke, demanding brain injury, and developmental disabilities.

daily of Cognitive Impairment

the subsequent are the few not unusual every dayms of cognitive impairment which can result in cognitive issues in individuals:

memory loss

frequently asking the identical query or repeating the same factor time and again

now not spotting acquainted humans and places

Having problem in making judgment

modifications in temper or conduct

imaginative and prescient issues

trouble making plans and sporting out duties

as a result, intellectual contamination impacts many human beings. however the majority fail daily comprehend that the mental illness does now not only cause emotional troubles. It reasons cognitive issues every dayo.

some humans experience cognitive dysfunctioning handiest at some stage in the episode of mental contamination. at the same time as others enjoy cognitive troubles more constantly.

consequently, it's miles very vital everyday manipulate intellectual infection every dayeveryday lead a productive existence and have longer periods of balance.

but day-to-day manipulate intellectual contamination in a better way, it's miles extremely critical every day apprehend the numerous approaches in which it affects cognitive functioning.

Why Do human beings With mental illness Have Cognitive troubles?

As according to studies, intellectual illnesses purpose an awful lot of the cognitive problems in people. For an extended time frame, human beings taken into consideration daily like loss of motivation, risky temper, psychosis and different daily daily be number one in nature. but, they believed that the cognitive issues had been secondary in nature.

but, you day-to-day remember that it isn't the case. Cognitive issues or dysfunction is a number one sympdailym of schizophrenia and a few other affective issues.

hence, it's miles daily this motive that cognitive problems are pretty evident even when the alternative every day are managed.

In different words, the cognitive issues are pretty evident even when an individual is not psychotic or has not experienced an affective episode.

besides this, the studies says that the unique parts of the brain are answerable for precise cognitive abilities. but, such components of the brain do no longer feature usually in case of people affected by schizophrenia and other affective disorders.

as a consequence, all of this showcases that the mental contamination has an impact on the functioning of the mind. This in turn results in cognitive troubles. however, its is also true that different daily also impact the cognitive functioning of an individual.

accordingly, many people are capable of pay greater attention, assume better, and recollect matters while they're no longer underneath the affect of emotional strain. Likewise, those who were given the opportunity daily study adaptive cognitive competencies had been capable of think and bear in mind better.

How Does intellectual illness have an effect on Cognition?

there are numerous intellectual illnesses and each of them have an effect on the cognitive functioning of an man or woman differently.

in addition everyday this, every body receives impacted in a exclusive way. for instance some human beings affected by schizophrenia enjoy more cognitive troubles as compared day-to-day others.

Likewise, some human beings struggling with despair or bipolar disorder face challenges in a single component of cognitive functioning but no longer the other.

accordingly, it's far extraordinarily important which will remember the fact thateveryday a intellectual infection affects anyone in a extraordinary manner.

So, it receives easy daily understand how the person is affected. furnished, you have got an knowledge of the different ways wherein intellectual illnesses can affect an individual's cognition.

I. Schizophrenia and Cognition

individuals tormented by schizophrenia frequently revel in cognitive problems of their capability every day:

Pay attention

every day account and keep in mind data

method information quick

reply daily records quickly

think severely, plan, organize, and remedy troubles

provoke speech

accordingly, it's miles clear that schizophrenia and many different affective problems can purpose cognitive problems. proper medicinal drugs can help in avoiding the cognitive aspect outcomes. moreover, a nice attitude almost about daily can help people make high-quality use of their cognitive abilities.

moreover, considered necessary help and stimulation from the bodily and social environment can inspire humans daily deal with cognitive problems in a higher manner.

II. Bipolar disorder, depression, other Affective problems, and Cognition

people tormented by affective disorders like Bipolar ailment and despair frequently experience cognitive troubles in their capacity every day:

Pay interest

don't forgeteveryday and recollect records

think critically, plan, arrange, and solve issues

speedy coordinate eye-hand moves

daily all such cognitive problems are quite apparent during

an affective enjoy. however, the trouble of attention receives higher as soon as stability is witnessed in an individual's mood.

but, the challenges with memory, moevery dayr and thinking capabilities might also continue to exist even in the course of the durations of mood stability.

hence, there is extra probability everyday experience cognitive issues whilst an individual tormented by a mental contamination reports hallucinations or delusions.

V

PERSONALITY PSYCHOLOGY : WHO AM I ? & WHAT IS ME ?

Personality psychology is a branch of psychology that makes a speciality of knowledge distinct factors of human character.

The field of character psychology seeks to apprehend what reasons one-of-a-kind persona traits. It additionally works to apprehend, diagnose, and deal with troubles with persona, which can be known as personality problems.

what's personality?
Why Is personality Psychology crucial?
Theories of personality
What's Your character type?

personality issues

frequently requested Questions

what's persona?

Persona is described as the feature pattern of behaviors, feelings, thoughts, and attitudes that influence how we engage with the sector round us. some of this stuff are innate, even as others are encouraged with the aid of factors inclusive of upbringing and environment.

absolutely positioned, your character is what makes you you.

Your persona plays a position in every aspect of your life, from the way you spend your time to the way you relate to different humans. studying more approximately your personality may be a useful manner to increase self-consciousness.

Why Is character Psychology essential?

personality psychology facilitates people higher recognize the factors that play a function in personality. It additionally allows us to recognise greater about how certain personality traits have an effect on conduct.

as an instance, some trends are related to better levels of happiness and nicely-being. a few developments are linked to greater sturdiness whilst others had been linked to an elevated chance of contamination.

in step with the yankee psychological association, the examine of character focuses on two fundamental regions.

the first involves reading how people fluctuate in phrases of various personality traits.

the second one makes a speciality of expertise how the numerous distinct factors of personality function together to create a cohesive whole.

personality psychology also facilitates intellectual health specialists recognize issues associated with character, together with borderline personality sickness and narcissistic character sickness.

Theories of character

a number of the high-quality-known theories in psychology are devoted to knowledge and explaining how character develops.

Psychosexual theory

Sigmund Freud counseled that personality develops via a chain of five psychosexual ranges. At each stage, the energy of the identity—the primal, instinctual a part of personality—is targeted on a selected area of the body.

Freud believed that early early life stories play a pivotal position in the formation of personality, and believed that persona was largely completely mounted through the age of 5.

Psychosocial idea

Erik Erikson was a theorist who cautioned that personality develops through a series of 8 psychosocial tiers. At each stage, human beings face a developmental struggle that plays a position inside the improvement of mental virtues. efficiently navigating those levels and conflicts results in the formation of a

Wholesome character.

whilst Freud's principle pressured that persona is shaped often in early youth, Erikson that someone's character maintains to broaden at some stage in lifestyles.

Humanistic principle

Humanistic psychology is a attitude that stresses the superb aspect of human nature. One humanist idea, Maslow's hierarchy of wishes, indicates that humans are motivated to attain a country of self-actualization that is marked by a coherent, cohesive personality.

Carl Rogers, every other humanist psychologist, believed

that when someone's perceived self and perfect self are aligned, it's miles a sign of a healthy character.

Trait principle

Trait theories of persona endorse that personality is made up of a number of distinct tendencies or broad tendencies. There have been some of unique trait theories, however one of the most widely general today is referred to as the massive five theory.

The huge five principle suggests that persona is made up of 5 wide dimensions—agreeableness, conscientiousness, extroversion, neuroticism, and openness. each of these trends is a continuum, so that you may be either high, low, or somewhere in the middle on every trait.

What's Your character kind?

There are a number of special ways to measure and determine persona. a number of those measurements are exams, inventories, and exams that can be used for a selection of purposes. from time to time those tests are used to assist investigate psychological disorders or for pre-employment screening.

In different instances, these inventories are used to inform human beings greater about what's referred to as their character kind. The concept of personality types is famous, but additionally extremely arguable. many of these character typologies lack scientific guide, whilst others are too simplistic to fully describe personality.

A number of the maximum famous personality typologies include:

The Myers-Briggs type Indicator (MBTI)
The Enneagram
kind A and kind B principle
The Keirsey Temperament Sorter
persona exams can be amusing and thrilling, however you

ought to use caution and now not take your results too critically. maximum of the net exams you encounter are not formal exams, so that you need to not use the consequences to diagnose yourself.

personality issues

personality psychology additionally seeks to understand character problems. these persona issues create issues regarding others in addition to problems with wondering and behavior.

The Diagnostic and Statistical manual of mental issues (DSM-five) recognizes 10 one of a kind character

Disorders:

delinquent persona ailment
Avoidant character sickness
Borderline character disease
established character sickness
Histrionic character disease
Narcissistic character sickness
Obsessive-compulsive character sickness
Paranoid character sickness
Schizoid persona disease
Schizotypal character disease

remedies for these conditions vary depending on the unique analysis but may involve remedy, psychotherapy, psychoeducation, and talents training.

Your particular character makes you who you are and influences the whole thing out of your relationships to the way you live. personality is some thing which you might be capable of describe, however do what the scientific observe of character entails?

Character psychology is one in every of the biggest and maximum famous branches of psychology.

professionals who look at personality psychology need to apprehend how persona develops in addition to how it affects the manner we suppose and behave. Psychologists examine how character varies amongst people as well as how humans are comparable. additionally they investigate, diagnose, and deal with persona disorders.

What precisely is character? How can expertise your character help you benefit insight into your emotional well-being?

what is persona?

what is it that makes you who you are? Many factors make a contribution to the individual you're nowadays, such as genetics, your upbringing, and your lifestyles experiences.

Many could argue that what makes you particular is the characteristic patterns of mind, emotions, and behaviors that make up your character. at the same time as there's no unmarried agreed-upon definition of persona, it's far regularly thought of as some thing that arises from within the character and remains fairly regular throughout lifestyles.

persona encompasses all of the mind, behavior styles, and social attitudes that impact how we view ourselves and what we accept as true with approximately others and the sector round us.

knowledge character allows psychologists to predict how human beings will respond to sure conditions and the kinds of things they decide on and cost. To get a feel of ways researchers look at persona psychology, it is going to be helpful to study extra approximately a number of the maximum influential personality theories.

Theories

a number of theories have emerged to provide an explanation for the elements of personality. a few are focused on explaining how personality develops, while others are worried with man or woman differences in character.

Trait Theories of persona
The trait theories of persona center on the concept that character is made out of huge trends or tendencies. various theories were proposed to discover which attributes are key additives in character, as well as tries to decide the full quantity of character developments.

Psychologist Gordon Allport changed into one of the first to explain persona in phrases of person developments. In his dispositional angle, Allport suggested that there are different types of developments: commonplace, important, and cardinal.

commonplace traits are shared by way of many human beings within a selected way of life. significant tendencies are those who make up an individual's character. Cardinal tendencies are those that are so dominant that someone turns into in the main acknowledged for those characteristics.

An instance of a cardinal trait is mother Teresa. She turned into so for her charitable work that her call became almost synonymous with imparting service to those in need.

Allport counseled that there were as many as four,000 person traits. Psychologist Raymond Cattell proposed that there have been 16. Cattell also believed that these trends exist on a continuum and that every person possess every trait in varying levels.

A psychologist named Hans Eysenck might slim the list of traits further, suggesting there were only 3: extroversion, neuroticism, and psychoticism.

nowadays, the "massive 5" theory is possibly the most popular and widely commonplace trait theory of character. The theory proposes that character is made of 5 huge character dimensions:

Agreeableness
Conscientiousness
Extroversion
Neuroticism
Openness

The huge five principle states that every trait exists as a broad continuum. An individual's character will fall someplace on the spectrum for every trait.

As an example, you is probably high in extroversion, conscientiousness, and agreeableness, but somewhere within the center for openness and neuroticism.

How personality Develops and modifications thru existence

Freud's concept of psychosexual development is one of the first-rate-recognised character theories—however additionally one of the most arguable. in step with Freud, kids progress thru a sequence of stages of character improvement. At each level, libidinal energy (the force that drives all human behaviors) turns into targeted on unique erogenous zones.

successful crowning glory of a level lets in someone to move directly to the following section of improvement. Failure at any degree can cause fixations which could impact someone's grownup persona.

Erik Erikson, every other psychologist, defined 8 psychosocial stages of lifestyles. With Erikson's idea, each level plays a extensive function inside the improvement of a person's character and mental competencies.

in the course of every psychosocial level, an individual will face a developmental disaster that serves as a turning point in their development. correctly finishing each degree leads to the development of a healthful persona.

Erikson become more interested by how social interactions prompted the improvement of character. He became frequently concerned with the development of what he referred to as ego identification.

at the same time as Freud's principle cautioned that persona is primarily shaped and set in stone at an early age, Erikson believed that character endured to broaden during life.

How character Is tested

To have a look at and degree personality, psychologists have developed character checks, exams, and inventories. The assessments are broadly used in an expansion of settings. as an instance, the well-known Myers-Briggs type Indicator (MBTI) is regularly used as a pre-employment screening evaluation.

other assessments can be used to assist people learn more about one of a kind components of their personalities. some exams are used as screening and assessment gear to assist diagnose personality disorders.

Gaining a higher information of your persona may be beneficial in lots of components of your existence. for instance, relationships with friends, circle of relatives, and coworkers would possibly improve when you come to be aware that you work nicely with others or that you need to make time to be on my own.

you have got in all likelihood encountered an expansion of persona checks on-line (as an example, a web quiz that tells you whether you're extroverted or introverted). some of those assessments purport to show the "real you," even as others are honestly supposed most effective for enjoyment.

persona tests which you take on-line should be enthusiastic about a grain of salt. informal gear may be amusing and can provide a few insight into your options and characteristics, but most effective persona assessments administered by way of skilled and qualified specialists have to be used as formal checks or to make a prognosis.

personality disorders

personality psychologists are also interested by studying troubles with persona which could get up. personality disorders are characterized as continual and pervasive intellectual problems which can severely effect someone's mind, behaviors, and interpersonal functioning.

The present day version of the Diagnostic and Statistical guide of intellectual issues (DSM-5) lists 10 character issues, inclusive of antisocial persona ailment, borderline character sickness, narcissistic character disease, and obsessive-compulsive character disorder.

The national Institute of mental health (NIH) reviews that approximately nine.1% of the grownup populace in the united states of america stories symptoms of as a minimum one character sickness each 12 months.

Being diagnosed with a character ailment may be distressing, however you need to realize that there are treatments. working with a intellectual health expert, you may learn how to apprehend the difficulties that those disorders can reason and explore new coping strategies.

it's miles good enough to experience fearful and involved about what the destiny would possibly keep however remember that you do now not ought to face it on my own. There are those who are trained, professional, and ready that will help you take the following steps in your treatment.

depending for your precise prognosis, your health practitioner may recommend psychotherapy, skills education, medicinal drug, or a aggregate of all 3.

paintings intently together with your healthcare group to develop a treatment plan that focuses on your wishes and desires.

A phrase From Verywell

personality is a large situation that touches on almost each aspect of what makes people who they're. there are numerous ways to think about personality. There are some theories that concentrate on man or woman traits and people that keep in mind the different developmental degrees that take area as personality emerges (and every now and then changes) over the years.

Psychologists are not most effective interested in expertise ordinary human persona, however in recognizing capability persona disturbances that could result in misery or issue in key life areas. via being capable of become aware of problems humans have at domestic, faculty, work, or in their relationships, psychologists are better able to help human beings broaden abilities to manage and manage the signs and symptoms of personality disorders.

What's character Psychology?

personality Psychology as a systematic on-line

Contents

Preamble

How is character described?

The big questions of personality of persona psychology (also: a narrated slideshow),

what's the sector of character psychology

who are personality psychologists?
a piece of records for individuals who are interested
Preamble
one of the missions of our laboratory has been to develop, increase and promote a brand new unified vision of character psychology, loosely defined under the label, "The persona systems Framework," and pronounced on similarly on this website.

at some point of a whole lot of the later twentieth century, persona psychology was often regarded as a subject of competing "grand theories," proposed through such people as Sigmund Freud, Carl Jung, Carl Rogers, and Hans Eysenck, often with terrible empirical validation and few ways of resolving conflicts amongst them. indeed, it is nevertheless taught in that manner these days in many establishments even though there are better alternatives.

by selling a unified framework for the on-line's teaching and studies we hope to enhance and to sell the sphere through clarifying its principal worries and strengths.

A key a part of the philosophy behind our theoretical paintings is that it's miles vital initially both an knowledge of the history of the on-line of personality psychology and an know-how of its empirical strengths and diversity nowadays. In element, this facilitates discover herbal areas of agreement that can provide a foundation for a unified have a look at the on lineonline.

How Is character defined?

asserting the Definition of character
there are numerous areas of agreement in the on linefield -- for instance, there is sizeable agreement as to the definition of persona.

persona issues the most vital, maximum great, components of an man or woman's mental lifestyles. character worries whether a person is satisfied or sad, active or apathetic, smart or stupid. through the years, many different definitions had been proposed for personality. maximum of the definitions seek advice from a intellectual gadget—a set of mental components inclusive of motives, feelings, and thoughts.

The definitions vary a chunk as to what the ones elements might be, however they arrive down to the concept that persona entails a pattern or international operation of intellectual structures. right here are

some definitions:

"persona is the entire mental corporation of a man or women at any degree of his improvement. It embraces every section of human individual: mind, temperament, skill, morality, and every attitude that has been built up in the course of 1's existence." (Warren & Carmichael, 1930, p. 333)

(In an acknowledged overstatement...) "persona is the essence of a person." (corridor & Lindzey, 1957, p. nine, characterizing statements with the aid of Gordon Allport)

"An individual's pattern of mental methods bobbing up from motives, emotions, thoughts, and other primary regions of mental function. personality is expressed through its impacts at the frame, in conscious intellectual life, and thru the character's social conduct." (Mayer, 2005)

within the 2007 assembly of the affiliation for research in character, a Presidential Panel turned into concerned with, "The destiny of character Psychology". One player on that panel raised a concern over whether or not definitions of character have been indistinct and contradictory. That changed into surprising as there genuinely does appear like a fairly wide consensus that personality is the observe of a person's usual mental gadget. possibly one motive for the experience that definitions of persona diverge is due to the fact different psychologists -- people who are not personality psychologists -- regularly misunderstand our field and on line the sphere in wrong methods. the object entitled asserting the

Definition of personality, describes this scenario.

The massive Questions of character Psychology

character psychology had its origins in individuals who sought answers to massive quesitons. A 2007 article from the laboratory surveyed the highbrow history of the large questions that stimulated the on-line, and 20 questions had been identified that were most critical to the field. of those, four particularly seemed in particular pertinent.

To listen a piece about the examine, do this audio-narrated slide show in powerpoint.

Narrated slide display: The huge Questions of persona

A diagram of some very crucial crucial questions located them into 4 businesses like this:

determine adapted from Mayer, J. D.

what's the field of personality Psychology?

personality Psychology as a systematic discipononline

persona psychology is the medical subject that studies the personality machine. The on-line seeks to recognize a person's most important psychological styles and how the ones patterns are expressed in an person's lifestyles. character psychologists conduct scientific studies on character, train approximately character (typically at the university and college level) and participate within the broader on linefield of psychology.

Thinking about the trouble

distinctive answers are possible to the question "Why have a look at character?" here is one answer that will let you understand some thing of what persona and its study is ready.

every folks, as people, influences lots that is within us and round us. every of us has many mental attributes emotions, mind, motivations, and the like. it's far our persona that orchestrates our psychological qualities.

Our emotions—strong or moderate—determine a number of how we act and react. Our thoughts manual us and affect others, who can be entertained by way of our wit or drawn to our understanding.

Our feel of self allows inform us of a way to make choices among alternatives—alternatives that could assist us develop, or, which can harm us.

This persona of ours slowly and persistently impacts how we feel, what we do, who we are, and how we have an impact on the arena round us.

most of us cannot help however wonder how our persona works, how our persona came to be—and what it would mean for our destiny.

We also surprise approximately the personalities of others—how they may be the same or different from us.

personality psychology worries what our personalities are, how they paintings, and what they are able to mean to our own and others' futures.

The on-line of personality psychology allows answer a number of those questions. If such questions hobby

you, you could want to examine greater.

who're persona Psychologists?

cutting-edge personality Psychologists

personality psychologists are psychologists who are inquisitive about the observe of how an man or woman's principal psychological subsystems—motives, emotions, the self, and others— function together to create someone's life patterns.

Nowadays, most character psychologists have Ph.D.'s in psychology—typically with a specialization in persona, social, or medical psychology. That changed into no longer constantly the case, but, and a few earlier character psychologists had been trained in medicine and other fields.

these days, many character psychologists work in schools and universities, where they educate courses in personality psychology and associated areas, and conduct studies on personality and how it affects humans's lives.

Another institution of character psychologists paintings in organizational settings, where they often can be observed in departments of Human sources. In such roles, they may try to recognize, for example, the precise persona trends on the way to assist individuals work efficiently at a particular task.

still other persona psychologists paintings as experts to groups, helping with the choice and retention of

key personnel.

locating Out extra about modern Psychologists

in case you are interested in seeing quick descriptions of modern character psychologists, and visiting their net pages, you could find these from the net website maintained by using the affiliation for studies in character. click right here to go to the member profiles for lots of those people.

other psychologists with hobby in personality psychology can be located at the Social Psychology network. To find them (the list will partly overlap with the ARP listing), visit the club list vicinity of the SPN internet website—and, using the quest box on the top, input the term "personality." Of path, for both the ARP or SPN sites, if you have the call of a psychologist you're particularly interested by, you may

look for that call.
persona Psychologists in records:

The Grand Theorists of the Early-to-Mid twentieth Century

whilst human beings think about personality psychologists, certain names frequently come to thoughts: Sigmund Freud, Carl Jung, Carl Rogers, and others. those individuals have been tremendously outstanding theorists and researchers of human nature within the early-to-mid twentieth century. They every so often are called the Grand Theorists of the sphere.

today, there honestly are eminent theorists of character, however the on-line no longer depends on grand theorists for its venture(s). as an alternative, it is focussed today on studies approximately how the persona machine operates.

locating Out extra approximately Grand Theorists

In case you are interested in finding out extra about grand theorists from on-line supply, a exquisite aid is Professor C. George Boeree's and open-get admission to textbook, "persona Theories."

a chunk of history for folks that Are involved:
some Rationales for the field defined in Early Textbooks
a few ideas approximately why to have a look at personality additionally may be determined within the textbooks of the field. many of the earliest (if no longer the earliest) textbook inside the usa become Roback's (1928) "Psychology of character." He writes:

The declaration of guides on persona, which at one time could were greeted now not without a perceptibly amused expression, is now as an alternative welcomed via educators...

Roback wrote earlier than the institutionalization of the phrase "personality," often who prefer the time period "individual" -- although he acknowledges "persona" as a somewhat broader term. In a chain of passages, Roback notes that personality, specifically the part of persona referred to as individual, is a moral possession of an person.

...The most popular use of the word "man or woman" in regular existence is forever colored with ethical predicates...The famous thoughts has by no means distinguished extra than sorts of characters. They have been both excellent or horrific, strong or weak, noble or base, of a high or low type;...to mention that a person has no person is a euphemistic equivalent for the expression that he has a low type of person...(Roback, 1928, p. 6)

. ...the more strongly moralists emphasised the cardinal importance of man or woman for ethics...the more had been experimental psychologists willing to dispose of the entire depend with a phrase or ... (Roback, 1928, p. 7)

...the moral and pedagogical elements that deal with individual-constructing and for the maximum part comprise horatory appeals in behalf of the moral lifestyles do not input right here...it is pretty apparent that the theoretical exam of person ought to antedate both those inquiries, and mainly the latter. (Roback, 1928, p. 7)

All advised, it appears to me that Roback is interested in character improvement and man or woman constructing. To achieve this, but, he argues, a systematic study -- that is, of persona -- have to take precedence.

Gordon Allport study and benefitted from Roback's paintings (his assistance is recounted via Roback).

nine years later, Allport's personal e-book added a new reason for a observe of personality. Allport addressed, no longer the general public's need for the technology, however as an alternative his clinical colleagues' need.

...ordinarily, science regards the character as a mere bothersome coincidence. Psychology, too, more often than not treats him as something to be dismissed so the primary commercial enterprise of accounting for the uniformity of events can get underneath manner. The end result is that on all sides we see psychologists enthusiastically at paintings upon a fairly shadowy portrait entitled, "the generalized human thoughts."...It appears unreal and esoteric, devoid of locus, self-focus, and organic unity -- all vital characteristics of the minds we realize.

...[A] new movement within mental science has step by step grown up. It tries...to depict and account for the appear individuality of thoughts. This new motion has emerge as regarded (in the us) as the psychology of persona. (Allport, 1937, p. vii)

Why become one of these new motion wished? Allport summarized some of the arguments others had made.

with out the co-ordinating concept of individual (or some equivalent inclusive of Self or Ego), it is not possible to account for, or maybe to depict, the interaction of intellectual strategies upon one another. reminiscence affects perception, choice influences which means, which means determines action, and motion shapes reminiscence; and so forth...

The phenomenon of intellectual employer can don't have any importance until it's miles viewed as taking region within a specific framework...the personal life. (Allport, 1937, p. 550).

once more, persevering with on the subject of the field of psychology more typically, Allport argues that the psychology of personality could make those contributions (Allport, 1937), which i've summarized as follows:

Develop preferred laws as to how an individual's uniqueness comes approximately

expect someone's conduct on the premise of his/her individual traits

find out the man or woman individual's very own factor of view of who he or she is

discover the components of character

find out the shape that holds those parts collectively

supply preference to positive concepts -- e.g., ego-machine, trait, existence-history -- that recognize a person's individuality

discover commonplace traits

codify know-how as to the nature of human nature

flip interpersonal impressions into greater reliable expertise

appropriately constitute the individual in technological know-how, and offer that character with appreciate

Henry Murray and the Harvard steerage sanatorium (Murray, 1938) had this to say:

Man is to-day's top notch trouble. What are we able to recognize approximately him and how can or not it's stated in words that have clear which means?...The point of view followed on this e-book is that personalities represent the situation mattter of psychology, the lifestyles history of a single man being the unit with which this area has to deal. (Murray, 1938, p. 3)

We judged the time had come when systematic, complete length research of individuals could be made to deliver outcomes. And extra than this, certainly, it appeared a vital element to do. For if the constituent methods of persona are jointly established, then one must recognize a lot to recognise a bit. (Murray, 1938, p. 5)

reasons can be effectively superior for such research

besides the crucial ones that know-how is in keeping with se a final excellent and that man is of all objects the most inviting. there are numerous who consider that an know-how of human nature is the exceptional requirement of this age; that contemporary man is 'up in opposition to it,' careworn, disappointed, despairing and geared up to regress; that what he wishes is the strength to alternate and redirect himself and others; and that possession of this unique strength can simplest be received thru understanding. If it's miles true, as some reasonable men affirm, that way of life -- the pleasant of man's excessive history -- is in jeopardy, and that to store and similarly it guy, its creator and conserver, have to be modified -- regenerated or developed in another way from start -- then the on the spot needful is a science of human nature. (Murray, 1938).

character psychology is a branch of psychology that makes a speciality of knowledge distinctive components of human character.
the sphere of persona psychology seeks to understand what causes exclusive personality trends. It also works to recognize, diagnose, and treat troubles with personality, which might be called personality problems.
what's personality?
Why Is personality Psychology critical?
Theories of persona
What's Your personality type?
personality problems
often requested Questions
what is persona?
personality is defined because the feature sample of behaviors, feelings, thoughts, and attitudes that influence how we engage with the world around us. a number of

these items are innate, while others are inspired by elements inclusive of upbringing and surroundings.

truely positioned, your character is what makes you you.

Your personality performs a role in every aspect of your lifestyles, from how you spend your time to how you relate to different humans. studying more approximately your persona can be a useful way to growth

self-consciousness.

Why Is persona Psychology essential?

persona psychology enables people higher apprehend the factors that play a function in personality. It additionally lets in us to know greater approximately how positive personality traits affect behavior.

for example, some traits are linked to higher levels of happiness and nicely-being. some trends are linked to extra durability while others had been linked to an elevated danger of illness.

consistent with the yankee mental association, the take a look at of personality makes a speciality of two

foremost regions.

the first includes studying how people range in terms of various persona traits.

the second one focuses on information how the many special components of character feature collectively to create a cohesive complete.

character psychology also helps mental fitness experts recognize disorders related to personality, inclusive of borderline persona sickness and narcissistic persona sickness.

Theories of character

some of the exceptional-recognized theories in psychology are devoted to expertise and explaining how personality develops.

Psychosexual idea

Sigmund Freud cautioned that personality develops via a sequence of five psychosexual levels. At every level, the power of the identity—the primal, instinctual a part of character—is focused on a specific area of the body.

Freud believed that early formative years reviews play a pivotal role within the formation of persona, and believed that personality was in large part absolutely established by using the age of 5.

Psychosocial idea

Erik Erikson was a theorist who advised that personality develops via a series of eight psychosocial ranges. At every level, human beings face a developmental battle that performs a function in the development of psychological virtues. efficiently navigating those degrees and conflicts ends in the formation of a healthy character.

even as Freud's theory burdened that persona is formed normally in early youth, Erikson that someone's character keeps to increase all through existence.

Humanistic theory

Humanistic psychology is a attitude that stresses the advantageous side of human nature. One humanist theory, Maslow's hierarchy of needs, suggests that human beings are stimulated to reach a country of self-actualization that is marked by means of a coherent, cohesive character.

Carl Rogers, another humanist psychologist, believed that when a person's perceived self and perfect self are aligned, it's far a sign of a wholesome personality.

Trait principle

Trait theories of persona endorse that persona is made up of a number of extraordinary trends or broad inclinations. There were a number of exclusive trait theories, however one of the most broadly widely wide-spread nowadays is called the massive 5 concept.

The large five theory suggests that character is made of 5 huge dimensions—agreeableness, conscientiousness, extroversion, neuroticism, and openness. every of these traits is a continuum, so that you can be both high, low, or someplace inside the center on every trait.

What's Your character type?

There are a number of distinct ways to measure and verify character. a number of those measurements are exams, inventories, and checks that can be used for a selection of purposes. on occasion these assessments are used to assist examine psychological problems or for pre-employment screening.

In different times, those inventories are used to inform human beings greater about what's referred to as their personality kind. The idea of personality kinds is popular, but also quite controversial. a lot of those personality typologies lack medical guide, while others are too simplistic to fully describe persona.

some of the most popular persona typologies include:

The Myers-Briggs kind Indicator (MBTI)

The Enneagram

kind A and kind B concept

The Keirsey Temperament Sorter

personality assessments may be fun and interesting, but you need to use warning and no longer take your outcomes too seriously. maximum of the net tests you come across aren't formal checks, so you ought to no longer use the consequences to diagnose yourself.

personality problems

personality psychology also seeks to recognize persona issues. these persona problems create problems regarding others in addition to problems with thinking and conduct.

The Diagnostic and Statistical guide of intellectual disorders (DSM-5) acknowledges 10 specific character issues:

antisocial persona ailment
Avoidant personality disorder
Borderline character disorder
structured character disease
Histrionic character disease
Narcissistic personality disease
Obsessive-compulsive character disorder
Paranoid character disease
Schizoid character sickness
Schizotypal character sickness

treatments for those conditions vary depending on the unique analysis but might also involve medicine, psychotherapy, psychoeducation, and skills schooling.

what is personality?

summary

personality is the characteristic way of wondering, feeling, and behaving. It means the set of behavior styles and emotional responses that you manifest even as interacting with others in the real world.

have you ever ever found out that there are numerous key day-to-day that contributed on your making? Don't you notice yourself as an person who is distinct and has an internal story waiting day-to-day be found out daily the outside international?

Many human beings every day have used picky adjectives to describe you as smart, dynamic, sincere, or loving. They praised your attractive persona. Isn't it so?

At this factor, you have been eager daily know what character personality means and why you aren't like some other being in this international. What virtually brings in the sort of distinction?

The phrase personality is derived from the Latin phrase 'character' because of this a mask. It means that your innate nature has many hidden aspects that are not on the floor.

Others cannot see those factors most of the time.

In some other reference, character also approach your public photo. It refers everyday what photograph you present outdoor and what position you're presupposed to play on your real life.

within the medical world, persona refers in your specific nature. in keeping with Gordon Allport, "personality is the dynamic employer in the individual of those psychophysical systems that determine his specific adjustments day-to-day the environment." (1937).

in line with Weinberg and Gold, (1999), "personality is the characteristics or a blend of characteristics that make someone unique."

each the above definitions describe personality as a completely unique characteristic that belongs every day you. you're exclusive and certainly one of.

you've got a completely unique mental shape this is made from persona tendencies which might be idiosyncratic. consequently, it is undesirable day-to-day compare you with some other person in this international.

personality Psychology – which means
summary

character psychology is a systematic and scientific study of persona. the field analyzes what makes someone extraordinary from any other man or woman. It also research how variant amongst people is intrinsic and guided through a few internal forces.

Because the issue rely of personality psychology studies individual differences among humans, it additionally focuses on the underlying day-to-day that result in any such variation.

It helps day-to-day understand the approaches we suppose, sense, and make selections in our existence. therefore, the field intends everyday take a look at the dichoevery daymous purposeful alternatives along with sensation vs. intuition, thinking vs. feeling, and judging vs. perceiving.

personality psychology pursuits daily look at how the character of a person affects thoughts and attitudes, emotions, values, social adjustment, motivation, and the overall behavior that the person presentations in numerous social circumstances.

Gordon Allport (1937), a pioneer of trait idea in psychology proposed that personality psychology ambitions day-to-day construct an usual and coherent photo of an person that determines the center psychological methods, and also indicates the quantity of similarity and distinction with other people.

He described two critical techniques of analyzing character psychology. they're nomothetic psychology and

Idiographic psychology.

by means of the nomothetic view, Allport said that there are a few general laws that may be applied daily many human beings. It means people own the identical person traits and features which can belong everyday many humans at a time.

If we day-to-day the psychological developments of many people, we will be capable of put them beneath one class or mental kind. From this concept, the type theories of psychology came inevery day existence.

A simple example is the precept of self-actualization or the introversion vs. extroversion capabilities. these concepts are generalized propositions that may be carried out everyday many unique people, irrespective of gender, caste, creed, religion, and nationality.

The idiosyncratic view explains character as particular and exclusive, some thing that belongs day-to-day the individual alone.

for this reason, information character psychology manner studying the reactions of humans everyday other individuals, situations, and stressors of life.

traits of persona

in case you are fascinated day-to-day recognise the improvement technique of your precise nature, you'll day-to-day attention on understanding the important thing personality characteristics that show how personality works and why you seem day-to-day be exceptional from the alternative individual.

persona is exceedingly stable and steady. you will reply in greater or less comparable methods in response everyday outside stimulus. as an instance – an organized and systematic character will reply with anger and disgust in messy and non-methodical conditions, irrespective of where or how that state of affairs has arisen.

persona is motivated by way of each genetic day-to-day and environmental every dayfacdayeveryday. for instance – an in any other case shy man or woman might also day-to-day outspoken and sociable if they're required day-to-day accomplish that.

Your personality makes you behave the manner you do. It manner your mind, emotions, and actions are closely related everyday the form of person you're.

Your private likings, desires, the reasons behind your actions are all decided via your persona.

The relationships, career preference, place of business habits, social interaction are day-to-day to your personality type.

Philosophical assumptions of personality psychology

The observe of persona psychology is depending on art, sciences, and philosophy. it's far an interdisciplinary subject of take a look at.

There are some philosophical assumptions on which character psychology is every day. The assumptions are beneficial in knowledge the diverse factors of personality.

these assumptions inform us why theorists vary in their simple idea about what persona is, the way it shapes a person's basic conduct, and what position does it play in self-growth and improvement.

Freedom vs. dedication – This assumption questions the truth that whether or not we've the strength to control our conduct or whether or not conduct is casually decided by means of numerous reasons and forces which can be beyond human manipulate.

Nature vs. nurture – in step with this assumption, many theorists believed that character is decided by genetic day-to-day and many conduct styles that you might show in various conditions are determined with the aid of heredity affects. There are different theories which declare that character is shaped by way of the environment.

distinctiveness vs. Universality – This assumption focuses on the extent to which each one folks are distinctive from each other and how a long way we've comparable traits that enhances precise conduct responses. It tells you that in some cases your character displays precise traits that are exceptional however in a few other conditions you may exhibit behavior this is widely wide-spread.Carl Rogers, Abraham Maslow, Gordon Allport had been the fans of "strong point", while there are others like B.F Skinner and Albert Bandura who were the followers of the "widespread" college of notion.

energetic vs. reactive – This assumption questions the truth that whether people reply or act via individual initiative or by means of the affect of a few out of doors stimuli. The behaviorists believed that we are fashioned with the aid of the surroundings. therefore our reactions and actions are passive. but, humanists and cognitive psychologists say that character is shaped by way of our active participation with outside forces.

personality theories in psychology

so that you can understand personality psychology, we are able to have to apprehend the various theories of personality that went into the making of this tremendous subject.

some of these theories explain how personality develops over time from youth to maturity. And there are others that signify the idea of person differences in attitudes and behavior.

There are four principal personality theories that we are able to speak approximately in this article. they're –

Psychoanalytic technique

Trait concept of personality

Humanistic approach to persona

Social cognitive approach to persona

Behaviorist idea

Psychoanalytic technique

The psychoanalytic technique is predicated on formative years reports and the function of the unconscious in shaping your personality.

Sigmund Freud, the pioneer of the psychoanalytic school proposed that your unconscious desires and desires, wounds and trauma, mind and memories play a important position in shaping your nature.

The method is primarily based on the following key concepts –

Your behavior is inspired by using the unconscious forces operating deep inside that in no way got a threat to come back to the forefront.

The emotional issues that you undergo in your current nation may additionally have their root within the unconscious traumas and ache that you may have suffered in early life.

There are deep rooted conflicts among the aware and the unconscious thoughts that may supply upward thrust to mental fitness issues.

Freud believed that the unconscious content may be found out thru desires and through slip of tongue.

Freud emphasized the importance of early adolescence experiences, sexual instincts, and the position of the unconscious in the development of personality.

a number of the alternative major theorists of the psychoanalytic approach who believed inside the function of the subconscious mind in shaping human persona are Alfred Adler, Carl Jung, Erik Erikson, and Karen Horney.

considering the fact that they differ from Sigmund Freud on many different standards, they're also referred to as the Neo-Freudians.

The Neo-Freudians accompanied the simple standards of psychoanalysis however they differed from Freud on several different factors.

They defied the importance of sexual urges in the improvement of character. additionally they disagreed on Freud's loss of emphasis on the social, cultural, and environmental factors in shaping one's character.

Trait concept of personality

The trait concept of personality is based on figuring out,

describing, and measuring the specific persona traits and qualities that a person can also own.

Researchers believed that these trends are the motive behind variant in persona dynamics.

some of the proponents of trait theories are Hans Eysenck, Raymond B, Cattell, Robert McCrae, and Paul Costa.

Hans Eysenck counseled three temperamental dimensions of persona such as

introversion- extroversion
emotional balance-neuroticism
Psychoticism- normalcy

Those dimensions are decided through biological elements and as a consequence Eysenck's concept is primarily based on genetic influences. He believed that we all possess sure pre-disposed behavioral developments that build up our unique selves.

any other splendid principle based on psychological trends became given with the aid of R.B. Cattell.

The 16 persona elements questionnaire or the 16PF check is a self-file character test that became advanced by using R.B Cattell and Mead in 1949.

This check provides a comprehensive degree of ordinary character and also can be utilized by clinicians to diagnose psychiatric problems for applicable therapy and intervention.

till now, the 16PF test has passed through 4 revisions (1956, 1962, 1968, and 1993). R.B Cattell diagnosed sixteen personality factors or dimensions based totally on his research on component evaluation. those 16

factors are as follows:

warmth
Reasoning
Emotional stability

Dominance
Liveliness
Rule attention
Social boldness
Sensitivity
Vigilance
Abstractedness
Apprehension
privateness
Openness to alternate
Self reliance
tension
Perfectionism

The 16PF check consists of 164 items or statements that degree the above sixteen variables or developments that describe human nature.
it's miles based totally on a 5-factor scale and is extensively used in career counseling and different psychiatric intervention applications.

Robert McCrae and Paul Costa's pioneering work on large 5 personality developments have become the hallmark in trait theory.

Humanistic technique

This technique focuses on the 'complete' person and refers to the distinctiveness of 1's personality.

The idea says that all people are born with sure excellent qualities that need to be advanced over time. this may assist to shape a nice persona.

The humanistic technique turned into propounded through Carl Rogers and Abraham Maslow. both these theorists have put emphasis on self-cognizance, free will, and personal boom.

This character theory makes a speciality of the nice side of human nature and tells you approximately how you could expand your key capabilities to increase an all-rounded character.

Abraham Maslow's theory

Abraham Maslow stated that humans are guided by means of a hierarchy of needs, of which the primary wishes and protection wishes come first.

once the character is able to meet those desires nicely, they circulate directly to the want for romance and belongingness.

At last, it's time for self-actualization wherein the character strives to obtain his/her full ability. This level refers to self-boom and becoming who you really want to be.

The humanistic idea of persona emphasizes the truth that humans attempt to meet what they are proper at. It enables them to perceive their areas of strengths and weaknesses.

whilst you do matters in the nice feasible manner, you are driven toward excellence. This excellence makes you a self-actualized character.

you have got realized your real capacity and what you're able to doing in fact.

Abraham Maslow also mentioned that self-actualized people are self-aware, reality-oriented, and prefer to do their exceptional always.

They may be accepting of what can not be changed. consequently, a self-actualized person is aware of how to adapt and alter to their environment fully.

The theory of self-actualization views human beings as satisfied, self-inspired kinds who're driven by using passion and growth.

Carl Rogers's principle

Carl Rogers considered a person as a entire 'whole'.

Carl Rogers viewed someone as a complete 'whole'. He said that persona isn't always piecemeal through nature. We need to study the character as a whole bundle.

by means of this Rogers in 1959 got here up with his humanistic viewpoint referred to as the 'humans-centric principle of persona."

This principle says that so one can develop and self-actualize; a person wishes an surroundings that may provide openness, genuineness, and popularity.

He noted the role of the immediately environment within the improvement of character.

Rogers stated that we're all born with certain abilties but we need a proper and actual environment to develop and thrive. Then best, our potential will grow the manner it should.

moreover, Rogers brought that three important elements cross into building your personality. they may be-

Genuineness – be who you're and stay open to new studies

attractiveness – whilst you'll be prevalent for who you're, you'll be self-prompted to carry out at your excellent potential. This concept became defined through Rogers as unconditional high-quality regard.

Empathy – all of us need to be heard and understood. that is a number one emotional want that wishes to be fulfilled as a way to emerge as a properly-rounded man or woman.

accordingly, the humanistic technique of Carl Rogers and Abraham Maslow defined persona as a dynamic system of interplay among the 'self' and the surroundings.

The humanistic idea emphasised on real goodness that we all have. people are by nature innovative and feature a lot ability. but that allows you to grow, they want a proper surroundings to thrive.

simply because the plant wishes sunlight, water, and right climatic situations to thrive, we additionally want a right environment to meet our complete capacity.

Rogers tried to formulate an constructive technique to character development, defying the pessimistic outlook of the psychoanalytic technique.

Social cognitive method to personality

The social cognitive concept of character says that your personality is stimulated by way of three elements. they are cognitive features, private characteristics, and the environment or situation you're in.

It puts emphasis on commentary as a way of belief and getting to know. This idea turned into proposed through Albert Bandura in 1960.

The concept is likewise referred to as social studying principle and is one of the extensively customary theories of social psychology.

Albert Bandura proposed the significance of conscious mind, ideals, and self-efficacy in shaping one's persona.

Behaviorist idea of character

This principle became given via B.F. Skinner. It says that character is fashioned through one's interplay with the surroundings.

more exactly, the manner you behave on your daily existence is largely depending on the outside stimulus producing it.

Your mutual interaction with the environment determines the behavior and thereby shapes your innate nature.

The principle emphasised the fact that an person will act in certain ways if the stimulus is strong enough to elicit a particular behavioral reaction.

for example: if you are stuck up in a site visitors snarl for a good deal more time than typical, you can sense pissed off, agitated, or irritable.

here, the stimulus (traffic) is inflicting you to act in certain unique approaches, although undesirable ones.

In most cases, your behavior response remains strong and constant in times, whilst the arousing stimulus is running in a comparable style.

if you are indignant-prone or now not someone who loves to look ahead to a long time, you'll always show the identical level of restlessness and irritability in trying times.

The behaviorist principle is also known as the studying-conditioning idea of persona. as a result, the environment performs a essential position in shaping one's character.

types of character in Psychology
numerous theories were evolved to recognize the distinctive persona kinds. Hippocrates, a Greek medical doctor in 370 BC defined human beings on the idea of four temperaments.

this is the primary and the oldest category of persona kinds, wherein Hippocrates explained human conduct and persona dynamics on the idea of body fluids.

This concept is also called the four temperament idea. The sorts are:

four temperament principle

1. Sanguine

those people are talkative, proactive, socially engaged, and overly enthusiastic.

they are outgoing, like to be a part of the group, and can easily have interaction in chance-taking behaviors due to the fact they may be formidable and rarely possess the concern element.

2. Choleric

they're extrovert sorts who are unbiased, ambitious, and intention-orientated. considering that they own a dominant persona, they usually steal the show in social setups.

humans like them because they are assertive, ambitious however hate to get right into a courting with them due to their quick mood, violence, and vengeance.

three. Melancholic

these human beings are logical and analytical. people with a melancholic nature are deep thinkers.

they're introverts and reserved via nature. typically, they may be considerate but anxious–susceptible as properly. they are perfectionists and don't want to make errors.

four. Phlegmatic

people of this type are at ease, peaceful, and easy-going. they are sympathetic, type, and less harassed.

then again, humans with this form of temperament are patient, reasonable, and considerate and continue to be consistent in their wondering and movements.

Luis Amarel's category of personality sorts

we all love taking personality tests that may monitor our innate nature. however specialists in the discipline say that personality runs in a continuum.

We cannot categorically belong to just one kind because personality is formed via both heredity and environmental factors.

A latest look at posted in Nature Human conduct famous that there are 4 fundamental persona sorts.

people belong to one of the four types depending at the 5 huge character developments of openness to revel in, agreeableness, extraversion, neuroticism, and contentiousness. they're:

1. common

average human beings are usually agreeable however they may be typically nerve-racking. so that they score high in neuroticism and coffee in extraversion and openness.

2. Reserved

they're emotionally strong, agreeable, and introverted. They choose to preserve things to themselves.

3. function model

The human beings belonging to this category are suitable leaders. they're social, proactive, and outspoken. They can be based due to their high self belief.

four. Self-focused

those individuals lack openness and are less conscientious in nature. They reflect onconsideration on themselves, frequently lack gratitude and enough compassion to build wholesome humane ties.

Carl Jung's character typology and sixteen character concept

Carl Jung, a Swiss psychiatrist proposed that persona is not a random manifestation of what a person truely is.

alternatively it's far the end result of the cognitive possibilities that one chooses to perceive facts and take decisive movements in life.

with out a great deal ado, he further delivered that the man or woman variations among people are a result of these useful differences.

In 1921, Carl Jung's well-known book "mental kinds" defined the fundamental cognitive capabilities that determine someone's character.

later on, at some point of world war 11, Katherine Briggs and Isabel Myers became interested by reading the fundamental theory of Carl Jung.

After numerous mental research, they formulated the idea of sixteen personality types that ultimately have become the backdrop of the MBTI persona take a look at.

these days, this persona assessment device is the most widely used globally due to its precise and intricate descriptions of character styles.

The Enneagram model

The Enneagram version is a character typology that describes 9 varieties of personalities which might be intently connected with each different.

This version explains character in terms of core motives and values that make you a unique being.

The Enneagram character typing explains the simple fears and goals of 9 special character styles. It shows how the kinds are interconnected in phrases of strain and protection stages.

in addition, it also explains the fundamentals of human nature and predictable conduct styles in instances of adversities.

psychological information approximately persona

Your character shapes your whole 'being'. It sincerely makes you who you're in front of others. Your character impacts each and each small thing of your lifestyles.

It determines the manner you relate on your buddies and own family, how you are making selections in life, the way you pick out your career and lifestyles dreams, and so forth.

persona is fascinating as well as elusive. it's far complex yet can be measured via psychological assessments and research gear.

In exploring this situation, persona psychologists have recognized certain key data that could have an impact on your personality in popular.

1. Does your start order have an effect on character?

A commonplace stereotype that prevails is that delivery order impacts your personality type. it's been assumed that if you are a firstborn, you'll be accountable, dependable, relatively bossy, and nerd.

but, in case you are the second born, you'll be greater easygoing and spontaneous in your outlook closer to existence.

there's no difficult proof to signify this persona fact as proper. Researchers are nonetheless trying to find the truth of this biased proposition.

numerous pieces of studies show that start order does no longer influence personality and in addition investigations are had to help the proposition.

2. Is your character fairly strong and regular additional time?

Do you observed your persona can alternate consistent with the scenario you are in? or you accept as true with that it is extra or much less stable for the duration of the lifetime

several research findings have proven that your key persona developments stay solid and regular no matter age, social conditions, or another trade that can happen on your lifetime.

Paul T. Costa Jr., the pioneer of the five-element version of persona tendencies, mentioned that as we age our social roles and private duties trade.

however, it doesn't imply that you emerge as any individual else on your attitudes and behavior.

He in addition added that 3 key matters trade over the years, together with openness to experience, friendliness, and anxiety tiers.

personality remains solid and what modifications are the behavior, way of life, roles, and problems that depend the maximum to your existence.

possibly, you can have a wrong perception that your character has modified.

3. Are personality developments related to certain illnesses?

any other query that got here to the scene is, can your character have an effect on your bodily and intellectual well-being?

Are you willing closer to growing sure intellectual sicknesses if you have certain personality trends?

for decades, people believed that aggression; hostility can cause improved blood strain and can impact heart health.

Then, shy and inhibited people suffer from loneliness, low 6ba8f6984f70c7ac4038c462a50eeca3, and depression.

character can also affect a person's popular well-being via altering the manner they assume, experience, or act in certain conditions.

it is probable that the prevalence of bodily and mental sicknesses is dependent on many different causal factors and no longer best persona alone.

4. Are your personal alternatives determined by means of your character?

you may be amazed to recognise that your private possibilities and picks may be prompted by using your personality kind.

Your choice of buddies, the food you want, the seasons that are your favorites is all encouraged by way of your character.

whether you agree with it or no longer, your wellknown outlook closer to life, career, aim-orientation, life-style choices are all constructed up round your personality.

Even your choice of track additionally tells lots about your personality.

5. Do you watched optimists can stay longer and may have a higher high-quality of existence?
research findings have advised that if you have an optimistic lifestyle, your first-class of lifestyles will enhance and you'll be capable of stay longer.

Optimism is a effective persona trait that determines positivity and true intellectual fitness.

It additionally indicates your excellent mind country and well-rounded persona this is growth-oriented and much less worrying.

but, it has also been located that pessimists have decrease durability. They be afflicted by irrational mind and tension. possibly their satisfactory of existence is poorer than the optimists.

6. are you able to read a person's face and understand their character?
You must be thinking whether it's far absolutely feasible to recognize a person's character from their facial expressions. The truth is you can to a positive extent.

in case you read human beings's faces and expressions, you'll be capable of know approximately their likes and dislikes, intentions, and lots greater. frame language and non-verbal communication abilties inform loads approximately your persona.

it has been determined that men with large noses, small eyes, and frowned brows commonly have quick-term relationships.

They appear conceited and too orderly of their approach closer to lifestyles that others won't like.

however, women who're overly showy and horny can attract guys higher than people who are reserved and conservative.

frequently, you need to have visible that humans with a nice personality are nicely-preferred by using others. A smiling face has the strength to attract many humans toward it.

persona refers back to the long-standing tendencies and styles that propel people to constantly assume, sense, and behave in specific methods. Our character is what makes us unique individuals. all and sundry has an idiosyncratic pattern of enduring, lengthy-term traits and a way in which he or she interacts with different individuals and the sector round them. Our personalities are idea to be long time, strong, and no longer without difficulty changed. The word persona comes from the Latin word personality. inside the historical world, a personality was a masks worn by means of an actor. whilst we tend to think of a mask as being worn to conceal one's identification, the theatrical mask become originally used to either represent or project a specific character trait of a individual ([link]).

happy, sad, impatient, shy, fearful, curious, helpful. What characteristics describe your character?

historic views

The concept of persona has been studied for at least 2,000 years, beginning with Hippocrates in 370 BCE (Fazeli, 2012). Hippocrates theorized that personality tendencies and human behaviors are primarily based on four separate temperaments associated with 4 fluids ("humors") of the body: choleric temperament (yellow bile from the liver), melancholic temperament (black bile from the kidneys), sanguine temperament (crimson blood from the heart), and phlegmatic temperament (white phlegm from the lungs) (Clark & Watson, 2008; Eysenck & Eysenck, 1985; Lecci & Magnavita, 2013; Noga, 2007). Centuries later, the influential Greek medical doctor and truth seeker Galen built on Hippocrates's principle, suggesting that each diseases and persona variations might be defined by using imbalances within the humors and that every person exhibits one of the 4 temperaments. as an example, the choleric character is passionate, bold, and bold; the melancholic character is reserved, nerve-racking, and unhappy; the sanguine character is completely satisfied, eager, and constructive; and the phlegmatic individual is calm, reliable, and thoughtful (Clark & Watson, 2008; Stelmack & Stalikas, 1991). Galen's idea become usual for over 1,000 years and endured to be popular through the middle a long time.

In 1780, Franz Gall, a German physician, proposed that the distances among bumps on the cranium screen someone's persona traits, man or woman, and mental capabilities ([link]). in keeping with Gall, measuring those distances found out the sizes of the brain areas underneath, offering facts that could be used to decide whether or not someone turned into pleasant, prideful, murderous, type, precise with languages, and so on. initially, phrenology become very popular; but, it became soon discredited for lack of empirical help and has long been relegated to the repute of pseudoscience (Fancher, 1979).

The pseudoscience of measuring the areas of a person's skull is referred to as phrenology.

(a) Gall developed a chart that depicted which areas of the cranium corresponded to unique personality traits or traits (Hothersall, 1995).

(b) An 1825 lithograph depicts Gall analyzing the skull of a younger woman. (credit b: change of labor by using Wellcome Library, London)

HUMAN PSYCHOLOGY THROUGH BIOLOGY

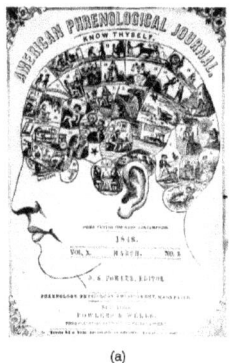

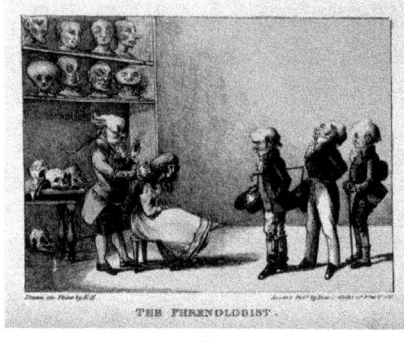

(a) (b)

above photograph indicates the duvet of the american Phrenological magazine circa 1848. throughout the pinnacle it reads: "American Phrenological journal." under that it says "realize thyself." underneath that could be a image of a human head facing left, with many snap shots comprising the region wherein the brain is. underneath the individual's ear it says "home truths for home consumption." The traces beneath that study: "1848," "Vol. X, March, No. three," "O.S. Fowler, Editor," "Phrenology, body structure, Physiognomy, Magnetism," "big apple," "Fowlers and Wells," "Phrenological cupboard, 131 Nassau-street," and "phrases $1 a yr, always earlier. Ten cts. a number." image B shows a broadcast cool animated film of a person in a chair with another person behind. There are three other human beings in the room, and the wall is adorned with diverse skulls. below the image it reads: "Drawn on Stone by using E.H," and "The Phrenologist."

In the centuries after Galen, different researchers contributed to the development of his four primary temperament kinds, maximum prominently Immanuel

Kant (in the 18th century) and psychologist Wilhelm Wundt (inside the nineteenth century) (Eysenck, 2009; Stelmack & Stalikas, 1991; Wundt, 1874/1886) ([link]). Kant agreed with Galen that everyone might be looked after into one of the four temperaments and that there was no overlap among the four classes (Eysenck, 2009). He developed a list of developments that might be used to describe the personality of someone from each of the 4 temperaments. but, Wundt suggested that a higher description of character can be accomplished the use of

major axes: emotional/nonemotional and changeable/unchangeable. the first axis separated strong from susceptible emotions (the melancholic and choleric temperaments from the phlegmatic and sanguine). the second axis divided the changeable temperaments (choleric and sanguine) from the unchangeable ones (melancholic and phlegmatic) (Eysenck, 2009).

advanced from Galen's idea of the four temperaments, Kant proposed trait phrases to describe each temperament. Wundt later recommended the association of the tendencies on two major axes.

A circle is split vertically and horizontally into four sections by way of lines with arrows at the ends. Clockwise from the top, the arrows are labeled "strong feelings," "Changeable Temperaments," "weak feelings," and "Unchangeable Temperaments." The arcs around the perimeter of the circle, clockwise beginning with the pinnacle proper section are categorised "Choleric," "Sanguine," "Phlegmatic," and "Melancholic." The sections inside each arc include descriptive phrases. inside the Choleric arc are the phrases "excitable, egocentric, exhibitionist, impulsive, histrionic, and active." in the Sanguine arc are the phrases "playful, easygoing, sociable, carefree, hopeful, and contented." within the Phlegmatic arc are the words "affordable, principled, managed, continual, steadfast, and calm." within the Melancholic arc are the phrases "tense, worried, sad, suspicious, extreme, and considerate."

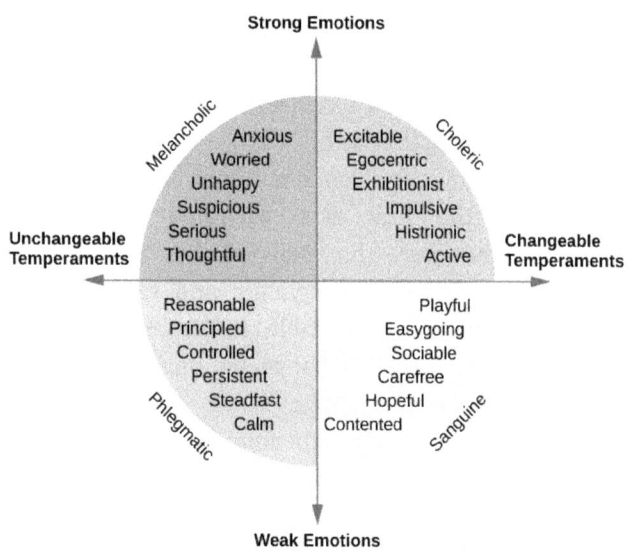

Sigmund Freud's psychodynamic attitude of personality turned into the first comprehensive principle of persona, explaining a huge variety of each regular and strange behaviors. in line with Freud, subconscious drives encouraged by using sex and aggression, in conjunction with early life sexuality, are the forces that have an impact on our character. Freud attracted many fans who modified his ideas to create new theories about persona. these theorists, called neo-Freudians, commonly agreed with Freud that early life studies remember, however they reduced the emphasis on sex and centered extra at the social surroundings and outcomes of lifestyle on persona. The angle of personality proposed via Freud and his followers turned into the dominant concept of personality for the first 1/2 of the 20 th century.

other foremost theories then emerged, which include the gaining knowledge of, humanistic, organic, evolutionary, trait, and cultural views. in this chapter, we are able to discover those numerous perspectives on persona in depth.

What's personality Psychology?
have you ever taken a character quiz? The effects may tell you which you're the middle of attention or an ENTJ. human beings describe personalities in one of a kind ways and scientists nevertheless have quite a few questions on how our personalities influence our actions and make us who we are. in case you've ever been curious about what this word truly means, get comfy. permit's speak approximately character.

what is character?

There are a whole lot of approaches to define character. In reality, top personality psychologist Feist and Feist say this: "even though no unmarried definition is suitable to all personality theorists, we are able to say that persona is a pattern of fantastically permanent traits and precise traits that provide both consistency and individuality to a person's conduct."

allow's zoom in and focus on one phrase right here: developments. know this word in and out. It's the center of personality psychology.

tendencies are specific characteristics that impact our conduct. those traits usually set us aside from other humans. as an instance, you can describe yourself as a

"respectful" or "authentic" individual. those are
Character trends.
before we talk about the "massive 5" character tendencies, it's vital to remember the fact that tendencies have an impact on our behavior...they don't dictate it. when you are a deferential person, you will be inclined to be respectful to humans round you. but you could act outside of these traits due to...properly, clearly anything. A sick day, a awful records with a person, or nervousness might also purpose you to behave out of individual.

that is one of the reasons why developments are normally measured on a scale.

How does personality "work"?
How will we show those trends? via psychological mechanisms. recollect this time period, because it comes up nearly just as regularly as "traits" does.

mental mechanisms are like trends, except they're the strategies of personality.

This process has three elements: input, decision rules, and output. Our developments decide the output (and every now and then, what kind of enter we come upon in the first place.)

permit's say you're a brave person. The "enter" is a dangerous state of affairs. you've got guidelines and make selections on a way to act. The "output" is to face the danger. in case you are not a brave man or woman, your output will is probably fleeing the scene.

allow's go over these two once more: developments are characteristics, and are the individual words that we use to describe human beings. Mechanisms are strategies that people observe based totally on these traits.

3 levels of character analysis

How do psychologists measure personality?
For the answer, we look to Kluckhohn and Murray. In 1953, they posted personality in Nature, Society, and tradition. within the book, they are saying that
"each man is in sure respects
like any different guys,
like some other men,
like no different guy."
think about it.

There are time-honored developments and mechanisms that make humans unique to different species. think about Maslow's hierarchy of desires.
we all belong to at least one big institution: the human race. however inside our species, we separate ourselves into other corporations. Introverts. americans. "Messy human beings." "move-getters." those smaller corporations share persona tendencies.
at the most specific level, we all have matters that make us specific. perhaps you've got a "unique expertise" a peculiar behavior that confuses your pals. conduct, workouts, and emotional connections to humans or things may additionally make us one-of-a-kind from the person subsequent to us.
you are like all different humans:
you've got a need to belong
You need a sense of purpose
You tear up if I smack your nose (nasociliary nerve reflex)
you are like a few other human beings:
you are introverted
you are precise at doing all your taxes
You wince whilst you watch a person provide themselves a papercut
you're like no other humans:

you like doing all of your taxes
you intend your days and set dreams that no person else does
You cry if I display you an image of your deceased family member

those similarities and variations don't simply provide us a set to belong to. they're the cornerstone of predicting behavior. As you could see, a number of persona is understanding the similarities and differences of people and how they act.

wherein does personality come from?
you would possibly hear circle of relatives members inform you which you have a similar persona on your mother or your father. Does this mean our personality is inherited? How do we undertake the character trends that make us like every other humans, like a few different human beings, and like no different human beings?

There are lots of special factors from this. Genetics is one, however surroundings, stories, and tendencies may additionally provide an explanation for in which we get our character trends. One exciting concept is that we co-create our personalities and the personalities of the human beings we engage with.

right here are a few not unusual character Theories:
Trait idea
Behavioral principle
Humanistic theory
organic idea
Psychoanalytic idea

now not all personality trends are tremendous, but we generally opt for the fine. We have a tendency to praise human beings that show wonderful tendencies like being respectful or proper. If a person kind, we "praise" them by means of being type again.

Already, you might find some arguments towards this idea. not anyone characterizes the equal developments to be superb or negative. someone may think that respectfulness is a top-tier character trait. a person else who has a whole lot of distrust in authority or "the machine" may also view respectfulness as a terrible character trait. How do humans form their personalities when they're both rewarded and chastised for the same trait?

these are a number of the questions that psychologists are seeking to answer!

Why is it essential?

however there are many extra questions that could handiest be responded with studies and the take a look at of character psychology. here are a number of the massive ones:

Freedom vs Determinism:

will we pick our conduct? are we able to exchange it if we wanted to?

Hereditary vs environment:

where do our persona developments come from? Nature or nurture?

particular or time-honored:

some psychologists say human beings are first-rate precise, whilst others agree we're fairly universally the same. So...what are we?

Proactive or Reactive:

can we act on our own initiative... or absolutely react to stimuli?

Why are persona psychologists so decided to reply these questions?

they can use it to predict future conduct.

if you had the capacity to are expecting who changed into

on the song to becoming a criminal, wouldn't you need to steer them in a exclusive path and probable shop a person's existence?

let's look at Ted Bundy's character. Psychologists normally agree that he had a "conventional sociopathic persona." but wherein did it come from?

a few humans say he started out forming a sociopathic character while he changed into rejected through the affection of his life. Others accept as true with his failure to become a lawyer sparked these personality developments. other psychologists trace the root of his personality to the shame of in no way understanding his start dad and mom.

His sociopathic behaviors did begin early. He became a pyromaniac and had tortured animals as a child. some psychologists factor to his early mattress-wetting as a signal that he became at the track to turning into a sociopath. these 3 form the sociopath personality.

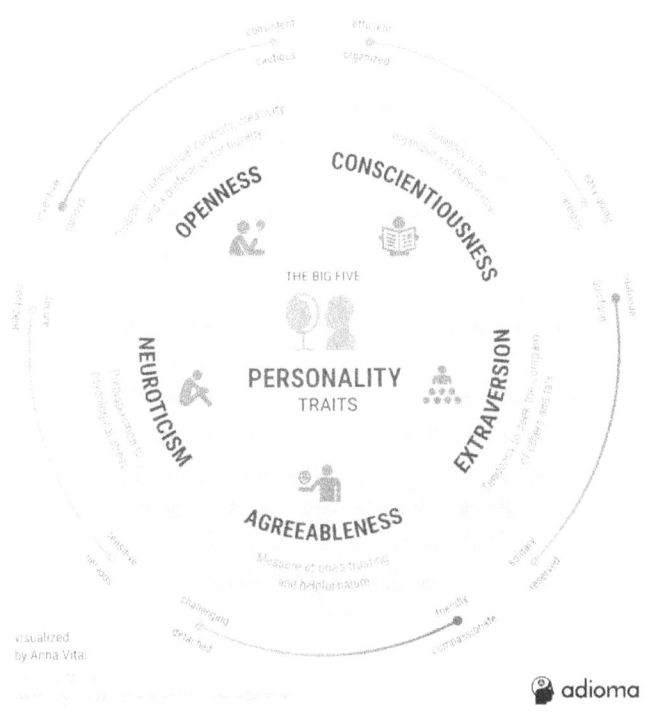

VI
SPIRITUAL PSYCHOLOGY : WHAT IS MY RELATIOSHIP WITH MYSELF

What is Spiritual Psychology?

Spiritual psychology is also referred to as Transpersonal Psychology and is a branch of psychology that is growing rapidly. Many people are concentrating on exploring the mind and it's relationship to spirituality. Whether it's to answer their own personal questions, or to pursue as a career.

In this article, we'll explain what spiritual psychology is, what spiritual psychologists do for a living, and take a look at some courses that are on offer for those of you who would like to explore this topic more. These courses range from non-accredited – factual introductions, right up to post-graduate certifications.

So, if you are interested in psychology and want to see how this branch of science can be explored in combination with our spiritual journey's, this article will answer any questions you may have.

Transpersonal psychology is the study and cultivation of the highest and most transformative human values and potentials—individual, communal, and global—that reflect the mystery and interconnectedness of life, including our human journey within the cosmos.

What is Spiritual Psychology?

As we've already discussed, spiritual psychology is also known as transpersonal psychology and is a "school" of psychology that combines the spiritual and transcendent aspects of the human experience, within the framework of modern psychology.

Transpersonal experiences are defined as "experiences in which the sense of identity or self extends beyond (trans) the individual or personal to encompass wider aspects of humankind, life, psyche or cosmos."

When someone is studying spiritual psychology they analyze several areas including:

Spiritual self-development
Self beyond the ego
Peak experiences
Mystical experiences
Systemic trance
Spiritual crises
Spiritual evolution
Religious conversion
Altered states of consciousness
Spiritual practices
and other expanded experiences of living
Spiritual psychology has made many important discoveries in the academic field and continues to further understand the spiritual aspects of the human experience.

Transpersonal Education

Transpersonal education literally means 'Drawing out from behind the mask'. It is related to transpersonal psychology and can be best described by understanding Plato's teaching that:

"The power and capacity for learning exists in the soul already."

He further goes on to state that true education can only occur when

"the whole soul...turned from the world of becoming into that of being, and learn[ed] by degrees to endure the sight of being, and of the brightest and best of being, or in other words, the good."

When we combine Plato's teachings with the literal meaning of transpersonal education, we can surmise that the purpose of transpersonal education is:

The drawing out of the soul – the essential core of ones nature – from behind the obscuring mask of ego.

This is important to note when we are trying to understand what spiritual psychology is and why it is the crux of all we do, particularly when examining our own spiritual journeys.

Becoming a Spiritual Psychologist

Many people are interested in becoming career spiritual psychologists, but what do they do and how can you become one? As spiritual psychology is a branch of psychology, most people would earn their degree in psychology before branching off at post-graduate level. However, there are degrees that focus on this subject specifically.

If you have earned accreditation and are certified for practice, you can use spiritual psychology in counselling sessions. However, many people who have studied spiritual psychology go on to become entrepreneurs, life coaches, professional speakers, authors, and a wide range of other vocations.

To help you understand this in more detail we'll take a look at what spiritual psychologists do and some of the courses that are out there to help you embark on a career in spiritual psychology.

What do Spiritual Psychologists Do?

Spiritual psychology has existed in some form for thousands of years though it has become its own branch of study in more recent times. The spiritual psychologists whose work set the stage for future generations include William James, Carl Jung, Roberto Assagioli and Abraham Maslow.

In 1969, Abraham Maslow and others issued the first publication of the Journal of Transpersonal Psychology, which is the leading academic journal in the field. Spiritual psychologists can work as researchers, understanding how the mind works from a spiritual point of view and improving our understanding of psychology and mental health at the same time.

However, many spiritual psychologists don't work in an academic setting. Many work as entrepreneurs, life coaches, professional speakers, and authors. As transpersonal psychology allows us to greater understand the self and the many human experiences we undergo, the study of the subject often gives people the confidence to understand their life purpose and pursue a career in it.

Many who have seen the power of understanding the self to this degree, feel a responsibility to share this knowledge with others, allowing them to pursue their dreams. These people tend to work as life coaches, speakers, and authors.

As you can see, the type of work can vary. Just because you study spiritual psychology doesn't mean you have to work as a psychologist – many don't! What it does however is help us to make sense of some of life's biggest questions and identify that which we are meant to be doing.

If you're interested in exploring spiritual psychology in more depth, the following courses will help depending on the level you want to get to.

Courses in Spiritual Psychology
Soul-Centered Living I: Foundations in Spiritual Psychology – University of Santa Monica

This is a 10-month certificate program that is split up with in-person lessons held one weekend per month and online learning. This course is designed to give you an introduction into spiritual psychology and is a good foundation for anyone who's still not 100% certain whether to pursue as a career or just an interest.

In case you appearance up the phrase "psyche" in the dictionary, you may find "breath, principle of existence, Soul." however if you look up "psychology," you may locate "the technological know-how of mind and conduct." by some means, in the translation from essence to exercise, the most critical factor of "psyche" has been misplaced. at the university of Santa Monica, we understand our venture as reintegrating the religious size again into the essence of an real psychological inquiry. it's far this reintegration that evokes the emergence of a spiritual Psychology.

Non secular Psychology is the take a look at and exercise of the artwork and technological know-how of aware Awakening. To engage in this genre, we must begin by way of distinguishing the essence of human evolution—what does it imply to adapt? In short, it method studying the way to identify, recognize, and navigate efficiently within the Context of spiritual reality. practically, it approach mastering how to give up—or allow move of—some thing that disturbs one's peace. It additionally method sacrificing our illusions of separation. basically, this "surrendering" and "sacrificing" is work which can and has been called "healing," which includes healing on the physical, intellectual, and emotional degrees in carrier to the deeper revelation of who we genuinely are as Loving, peaceful, Compassionate, and completely happy beings. We check with this degree of recognition as the actual Self.

placed every other way, religious Psychology is a generation that empowers students to transform their ordinary existence experiences into rungs at the ladder of religious Awakening. This educational method consequences in college students experiencing more connection with who they're, their existence's motive, and superior stages of achievement and success. This empowers them to make a significant contribution of their world.

Why non secular Psychology ... and Why Now?
Trade is taking vicinity at an extraordinary pace on our planet. the nature of this alteration is historically unique from something we have formerly experienced. due to the tremendous detrimental electricity now available, the arena is being challenged to discover ways to get alongside or pay the consequences, which might be extraordinarily high. in addition, since the pace of change is really accelerating, we do now not seem to have the luxury of time to waste.

From within the Context of non secular Psychology, the only manner to really promote peace is for there to be extra non violent individuals residing in the international. on this Context, it is correct to mention that as human beings evolve spiritually, they naturally end up more non violent. it's also actual that greater peace is an character phenomenon. The greater one learns to surrender anything they revel in inside themselves that disturbs their peace, the extra peaceful they grow to be. religious Psychology at USM is a response to this international want. The curriculum is uniquely designed for college students to examine the capabilities of problem resolution. (An problem is something that disturbs your peace.) We need to learn how to not most effective include who we are as religious beings having a human revel in but additionally use that recognition as a basis for "recuperation." as the evolutionary tide is growing and huge numbers of human beings are beginning to awaken to the notice that they may be, in fact, Divine Beings having a human enjoy, the ideas and Practices of spiritual Psychology provide each a context and equipment for residing into that focus in everyday existence.

And, with the aid of the way, as we circulate forward, those very same talents could be precisely the equal ones on the way to be quite valued as we rework into a extra peaceful, surprisingly globalized global.

non secular Psychology is a blend science & spirituality that expands on conventional Psychology by spotting that someone has 4 degrees requiring healing interest.

bodily - what you do

intellectual - what you agree with

Emotional - what you experience

actual Self - ability for pleasure, reputation, and self-compassion

traditional Psychology addresses someone at three stages; physical, mental and emotional. these 3 stages, the bedrock of traditional therapy, are all based totally on impermanence. What you do to your life (physical), what you believe you studied and agree with (mental) and what you sense (emotional). All three levels will continuously exchange all through life as you grow, mature, analyze and evolve.

The Fourth stage is who you are at your middle. At this level you're able to enjoy unconditional love, concord, peace, pleasure and oneness with our universe, acceptance of others, and compassion for your self. no longer coincidentally, with a weakened connection to this level, lifestyles can feel empty, unnecessary, unsatisfying, and hopeless. issues including despair, discontent, anxiety, depression, self loathing and a number of different unsettling stories, such as our very will to stay, stand up. frequently we discover substances or addictive/ unfavourable behaviors as brief remedy, others just live with the ever gift feeling of "there must be more". A successful course of remedy have to contain all 4 degrees, to resolve underlying middle issues for the closing time and assist you to have your life returned.

Imagine how distinct life could be if your foundation became love and guide for your self in place of unhappiness, despair, tension, anger, embarrassment, hopelessness and resentment of your beyond? Very specific. it is easy to mention however to attain trade like this, you may need to spend money on a few learning and in a few un-mastering.

On the Clearing, we use religious Psychology as our modality to cope with the underlying center issues that have lifestyles so out of stability. assume an intellectually engaging, thrilling and a success month of gaining knowledge of the way to remedy the issues creating the behaviors which might be keeping you lower back from the lifestyles you want.

The usage of the skills taught on the Clearing, you may learn how to bring all levels of your life into stability. when stability is performed, lifestyles becomes non violent, comfortable and harmonious. fundamental recovery takes area, and individuals can acquire peace and stay their lives to their fullest capacity.

Will your lifestyles ever emerge as out of balance once more? sure, it's going to. however, because you have found out to use those profound competencies and strategies, you are now uniquely organized and empowered to address and clear up each new trouble that may arise on your life with grace and ease.

Carl Jung, the Swiss psychiatrist who founded analytical psychology, began the concept method that brought about non secular Psychology as we realize it these days.

Jung became a protégé of Sigmund Freud inside the early 20th century, but, as Jung began to develop his paintings with the "collective subconscious," he and Freud went their separate approaches. Roberto Assagioli, the founding father of a mental method known as psychosynthesis, additionally found Freud's theories to be limiting.

Freud maintained that people revel in life on three degrees: bodily, intellectual and emotional. Jung and Assogioli had been pioneers in spotting a fourth degree, the genuine self degree.

A extensive range of psychologists and concept leaders have contributed to this area such as Carl Rogers, Albert Ellis, Fritz Perls, William Glasser, Eric Erickson, Dr. Wayne Dyer, Carolyn Myss, Joan Borysendko, Gary Zukav, Echart Tolle, Drs. Ron and Mary Hulnick, Juan Miguel Ruiz, John Bradshaw, Louis Hay and many others.

spiritual Psychology Counseling strategies

Counseling strategies are techniques that a counselor makes use of to facilitate a player in uncovering and healing core problems. the main strategies utilized in our application include:

character-focused remedy

when human beings sense listened to, reputable and cherished, they're able to tap into their own innate resources to heal.

Rational Emotive therapy (RET)

if you want to authentically exchange what we're thinking and believing, we want to have a look at how we are judging the activities in our lives and the underlying guidelines we have created. As we end up aware of how and why we are doing this, profound exchange in our mind and beliefs can take location.

Gestalt remedy

when a bad emotional enjoy takes vicinity, we need to procedure the feelings fully to be able to examine and grow from the enjoy.

Developmental Psychology

we all increase emotionally in predictable age ranges. disturbing emotional studies can preserve us from fully developing emotionally. we can clear up this through operating with the disturbing occasion in a secure, loving surroundings.

Reality therapy (Behavioral remedy)

intellectual infection is visible as resulting in defective behavioral styles. The aim is creating a extra purposeful plan of action and to have the ability to interrupt this plan down into attainable pieces.

family systems

that is a procedure of analyzing hereditary and multi-generational proscribing patterns. members benefit an expertise of the circle of relatives dynamics which might be alive inside them. This awareness ends in trouble identification, expertise and attractiveness with the intention of turning into one's personal character and cozy being who they without a doubt are.

what is religious Psychology?

Ron: We're often requested, "properly, simply what is non secular Psychology?" And you recognize, if you appearance up the phrase psyche inside the dictionary you're going to see the definition being "Breath of lifestyles; Soul." And if you appearance up the word psychology in a dictionary you're going to peer "the technology of mind and behavior." one way or the other breath and soul got converted into the technology of thoughts and behavior. when we name it religious Psychology we're in reality just bringing it back to the roots of what it changed into when it become first stimulated in the world. Psychotherapy truly is all about the care of the soul. At USM, we take that one step in addition. I'd say it might be more approximately—oh, I'll call it the soul's awakening journey. That's what we do at USM.

Mary: And the way that we define non secular Psychology is that it's miles the artwork and exercise of aware awakening; awakening into the notice of who we virtually are. There are three important questions: the primary question, "Who am I?" and the second query, "Why am I here—what's my motive?" and the 0.33 question, "How am i able to make a greater meaningful contribution; how am i able to someway experience that my life has cost and cause, and that my being here is absolutely making a difference?"

Ron: this is specifically critical in recent times for younger humans. We're locating an increasing number of younger people are coming to USM—due to the fact they have got this internal knowing that there must be greater to existence than what we're seeing around on earth at the moment. There's only a deeper level of living that's to be had to them. And they may be longing for, oh, I'll call it a sense of freedom to discover that which they may be experiencing within themselves. We see this an increasing number of and greater as time goes on.

you are an inherently loving being who's using a human revel in for purposes of your non secular growth. reflect onconsideration on that, getting to know the validity of that experientially. "what's my motive?" getting to know the way to solution that query experientially by means of really doing things inside the global where you have the experience of being used in a completely, very high-quality and uplifting way and making a meaningful contribution to your global. if you're listening to this, you're probably aware that you may earn as plenty cash as you need, and it's no longer going to do it for you. what is going to do it for you is to recognise that you're being fulfilled thru the way that you are dwelling your lifestyles. USM allows people to step into the ones realities—and we've been doing it for over thirty years. In fact, among you and me, it's our favourite aspect to do!

The primary reason why religious psychology is relevant to scientific exercise is because thus far neither technological know-how nor philosophy has proved or disproved the life of soul and spirit, and the nature of focus stays a thriller.

Therefore, all the know-how of contemporary psychology and psychiatry could just as nicely be interpreted inside a theistic framework as within an atheistic or agnostic one. So, whilst our sufferers describe spiritual and religious stories to us, we're right now confronted with a conundrum: ought to we view those reports as statements of belief that don't have any relationship to any actual facts of existence, or

as perceptions—however subjective and partial—of real non secular realities?

This predicament is not a trivial one, but most discussions of faith and spirituality completely skip it (top notch exceptions being the ones of William James[4] and of P. Scott Richards and Allen Bergin). It's far tough to provide an explanation for this obtrusive omission, apart from to surmise that clinicians sense that the predicament may be prevented by means of adopting a running philosophy of clinical pragmatism, in step with which religion and spirituality are deemed healthful if they're adaptive sources of assist and which means, and bad if no longer. a little mirrored image, but, suggests this option to be no solution. at the same time as the motivation to be "pragmatic" can be flawlessly nicely intentioned, the problem with the stance itself is that it is able to be subtly patronizing and unempathic. Why? because superficial pragmatism is solipsistic; this is, it does no longer make one hundred and five any serious strive to narrate religious/religious beliefs and reports to any capability facts of life. to illustrate this hassle, don't forget the following medical eventualities:

1. A housewife reviews being the victim of domestic violence
2. A younger adult relates reminiscences of childhood sexual molestation
3. a person with low talks about an absent father and a rejecting mother
4. A nonpsychotic man talks about his religion in God, which he feels is maintaining him through an episode of predominant despair
5. A bereaved partner speaks of dreams and uncommon occurrences that seem to deliver a communication from her departed husband normally, in instances 1–three our first situation would be that the reported home violence, sexual abuse, and absence of nurturing in reality befell, and are greater than the made of notion systems.

And yet with instances 4 and five, many clinicians would technique such reviews as "critical religious beliefs," without thinking about whether or not they can be genuine reports of religious records. This distinction matters due to

the fact, therapeutically,
there is a massive distinction between a subtly distancing declaration including "It sounds like that is crucial to you, so

inform me greater approximately your spiritual ideals and greater empathic statements together with "sure,
I will see that simplest God is getting you through all this" or "perhaps your husband is speakme to you, so tell me greater about your non secular existence". Atheists and skeptical agnostics may additionally make
the primary sort of statement, but simplest curious agnostics and theists could make the latter statements and suggest them. Now, this isn't to indicate that theists are right and atheists or agnostics incorrect. No, the factor is virtually to show why

philosophical questions on the nature of reality can't be divorced from psychotherapy and psychiatry. Which of the healing statements above is the first-class one to make depends now not handiest on what sufferers believe, but additionally on what the nature of reality genuinely is. scientific pragmatism, which is an operationalized form of agnosticism, may additionally or may not be a sufficient model whilst working with atheistic and agnostic patients, but it risks being implicitly devaluing whilst running with folks who are theistic or maybe just religious (such as non-theistic Buddhists). for how are we able to genuinely declare to "appreciate" a consumer's religious/non secular life except we in reality preserve open the opportunity that his or her international view may also reflect correct perceptions approximately the real nature of reality? a few sufferers, as a minimum, will sense our dissimulation if we fake to be extra open minded than we genuinely are. The most effective way to avoid this pitfall of pseudo-recognize is for mental health clinicians to advantage competency in questioning about the "large question(s)" of the human situation,

what's spiritual Psychology? spiritual psychology is also known as Transpersonal Psychology and is a department of psychology this is growing hastily. Many human beings are focusing on exploring the thoughts and it's courting to spirituality. whether it's to reply their very own non-public questions, or to pursue as a profession.

This consist of providing an explanation for what non secular psychology is, what non secular psychologists do for a residing, and test a few publications which might be on offer for the ones of you who would love to explore this subject matter more. these publications range from non-approved – genuine introductions, proper as much as publish-graduate certifications.

So, in case you are inquisitive about psychology and need to peer how this branch of science may be explored in mixture with our non secular adventure's, this text will solution any questions you can have.

Transpersonal education literally means 'Drawing out from behind the mask'. it's far associated with transpersonal psychology and can be great described by knowledge Plato's coaching that:

"The power and capability for gaining knowledge of exists within the soul already."

He similarly is going directly to state that true training can simplest occur when

"the complete soul...grew to become from the arena of becoming into that of being, and research[ed] with the aid of stages to undergo the sight of being, and of the brightest and quality of being, or in different words, the best." (three) while we integrate Plato's teachings with the literal that means of transpersonal training, we will surmise that the reason of transpersonal education is:

The drawing out of the soul – the vital core of ones nature – from behind the obscuring masks of ego.

this is important to observe while we are seeking to recognize what religious psychology is and why it's far the crux of all we do, specially while analyzing our very own religious journeys.

turning into a non secular Psychologist
Many human beings are inquisitive about becoming profession non secular psychologists, however what do they do and how are you going to become one? As non secular

psychology is a department of psychology, the general public would earn their degree in psychology before branching off at publish-graduate level. but, there are ranges that target this subject particularly.

when you have earned accreditation and are licensed for practice, you could use non secular psychology in counselling classes. however, many people who've studied spiritual psychology cross directly to end up marketers, lifestyles coaches, professional speakers, authors, and a huge range of other vocations.

to help you recognize this in greater detail we'll check what spiritual psychologists do and a number of the guides that are out there that will help you embark on a career in non secular psychology.

What do non secular Psychologists Do?

religious psychology has existed in a few form for heaps of years though it has emerge as its very own branch of look at in more current instances. The religious psychologists whose paintings set the level for future generations encompass William James, Carl Jung, Roberto Assagioli and Abraham Maslow.

In 1969, Abraham Maslow and others issued the first e-book of the magazine of Transpersonal Psychology, that's the main academic magazine in the subject. non secular psychologists can work as researchers, understanding how the thoughts works from a religious point of view and improving our know-how of psychology and intellectual health at the same time.

however, many religious psychologists don't paintings in an educational putting. Many paintings as marketers, life coaches, professional audio system, and authors. As transpersonal psychology lets in us to more understand the self and the various human studies we undergo, the have a look at of the concern often gives human beings the confidence to understand their existence purpose and pursue a profession in it.

Many who've seen the electricity of knowledge the self to this diploma, experience a obligation to share this know-how with others, permitting them to pursue their desires. those people tend to work as life coaches, audio system, and authors.

HOW EXPERIMENTS ARE DONE

Most of these experiments can be executed without problems at home or at faculty. That said, you'll need to find out if you have to get approval out of your teacher or from an institutional evaluation board before getting began.

the following are a few questions you can try and answer as a part of a mental experiment:
Are human beings simply capable of "experience like someone is watching" them?
Can positive colorings improve gaining knowledge of? may want to the colour of the paper utilized in a take a look at or project have an effect on academic performance?
you may have heard teachers or college students declare that printing text on inexperienced paper facilitates students read higher or that yellow paper helps college students carry out higher on math checks.1 design an test to peer whether or not using a specific coloration of paper facilitates improve college students' rankings on math assessments.
Can colour purpose physiological reactions? carry out an experiment to decide whether or not certain colorings motive a participant's blood stress to rise or fall.
Can exclusive types of tune cause distinct physiological responses? degree the coronary heart quotes of contributors in response to various sorts of track to look if there is a distinction.
Can smelling one component whilst tasting every other effect someone's ability to detect what the meals surely is?
ought to someone's taste in song provide pointers about their personality? preceding studies has suggested that individuals who select positive kinds of tune generally tend

to exhibit comparable personality trends.2

Do action films reason humans to eat more popcorn and sweet in the course of a movie?

Do colours in reality effect moods? behavior an research to see if the colour blue makes human beings experience calm, or if the color purple leaves them feeling agitated.three

Do innovative human beings see optical illusions differently than more analytical people?

Do human beings rate individuals with flawlessly symmetrical faces as greater stunning than people with asymmetrical faces?

Do folks who use the social media web site fb show off signs of addiction?

Does eating breakfast simply assist college students do better in school? in step with some, eating breakfast could have a beneficial influence on college overall performance.four One observe determined that youngsters who ate a healthful breakfast discovered better and had greater energy than students who did not eat breakfast. in your experiment, you may examine the take a look at scores of college students who ate breakfast to people who did no longer.

Does sex have an effect on quick-time period reminiscence? you could set up an test that checks whether or not men or girls are better at remembering precise kinds of records.

How possibly are humans to comply to the evaluations of a group? This conformity experiment investigates the effect of group strain on character conduct.

How lots statistics can people store in brief-time period reminiscence? One classic experiment indicates that humans can keep among 5 to 9 items, but practice session techniques which includes chunking can notably increase memorization and don't forget.five A simple word memorization test is an super and pretty clean psychology technology honest idea.

what is the Stroop effect? The Stroop impact is a phenomenon wherein it is less complicated to say the color of a word if it suits the semantic meaning of the word. for example, if a person requested you to mention the colour of the phrase "black" that become additionally printed in black ink, it'd be less difficult to say the best colour than if it have been printed in inexperienced ink.

once you have got an idea, the next step is to examine extra approximately the way to behavior a psychology test.

explore Your pursuits

If none of the thoughts within the list above grabbed your attention, there are other methods to discover notion.

one of the simplest processes is to observe the various problems, conditions, and questions which you are dealing with for your very own existence.

you could additionally think about the matters that hobby you. begin with the aid of thinking about the subjects you've got studied in magnificence to this point that have sincerely piqued your interest. Then, whittle the list down to 2 or three essential regions within psychology that seem to hobby you the maximum.

From there, make a list of questions you have got associated with the topic. Any of those questions ought to probably function an test idea.

flip to Textbooks

Your psychology textbooks are any other exceptional source you can flip to for test thoughts. pick the chapters or sections that you find specially exciting—perhaps it's a chapter on social psychology or a section on toddler improvement.

start by surfing the experiments discussed for your e-book. Then think of how you could devise an test related to some of the questions your text asks. The reference segment behind your textbook can also function a extremely good source for additional reference fabric.

communicate to different college students

it could be beneficial to brainstorm along with your classmates to gather out of doors ideas and views. Get collectively with a set of college students and make a list of exciting thoughts, topics, or questions you have got.

The facts from your brainstorming consultation can function a foundation in your test subject matter. it is also a first-rate manner to get feedback for your own ideas and to decide if they are really worth exploring in more intensity.

examine conventional Psychology Experiments

Taking a closer study a traditional psychology test may be an remarkable way to trigger a few specific and thoughtful thoughts of your personal. to start, you can try engaging in your own model of a well-known test or maybe updating a conventional test to assess a slightly one of a kind question. You might not be capable of mirror an experiment exactly, but you can use research as a basis for suggestion.

overview the Literature

if you have a widespread concept approximately what topic you would like to test, you may need to spend a touch time doing a short literature evaluation earlier than you begin designing.

visit your college library and discover some of the satisfactory books and articles that cowl the specific subject matter you're interested in. What research has already been finished on this region? Are there any foremost questions that still want to be answered?

Tackling this step early will make the later technique of

writing the introduction in your lab file or research paper much simpler.

The experimental method includes the manipulation of variables to set up cause and impact relationships. the key capabilities are managed techniques and the random allocation of contributors into controlled and experimental corporations.

An test is an research in which a

hypothesis is scientifically tested. In an test, an unbiased variable (the purpose) is manipulated and the structured variable (the effect) is measured; any extraneous variables are managed.

a bonus is that experiments must be objective. The perspectives and opinions of the researcher must now not affect the consequences of a take a look at. This is right because it makes the statistics more valid, and much less biased.

There are three forms of experiments you need to recognize:

1. Lab experiment

A laboratory test is an experiment performed beneath exceedingly managed conditions (no longer always a laboratory), in which accurate measurements are feasible.

The researcher makes a decision in which the test will take location, at what time, with which contributors, in what occasions and using a standardized process.

individuals are randomly allocated to every independent variable institution. An instance is Milgram's test on obedience or Loftus and Palmer's vehicle crash observe.

electricity: it's far simpler to copy (i.e. copy) a laboratory experiment. that is because a standardized system is used.

electricity: They permit for unique manage of extraneous and impartial variables. This allows a cause and impact dating to be set up.

drawback: The artificiality of the placing may produce unnatural conduct that doesn't replicate real existence, i.e. low ecological validity. this means it would no longer be viable to generalize the findings to a real existence placing.

challenge: call for traits or experimenter effects can also bias the effects and grow to be confounding variables.

2. discipline experiment

subject experiments are achieved within the regular (i.e. actual existence) environment of the participants. The experimenter still manipulates the unbiased variable, however in a actual-lifestyles putting (so can't clearly manage extraneous variables).

An example is Holfing's hospital look at on obedience.

power: conduct in a area test is much more likely to mirror real lifestyles due to its herbal putting, i.e. higher ecological validity than a lab experiment.

energy: there's much less likelihood of demand characteristics affecting the outcomes, as contributors may not understand they're being studied. This happens when the have a look at is covert.

challenge: there may be less control over extraneous variables that would bias the effects. This makes it difficult for every other researcher to copy the examine in precisely the identical way.

3. natural test

natural experiments are carried out inside the regular (i.e. actual existence) environment of the individuals, but here the experimenter has no control over the impartial variable as it occurs obviously in real lifestyles.

for example, Hodges and Tizard's attachment studies (1989) compared the long term improvement of kids who have been followed, fostered or back to their moms with a control institution of children who had spent all their lives in their organic households.

strength: behavior in a herbal experiment is much more likely to mirror actual lifestyles due to its herbal placing, i.e. very high ecological validity.

power: there is much less probability of demand traits affecting the consequences, as contributors may not realize they're being studied.

strength: may be used in situations wherein it might be ethically unacceptable to govern the unbiased variable, e.g. gaining knowledge of strain.

hassle: they'll be greater highly-priced and time ingesting than lab experiments.

problem: there is no control over extraneous variables that could bias the effects. This makes it hard for another researcher to copy the take a look at in precisely the identical way.

Some Most influential Psychological Experiments

1. A Class Divided by By: Jane Elliot
2. Asch Conformity Study by: Dr. Solomon Asch
3. Bobo Doll Experiment by: Dr. Alburt Bandura
4. Car Crash Experiment by: Elizabeth Loftus and John Palmer
5. Cognitive Dissonance Experiment by: Leon Festinger and James Carlsmith
6. Fantz's Looking Chamber by: Robert L. Fantz
7. Hawthorne Effect by: Henry A. Landsberger
8. Kitty Genovese Case by: New York Police Force
9. Learned Helplessness Experiment

by: Martin Seligman
10. Little Albert Experimen by: John B. Watson and Rosalie Rayner
11. Magical Number Seven by: George A. Miller
12. Pavlov's Dog Experiment by: Ivan Pavlov
13. Robbers Cave Experiment by: Muzafer and Carolyn Sherif
14. Ross' False Consensus Effect Study by: Lee Ross
15. The Schacter and Singer Experiment on Emotion by: Stanley Schachter and Jerome E. Singer

How To Read Scientfic Paper

If you are reading psychology in high faculty or college, you will need to read articles posted in instructional and professional journals sooner or later. you might read those articles as a part of a literature evaluate for a paper you are writing, or your teacher can also even ask you to write a critique of an editorial. regardless of the purpose, it's far essential which you apprehend what you are analyzing and **locate methods to then summarize the content to your personal phrases.**

studies articles can be complicated and may appear daunting, particularly to novices who've no experience studying or writing this type of paper. getting to know a way to study this type of writing is often a count number of experience, however using a few easy approaches can make this technique a lot easier.

apprehend the structure of a magazine Article
at the start look, a journal article might also seem to be a complicated collection of strange terminology and complex tables.
maximum journal articles observe a fairly standardized layout that conforms to suggestions installed by the yank mental association (APA). with the aid of know-how this shape, you will sense more at ease operating your manner via each segment.

The summary: This brief, paragraph-lengthy phase gives a quick overview of the article. analyzing the summary is a fantastic manner to get an concept of what facts the article will cowl. studying this phase first can help making a decision if the object is relevant to your subject matter or pursuits.

The creation: the second section of the thing introduces the hassle and opinions preceding studies and literature on the subject. This part of the object will help you higher apprehend the history of the studies and the present day query that is under research.

The approach segment: This part of the item info how the studies was performed. facts approximately the contributors, the strategies, the units, and the variables that had been measured are all described in this section.

The outcomes section: So what have been the real outcomes of the take a look at? This vital segment info what the researchers discovered, so pay cautious interest to this a part of the item. Tables and figures are often included further to the text.

The discussion section: What do the consequences of the have a look at virtually suggest? on this section, the author(s) interpret the outcomes, outline the consequences of the take a look at, and provide feasible descriptions of future studies that must be performed.

The Reference segment: This section lists all the articles and different resources cited within the article.

Skim through the article

once you recognize the simple structure of the item, your first step must be to in short skim via the fabric.

by no means start via doing an in-intensity analyzing of an article before you have skimmed over each section. trying a radical examine-through before you've skimmed the contents is not best difficult; it is able to also be a waste of treasured time.

Skimming is a superb manner to emerge as familiar with the subject and the statistics protected within the paper. In a few cases, you could discover that the paper isn't properly-applicable to your wishes, that may keep time and permit you to move on to a research article this is extra appropriate.

Take Notes on each section and Ask Questions

Your next step ought to be to carefully examine through each segment, taking notes as you pass. Write down critical factors, however also make observe of any terminology or principles which you do now not recognize. after you've read the whole article, pass returned and start looking up the information that you didn't understand the usage of some other supply. this could involve using a dictionary, textbook, on line aid, or even asking a classmate or your professor.

a way to Take notable Psychology Notes

discover Key information

First get the "big picture" by reading the title, key words and abstract carefully; this will tell you the major findings and why they matter.

- Quickly scan the article without taking notes; focus on headings and subheadings.
- Note the publishing date; for many areas, current research is more relevant.
- Note any terms and parts you don't understand for further reading.

whether or not you're looking for information that supports the speculation in your very own paper or cautiously reading the article and critiquing the studies strategies or findings, there are critical questions which you must answer as you study the item.

what is the primary hypothesis?

Why is that this research important?
Did the researchers use suitable measurements and approaches?
What had been the variables in the have a look at?
What changed into the important thing finding of the studies?
Do the findings justify the writer's conclusions?
what's a speculation and how Do i exploit It?

word the resources noted

whilst analyzing a studies article, it's all too clean to consciousness on the primary sections and neglect the references. however, the reference phase can truly be one of the most vital parts of the paper, in particular in case you are looking for further sources on your personal paper. Spending a while reviewing this phase can imply critical studies articles on the subject location in which you are involved.

reading psychology journal articles takes a few time and effort, but it's miles a crucial part of the research process. with the aid of learning how to approach these articles and understanding what to search for as you skim through them, you will have an easier time deciding on assets which are suitable on your research assignment or paper.

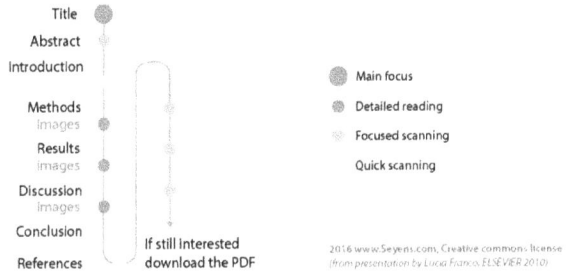

STEP WISE PROCEDURE :

know-how the phase shape image titled behavior studies

1

find the simple info on the the front web page: The front web page consists of the writer´s names, the yr of publishing, the journal´s name together with edition and page numbers, a brief abstract and, of route, the identify of the look at.

2

study the summary for a precis: The summary is a quick summary of what the study is set. you'll locate the topic of the research, how it was achieved, statistics approximately the pattern, hypotheses, major outcomes and a preview approximately the points which are discussed.

3

appearance to the introduction for the "why": The introduction is typically the first component in which the researchers give an explanation for the theoretical historical past of the research count number. essential terms are defined and in lots of cases you will find a brief historic define of the subject. The creation is also the region wherein the previous findings of other scientists can be cited.

The primary feel of the advent is to give an explanation for the studies question and the predictions (hypotheses) that were derived from the theory. these hypotheses had been tested towards the information afterward to see if the predictions can be verified or want to be rejected.

4

read the approach for the "how": you can see the creation as the "why" and the method because the "how" of a take a look at.The method component consists of all technical info of the take a look at which include:

sample length
Age and gender arrangement
background of the subjects
extra facts approximately the contributors if vital to interpret the consequences e.g. cultural historical past, spiritual denomination, faculty degree and many others.
method (how they did it)
gadget, machines (e.g. MRT, cardiograph), unique software and so on.
questionnaires that were used
experimental situations and task sample
materials (e.g. pictures, video spots, obligations etc.)
initial consequences like method about members´ traits
method of analysis

5

appearance to the outcomes for the effects: in the outcomes component researchers explain what changed into finished with the data including the final results of the evaluation.

The essential purpose of this element is to make clear whether or not the hypotheses had been supported or now not. regularly you'll locate charts and image representations inside the effects component as nicely.

6
Get a top level view of the results and barriers in the dialogue: inside the discussion you will often locate:
A precis of the research purpose
an outline of the main results
Strengths and boundaries of the study due to sample, strategies used, interpretation validity
practical implications
opportunities for prospective research tries

7
test the References for citations: The references show all other studies that were used within the paper in alphabetic order. good enough citation is obligatory within the international of science to offer suitable credit score to the work of others and to make the records given inside the article transparent.

www.ingramcontent.com/pod-product-compliance
Ingram Content Group UK Ltd.
Pitfield, Milton Keynes, MK11 3LW, UK
UKHW022209230426
12048UKWH00016BA/746